Generic and Energy-Efficient Context-Aware Mobile Sensing

Generic and Energy-Efficient Context-Aware Mobile Sensing

Özgür Yürür

Chi Harold Liu

CRC Press
Taylor & Francis Group
Boca Raton London New York

CRC Press is an imprint of the
Taylor & Francis Group, an **informa** business

MATLAB® is a trademark of The MathWorks, Inc. and is used with permission. The MathWorks does not warrant the accuracy of the text or exercises in this book. This book's use or discussion of MATLAB® software or related products does not constitute endorsement or sponsorship by The MathWorks of a particular pedagogical approach or particular use of the MATLAB® software.

First published in paperback 2024

Published 2015 by CRC Press
2385 NW Executive Center Drive, Suite 320, Boca Raton FL 33431

and by CRC Press
4 Park Square, Milton Park, Abingdon, Oxon, OX14 4RN

CRC Press is an imprint of Taylor & Francis Group, LLC

© 2015, 2024 Taylor & Francis Group, LLC

Version Date: 20141217

ISBN: 978-1-4987-0010-8 (hbk)
ISBN: 978-1-138-89451-8 (pbk)
ISBN: 978-0-429-16288-6 (ebk)

DOI: 10.1201/b18058

Dedicated to my parents Lütfiye Yürür and Zekeriya Yürür and to my elder brother Murat Yürür

Contents

Preface

This book presents up-to-date research and novel framework designs for context-aware mobile sensing, as well as introduces and elaborates the concept of context-awareness. The book supports proposed works by providing theory and equation derivations behind the concepts, design steps and tips for the implementation of smartphone programming, and MATLAB® use for the presentation of performance analysis.

Potential readers of this book are postgraduate students, engineers/researchers working on mobile computing/sensing, and industrial companies that would like to undertake mobile sensing research in order to produce mobile devices, such as activity-recognizing wristbands/watches. For postgraduate students, this is a good practical as well as theoretical reference book on mobile sensing. They will also learn modeling and analysis skills in given concepts. This book also contains many application examples to guide students step by step from a fundamental understanding to implementation of context aware–related algorithms/frameworks. For engineers, this book can help them understand the theory behind mobile sensing and provide insights into practical system design. The book includes some sections such as lightweight, online, and unsupervised pattern recognition methods; adaptive, time-variant, and optimal sensory sampling strategies; and energy-efficient, robust, and inhomogeneous context-aware framework designs, which are quite valuable design merits in this application domain for engineers. Researchers can learn the latest modeling and analysis research work on mobile sensing. The book is organized in a pyramid format to eventually create a generic context-aware framework. Therefore, researchers in this area can first grasp the instructed research material in this book, and then move on to more challenging problems found in future mobile sensing systems. Industrial people can adopt the covered topics for their commercial use to manufacture mobile devices in order to assist people.

Readers will be able to acquire the following benefits or knowledge: (1) A deeper understanding of the context-awareness in mobile sensing; (2) skills of modeling and analysis for context-awareness on resource-constrained mobile platforms; (3) insights and guidelines for designing and implementing practical context-aware frameworks in ubiquitous/mobile sensing.

Moreover, the book can be used as a textbook/supportive material for a postgraduate level course, and used as a comprehensive resource for researchers. The book is mostly suitable for readers who have majored in computer science, computer engineering, and electrical engineering or related areas, and for readers who have taken courses on probability theory, signal processing, machine learning, estimation theory, and game theory. The concept of the book includes the exciting and emerging research concepts of ubiquitous/mobile computing, artificial intelligence, sensor networks, Internet of Things, and mobile programming.

Currently, there is no textbook on the modeling, analysis, and implementation of mobile sensing from an energy efficiency, robustness, adaptability, and time-variant perspective. Being adaptive to the changing physical world through sensory sensing, time-variant user behaviors, robust response of context-awareness toward such conditions, and, more importantly, energy efficiency is important in context-aware mobile sensing. I strongly believe that combining all these key elements in order to create a generic context-aware framework would be a useful reference for readers working in research and application in this field. Many books in this domain focus primarily on abstract layer techniques of mobile/pervasive/ubiquitous systems. In contrast, this book also covers physical layer algorithm designs and analysis, including context transition through the cross-layer. Therefore, a comprehensive cross-layer design of mobile sensing is covered in the book.

Özgür Yürür, PhD
High Point, North Carolina

MATLAB® is a registered trademark of The MathWorks, Inc. For product information, please contact:

The MathWorks, Inc.
3 Apple Hill Drive
Natick, MA 01760-2098 USA
Tel: 508-647-7000
Fax: 508-647-7001
E-mail: info@mathworks.com
Web: www.mathworks.com

Authors

Özgür Yürür earned a double major from the Department of Electronics Engineering and the Department of Computer Engineering at Gebze Institute of Technology, Kocaeli, Turkey, in 2008, and an MSEE and PhD from the Department of Electrical Engineering at the University of South Florida (USF), Tampa, Florida, in 2010 and 2013, respectively. He currently works with RF Micro Devices, responsible for the research and design of new test development strategies and also for the implementation of hardware, software, and firmware solutions for 2G, 3G, 4G, and wireless-based company products. In addition, Dr. Yürür conducts research in the field of mobile sensing. His research area covers ubiquitous sensing, mobile computing, machine learning, and energy-efficient optimal sensing policies in wireless networks. The main focus of his research is on developing and implementing accurate, energy-efficient, predictive, robust, and optimal context-aware algorithms and framework designs on sensor-enabled mobile devices.

Chi Harold Liu is a full professor at the School of Software, Beijing Institute of Technology, China. He is also the deputy director of the IBM Mainframe Excellence Center (Beijing), the director of the IBM Big Data Technology Center, and director of the National Laboratory of Data Intelligence for China light industry. He earned a PhD from Imperial College, United Kingdom, and a BEng from Tsinghua University, China. Before moving to academia, he joined IBM Research, China, as a staff researcher and project manager and was previously a postdoctoral researcher at Deutsche Telekom Laboratories, Germany, and a visiting scholar at the IBM T. J. Watson Research Center, Armonk, New York. Dr. Liu's current research interests include the Internet of Things (IoT), big data analytics, mobile computing, and wireless ad hoc, sensor, and mesh networks. He received the Distinguished Young Scholar Award in 2013, the IBM First Plateau Invention Achievement Award in 2012, and the IBM First Patent Application Award in 2011. He was interviewed by EEWeb.com as the featured engineer in 2011.

Dr. Liu has published more than 50 prestigious conference and journal papers and owns more than 10 EU, U.S., and China patents. He serves as the editor for *KSII Transactions on Internet and Information Systems* and is the book editor for four books published by Taylor & Francis Group, Boca Raton, Florida. He has served as the general chair of the IEEE (Institute of Electrical and Electronics Engineers) SECON'13 workshop on IoT Networking and Control, the IEEE WCNC'12 workshop on IoT Enabling Technologies, and the ACM UbiComp'11 Workshop on Networking and Object Memories for IoT. He has also served as a consultant for Bain & Company and KPMG, United States, and as a peer reviewer for the Qatar National Research Foundation and the National Science Foundation in China. He is a member of the IEEE and the ACM (Association for Computing Machinery).

Introduction

The ever-increasing technological advances in embedded systems engineering, together with the proliferation of small-size sensor design and deployment, have enabled mobile devices (e.g., smartphones) to recognize daily-occurring human-based actions, activities, and interactions. Therefore, inferring a vast variety of mobile device user–based activities from a very diverse context obtained by a series of sensory observations has drawn much interest in the research area of ubiquitous sensing. The existence and awareness of the context provide mobile device users with the capability of being conscious of physical environments or situations, and this allows network services to respond proactively and intelligently based on such awareness. Hence, with the evolution of smartphones, software developers are empowered to create context-aware applications for recognizing human-centric or community-based innovative social and cognitive activities in any situation and from anywhere. This leads to the exciting vision of forming a society of the *Internet of Things*, which facilitates applications to encourage users to collect, analyze, and share local sensory knowledge for the purpose of large-scale community use by creating a smart network that is capable of making autonomous logical decisions to actuate environmental objects. More significantly, it is believed that introducing the intelligence and situational awareness into the recognition process of human-centric event patterns could give a better understanding of human behaviors, and it also could give a chance for proactively assisting individuals to enhance their quality of life.

Mobile devices supporting emerging computationally pervasive applications will constitute a significant part of future mobile technologies by providing highly proactive services that require continuous monitoring of user-related contexts. However, the middleware services provided in mobile devices have limited resources in terms of power, memory, and bandwidth as compared with the capabilities of PCs and servers. Above all, power concerns are major restrictions to the implementation of context-aware applications. These requirements unfortunately shorten the device's battery life due to high energy consumption caused by both sensor and processor operations. Specifically, continuously capturing user context through sensors imposes heavy workloads on hardware and computations and, hence, drains battery power rapidly. Therefore, mobile device batteries do not last long while operating sensor(s) constantly.

In addition to that, the growing deployment of sensor technologies in mobile devices and innumerable software applications utilizing sensors has led to the creation of a layered system architecture (i.e., context-aware middleware) so that the desired architecture can not only offer a wide range of user-specific services but also respond effectively to diversity in sensor utilizations, large sensory data acquisitions, ever-increasing application requirements, pervasive context processing software libraries, mobile device–based constraints, and so on. The ubiquity of these computing devices in a dynamic environment where sensor network topologies actively change yields creation of context-aware middleware that behave opportunistically and adaptively without a priori assumptions in response to the availability of diverse resources in the physical world as well as in response to scalability, modularity, extensibility, and interoperability among heterogeneous physical hardware.

In this sense, this book aims at proposing novel solutions to enhance the existing trade-offs in mobile sensing between accuracy and power consumption while the context is being inferred under the intrinsic constraints of mobile devices and around the emerging concepts in context-aware middleware framework.

The following is an overview of the book:

- Chapter 1 surveys the literature of emerging concepts to applications of context awareness in mobile platforms by providing up-to-date research in the literature and future research directions. Moreover, it points out the challenges faced in this regard and enlightens the reader about them by proposing possible solutions.
- Chapter 2 proposes a lightweight online classification method to detect user-centric postural actions, such as sitting, standing, walking, and running, using smartphones. These actions are called user states since they are inferred after the analysis of data acquired through the accelerometer sensor in smartphones. The study offers a computational lightweight and online classification method without knowing any a priori information. Moreover, the proposed method not only provides a standalone solution in differentiation of user states but also assists other widely used off-line supervised classification methods by generating training data classes and/or input system matrices. In addition, this chapter aims at improving these existing methods for online processing by reducing the computational burden. Finally, the proposed method still makes a solid differentiation in user states even when the sensor is operated under slower sampling frequencies.
- Chapter 3 presents a novel framework that includes an inhomogeneous (time-variant) hidden Markov model (HMM) and "learning from data" is a research area in signal processing. The framework either recognizes or estimates user contextual inferences within the concept of human activity recognition (HAR) for future context-aware applications. Context-aware applications

require continuous data acquisition and interpretation from one or more sensor readings. Therefore, device battery lifetimes need to be extended given that constantly running built-in sensors deplete device batteries rapidly. In this sense, a framework is constructed to fulfill the requirements of applications and to prolong device battery lifetimes. The ultimate goal of this chapter is to present an accurate user state representation model and suggest how to maximize power efficiency while the model operates. Most importantly, this research intends to create and clarify a generic framework to guide the development of future context-aware applications. Moreover, topics such as user profile adaptability and variant sensory sampling operations are examined.

- Chapter 4 studies mobile device–based battery modeling under the scope of battery nonlinearities with respect to variant loads. Also, the chapter models the energy consumption behavior of accelerometers analytically and then provides a simulation model and a context-aware smartphone application to examine this sensor behavior. With these models, the chapter aims at achieving a fine efficiency in power consumption caused by sensory operations while maintaining the accuracy of smartphone applications based on sensor usage. More importantly, this study aims at modeling battery nonlinearities and investigating the effects of different usage patterns in sensory operations in terms of power consumption and battery discharge, which may lead to the discovery of optimal energy reduction strategies to extend battery lifetime and facilitate a continual improvement in context-aware mobile services.

- Chapter 5 proposes a novel discrete-time inhomogeneous hidden semi-Markov model (DT-IHS-MM)–based generic framework to achieve a better realization of HAR-based mobile context awareness. In addition, the framework utilizes power-efficient sensor management strategies by providing three intuitive methods and optimal methods based on constrained Markov decision process (CMDP) and partially observable Markov decision process (POMDP). Moreover, a feedback control mechanism is integrated to balance the trade-off between accuracy in context inference and power consumption.

- Chapter 6 presents a generic probabilistic model in detail by representing both low- and high-level context behaviors accurately with respect to the heterogeneous physical world. The proposed generic model consists of a dynamic Bayesian network (DBN) constructed with various types of HMMs. On the one hand, the chapter aims at giving an inside-out summary of the topological structure within the proposed generic model; on the other hand, it attempts to give some new probabilistic assumptions around the proposed model.

Chapter 1

Context Awareness for Mobile Sensing

The continual development of small-size sensor design and deployment together with ever-increasing computing technologies in mobile device–based embedded systems platforms have enabled pervasive recognition of the individual and social contexts that device users touch with. Hence, the inference of daily occurring human-centric actions, activities, and interactions by a set of mobile device–based sensors has drawn much interest in the research area of ubiquitous sensing community.* It is believed that introducing intelligence and situational awareness into the recognition process of human-centric event patterns could give a better understanding of human behaviors, and it also could give a chance for proactively assisting individuals to enhance the quality of life [177,226].

1.1 Introduction

Ubiquitous sensing was first envisioned by Weiser [223] as in providing the right information to the right person at the right time through an effective kind of technology via physical environment, yet making the relevant computing elements and intercommunication invisible to the user. Then, the term of context-awareness first used in [195] where the ability of a mobile user's applications to discover and react to changes in the environment they are situated in. Also, the definition of context or context awareness was simplified and generalized first by [5] and later by [58]

---

* Paradigm of ubiquitous sensing is also described as pervasive computing, mobile computing, context-aware sensing, ambient intelligence, or more recently, everyware.

as being any information that can be used to characterize the situation of an entity, where an entity can be a person, a place, or a physical or computational object. In the latter, the complexity of context awareness was linked with individual user activities by [167] and also were modeled in [97]. In addition, the use of context awareness within mobile sensing and within the concept of smart spaces was introduced in [69,119,188]. Earlier attempts of context-aware applications were also presented in [33]. Now, the envisioned interaction between smart devices and users has become possible today and inevitable for future technologies. Therefore, the ubiquitous sensing has led to increase in the demand for novel applications and services to provide an interested context at anytime and from anywhere.

The integration of sensing and advanced computing capability in network-enabled mobile devices will produce sensory data and exchange information among local or system-wide resources by feeding the Internet at a social scale [197,209]. From this situation will emerge the concept of the Internet of Things (IoT, [10,240]) to shift into a collection of autonomous, ambient intelligent, and self-operated network nodes (e.g., independently acting smartphones), which are well aware of the surrounding context, circumstances, and environments. With these capabilities, the new network architecture would enhance data credibility, quality, privacy, and shareability by encouraging participation at personal, social, and urban scales and would lead to discovering the knowledge about human lives and behaviors, and environment interactions/social connections by leveraging the deployment capacity of smart things (e.g., smartphones, tablets) in order to collect and analyze the digital traces left by the users.

It is well known that the recognition of human behavior highly depends on perception, context, environment, and prior knowledge of the most recent event patterns. In other words, the understanding of human activity is based on the discovery of an activity pattern and accurate recognition of the activity itself. Therefore, researchers have focused on implementing computationally pervasive systems in order to create high-level conceptual models to infer activities and low-level sensory models to extract context from unknown activity patterns, as shown in Figure 1.1. At this point, the creation of a generic model to represent a true nature of human behavior stands as a major challenge. In this aspect, the construction of a framework using distinct middleware technologies has been put forward to provide a required model for the recognition of daily occurring human activities via observations acquired by various built-in smartphone sensors. These activities are inferred as the outcome of a wide range of sensory applications utilized in such diverse implementation areas ranging from environmental surveillance and assisting technologies for medical diagnosis/treatments to the creation of smart spaces for individual behavior modeling. The key challenge faced in this concept is to infer relevant activities in a such system that takes raw sensor readings initially and processes them until obtaining a semantic outcome under some constrictions. These constrictions mostly stem from the difficulty of shaping exact topological structure and also stem from

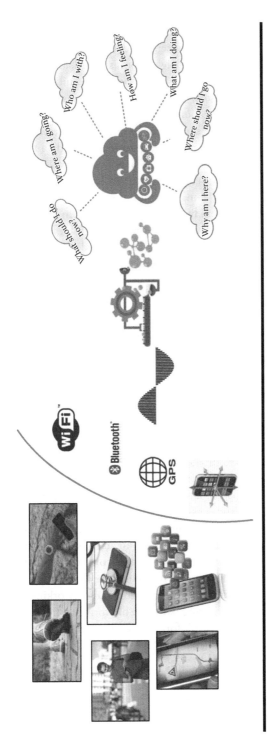

Figure 1.1 An overview of context awareness from low-level sensory models to high-level conceptual models: contextual information from heterogeneous physical world is acquired through built-in sensors and processed by middleware frameworks, finally resulting in a meaningful inference.

modeling uncertainties in the observed data due to saving the energy wasted during physical sensor operations and process of sensory data.

Today's mobile devices are becoming highly sophisticated, and the latest versions are now equipped with a rich set of powerful small-size built-in sensors such as accelerometers, ambient light sensors, GPS,* magnetic compass, and Wi-Fi.* These sensors can measure various information belonging to the physical world surrounding the mobile device; thereby, the ubiquitous use of mobile devices in the society creates a new exciting research area for context-aware sensory data mining applications. Specifically, smartphones could provide a large number of applications within the defined research area. Since human beings are involved in a vast variety of activities within very diverse contexts along with the usage of mobile phones that are getting more integrated into human lives and attached to them throughout the day, a specific context whose relevant data are acquired through built-in sensors can be extracted by a smartphone application. Eventually, desired information within the context is inferred by successful computing implementations.

Context-aware sensing applications can be classified under two different categories: *personal/human-centric* and *urban including participatory/community/group or opportunistic.*[†] In personal sensing applications, the device user is the point of interest. For instance, the monitoring and recognition of user-related posture and movement patterns for personal fitness log or for health-care reasons are an active research topic in this field. On the other hand, participatory sensing relies on the multiple deployment of mobile devices to interactively and intentionally share, gather, and analyze local knowledge that is not only based on a human activity but also based on the surrounding environment. Hence, participatory sensing requires the active participation of each user in collecting sensory data in order to result in large-scale phenomena, which cannot be easily measured by a single participation. For example, many users providing an intelligent traffic congestion report, information on their speed and location, while being in a transportation is a great implementation example of participatory sensing. On the other hand, unlike participatory sensing, opportunistic sensing accepts sensory data collection in a fully autonomous way without active user interaction. This type of applications runs in background mode without any user intervention in actual sensing, such as continuous location notification or ambient sound recognition. In summary, the generic idea of all possible sensing applications is to orchestrate the increasing capabilities of mobile devices (e.g., computing, communication and networking, and sensing) through running software on an existing hardware platform at a right time and place to enable services to infer meaningful information for the benefit of individual and community use.

---

* Their utilizations as sensors are described in Section 1.3.3.

[†] Opportunistic sensing slightly differs from participatory sensing due to the autonomous sensory data collection.

Besides the exciting development of context-aware applications, middleware systems and services in smart devices, however, have only very limited resources in terms of power, memory, and bandwidth as compared with the capabilities of PCs and servers. Especially, energy efficiency is a major restriction imposed on context-aware application developments since the extraction and inference of user-relevant sensory data require continuous sensor operations. This requirement unfortunately shortens the device's battery lifetime due to high energy consumption required by both sensor and processor operations. One solution is to take precautions on sensory operations while putting them into sleeping mode to reduce power consumption. However, it turns into an accuracy problem that middleware services may produce while providing information to the applications. This situation triggers the research into finding optimal solutions to balance the trade-off existing between power consumption and sensory data accuracy. Hence, the key goal lies in discovering the best characteristics of the target complex spatial phenomenon being sensed, meeting the demands of applications, and satisfying the constraints on sensor usage.

Toward this end, this chapter surveys the literature from the emerging concepts to applications of context awareness in mobile platforms by providing up-to-date research in the literature and future research directions. The chapter introduces context awareness in mobile platforms by pointing out and proposing solutions to the challenges in terms of recognition process of both low- and high-level contexts. More specifically, the chapter aims at finding novel solutions to enhance the existing trade-offs in mobile sensing, especially between accuracy and power consumption, while context is being inferred under the intrinsic constraints of mobile devices and around the emerging concepts in context-aware middleware framework. In addition, the chapter provides an overview of the context awareness in ubiquitous/mobile sensing and a comprehensive introduction to the definition, representation, and inference of the context. In this sense, it categorizes and gives an inside-out look into context-aware applications depending on the interested context under the limitation of mobile sensing and then identifies opportunities in this research area. Moreover, the chapter exposes the key elements that modern context-aware middleware and framework designs must have. Finally, the content and the flow of the chapter aim at seeking motivation, identifying drawbacks and the road map to possible solutions of the covered topics, and eventually summarizing and presenting findings by projecting future trends.

This chapter is organized as follows. Section 1.2 introduces the definition of context, context presentation, and the stages to infer context together with context modeling problem. This section also present the context-aware middleware and framework designs, and their key properties such as transparency, adaptability, and reflectiveness. Section 1.3 summarizes recently released significant context-aware applications and categorizes them under the interested context. Most importantly, Section 1.8 puts emphasis on the challenges that are faced during design process and system integration in the content and evaluates possible solutions.

1.2 Context Awareness Essentials

The context-aware systems aim at using a mobile device (e.g., a handheld smartphone or attached/wearable device) integrated with smart sensors in order to monitor and measure individual or environmental phenomena with the purpose of assisting or evaluating human life to achieve a desirable living standard. Figure 1.2 shows the architecture of a context-aware system including to extract low-level context from unknown heterogeneous physical world information acquired by sensors, and then to create high-level conceptual models based on such context inferences. In the following, we will provide the details of key components and modeling processes of the system.

1.2.1 Contextual Information

In the real world, being aware of context and communicating is a key part of human interaction. A context is defined as *a data source that can be sensed and used to characterize the situation of an entity.* In other words, context describes a physical phenomenon in a real-world environment. Hence, context can be described in a different way according to how the equipped sensors are being used. Context can also be defined as a characterization of a specific entity situation such as user profile, user surrounding, user social interaction, and user activity. For instance, we can define the entity by the user, and context by location information. In this sense, context becomes a much richer and more powerful concept, particularly for mobile

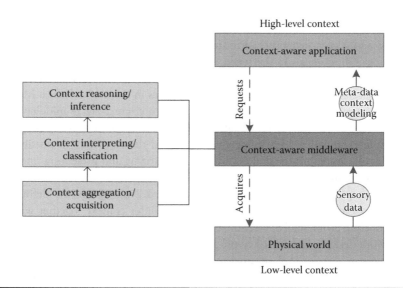

Figure 1.2   The architecture of context-awareness system.

users to make sensor network services much more personalized, and more useful. Therefore, context awareness refers to the capability of an application being aware of its physical environment or situation and responding proactively and intelligently based on such awareness [193].

1.2.2 Context Representation

The property of context awareness can be applied to mobile device–based applications and systems to reduce human intervention by enabling automatic proactive assistant services. Many context-aware applications provide this assistance by using logical context alone, which is obtained via data mining techniques (e.g., stored information in profiles, databases, or social websites). However, with the proliferation of wireless sensor–actuator networks, external physical factors (e.g., temperature, light, and location) are added into context-aware systems.

Figure 1.3 shows the hierarchical definition of context representation. As can be seen, sensors are accepted as low-level context which is directly referred to raw data. A sensor in context-aware applications is described not only a physical device, but also a data source which could be useful for context representation. The collected contextual information may range in a wide sense in terms of specification and representation of a phenomenon in the real world onto an entity in the cyber world. Hence, sensors can be classified as follows:

- *Physical sensors* refer to sensors that can capture almost any data belonging to the physical world (e.g., GPS: location; accelerometer: activity).
- *Virtual sensors* imply information source collected from software applications and services, or a semantic data obtained through cognitive inference (e.g., location info by manually entered place pinpoint through social network services or computation power of devices).
- *Logical sensors* define the combination of physical and virtual sensors with additional information obtained through various sources by user interactions (e.g., databases and log files).

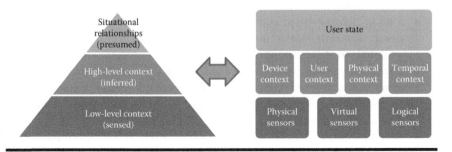

Figure 1.3   The hierarchical definition of context representation.

According to the levels of abstractions, high-level context is then inferred from low-level context. Hence, a definition of semantic meta-sensor/metadata/meta-context implies a level of abstraction [210]. Unlike sensors, context can be divided into the following:

- *Device context,* including net connectivity, communication cost, and resources.
- *User context,* including profile, geographic position, neighbors, and social situation.
- *Physical context,* including temperature, noise level, light intensity, and traffic conditions.
- *Temporal context,* including day, week, month, season, and year.

1.2.3 Context Modeling

Being associated with variant context sources, the accurate representation of context with high certainty under different conditions of measuring range and sampling methods is very important to ensure the quality of contextual information. In this sense, context modeling is required to reason and interpret dynamic context representations at a high-level abstraction in an unobtrusive way. A good context modeling aims at reducing the complexity of applications for robustness and usability and improving their adaptability and maintainability for future devolvement. To be able to do that, it has to consider heterogeneity (i.e., imperfectionist dynamic nature), comparability (i.e., coexistence of similar context from different sources), and mobility (i.e., asynchronous, timeless data capture) of a large variety of context sources at any level of abstraction. It also considers relationships and dependencies among semantic entities such as accuracy in context provisioning versus remaining battery power. In this regard, many context modeling schemes have been proposed [13,26,190,207,210]. Important ones are compared in Table 1.1 and listed in the following:

- Key-value models use a simplest matching algorithm that defines a list of attributes and their content/values describing specific context.
- Markup scheme–based context information models use a hierarchical data structure, mostly formed in XML [123], that consists of markup tags along with their attributes and contents. Therefore, it allows efficient data retrieval. Also, this type of schema can be used among different application domains to store temporary data and in–out data transfer. However, it is not feasible to make context reasoning in the presence of multi-markup schemes due to the lack of interoperability among different schemes.
- Graphical models, such as unified role modeling (UML) [98] and object role modeling (ORM)[90], make connections among context attributes and values based on relationships. Especially, this model is widely used within

Table 1.1   Important Context Modeling Schemes

Context Modeling	*Pros*	*Cons*
Key value	■ Simple text string matching technique ■ Easily manageable with small data size ■ Mostly application bounded	■ Not scalable, better in less complexity ■ Not applicable in hierarchical structure ■ Lack of enabling efficient context retrieval and validation
Markup scheme	■ Efficient data retrieval ■ Applicable in hierarchical structure ■ Provides partial validation	■ No design criteria ■ Complex context reasoning in multischemes ■ Lack of interoperability with similar models ■ Lack of richness and incompleteness
Graphical	■ Rich in context collection ■ Allows relationship modeling ■ Better in complex data management	■ Once designed, difficult to change later ■ No specific design structure ■ Lack of validation and interoperability with similar models
Object oriented	■ Allows more complex relationships and composition ■ Easily designed and run-time operable ■ Applicable through programming languages	■ No specific design structure, nontrivial to update and optimize ■ Difficult data retrieval ■ Mostly application bounded ■ Hidden to other apps due to data encapsulation
Logic based	■ High degree of formality ■ Easily designed and run-time operable ■ Co-operable with other models ■ Designed for checking and resolving context inconsistency	■ Lack of standardization ■ Provides context reasoning and validation at a certain level ■ Mostly application bounded ■ Lack of richness and incompleteness

(Continued)

Table 1.1 (*Continued*) **Important Context Modeling Schemes**

Context Modeling	Pros	Cons
Ontology based	■ Allows knowledge sharing, integration, and reuse ■ Provides well-defined, rich, quality, and re-expendable abstract model and explicit relations ■ Provides unique identification, redundancy, uncertainty handling, and partial validation	■ Complex and computational expensive data retrieval ■ Lack of handling heterogeneity, ambiguous, and quality-related issues

database management [91] that allows holding a massive amount of data and performs quick data retrieval. Also, complex context relations can be managed easily through database queries.

■ Object-oriented models [29] offer object-oriented techniques to be used in context modeling. Constructed object classes encapsulate or represent different context types; thereby reaching the context or processing its attributes is regulated with designed object-oriented class hierarchies and relationships. This model also provides reusability, inheritance, and polymorphism features into context or intercontext relationships. However, the model is suitable to be used for a dedicated application based that employs its own context reasoning structure.

■ Logic-based models include formality based on facts, expressions, and rules to set constraints, limitations, policies, or preferences while defining context reasoning. It is powerful to manage richness in context definitions by allowing adding, removing, or updating a new set of rules. Therefore, it could cooperate with other context modeling techniques to enhance context reasoning efficiency.

■ Ontology-based modeling [7,66,127] uses semantic technologies to represent context-related attributes and relationships. It is very widely used and is a promising instrument thanks to its highly formal expressiveness and conceptualization. Therefore, there are many development tools and engines, such as Resource Description Languange (RDF) [75] and Web Ontology Language (OWL) [100,219], available to apply ontology reasoning techniques. This model aims at providing simple, flexible, extensible, generic, and explicitly well-defined design objectives. However, with growing data size, context reasoning could be computationally expensive.

All context modeling approaches ultimately aim at providing solutions for context reasoning by capturing a variety of context types along with their relationships, dependencies, timeliness, and quality of content. They also support accurate reasoning and clear uncertainty on higher-level context abstractions. Therefore, there might be no single-context modeling technique to be used in a stand-alone fashion.

1.2.4 Context-Aware Middleware

The growing deployment of sensor technologies in smart devices and innumerable software applications utilizing sensors to sense the surrounding physical environment in order to offer a wide range of user-specific services has led to the creation of a *layered* system architecture (i.e., context-aware middleware). In this way, the desired architecture can response effectively for optimal sensor utilization, large sensory data acquisitions as well as meeting ever-increasing application requirements, leveraging the pervasive context-processing software libraries, and considering mobile device resource constraints. Due to the ubiquitousness of these computing devices in a dynamic environment where sensor network topologies actively change, the context-aware middleware yields applications to behave opportunistically and adaptively with no priori assumptions in response to the availability of diverse resources in the physical world, and also to scalability, modularity, extensibility, and interoperability among heterogeneous physical hardware [15].

As shown in Figure 1.4, within the ISO/OSI reference model, conventional middleware takes the place of the session and presentation layers by providing a higher

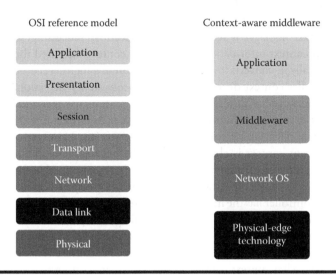

Figure 1.4 Comparison of ISO/OSI reference model and context-aware middleware.

level of abstraction built over the network operating systems (OS), offering fault-tolerant resource sharing, and masking out the problems to facilitate heterogeneity, stability, and efficiency of distributed systems. On the other hand, the context-aware middleware is defined as an abstract layer between OS and up-running applications. It aims at dealing with the heterogeneity of the physical world through edge technology, by adding more specialized mechanisms and services than an OS can provide. It is capable of wrapping (i.e., controlling physical devices and interacting with them to receive data), analyzing, and delivering the physical world information (e.g., through sensor networks, embedded systems, and RFID or NFC tags) to the application services in a transparent way, as shown in Figure 1.5. This degree of transparency separates the application layer from the internal middleware operations and from the detailed implementations of lower layers directly. In essence, the middleware creates a shielded interface by both enhancing the level of abstraction support needed by the application and hiding lower-layer operations between the physical layer (i.e., hardware and communications) at the bottom and the application layer at the top. Furthermore, it allows the computational burden required for context management to shift from the application to the middleware by letting the developers only deal with implementation logic and easily control the created entities (i.e., the characterized context) by context management. In this regard, robust optimization opportunities on many system constraints (e.g., relative computational cost associated with entity-relevant operations, limited battery power, and insufficient information storage) can be achieved. Moreover, the middleware will take the responsibility of all context-related entity management and provide a complete global access to the common resources needed by all applications residing on the same host without any conflict [121,122].

Figure 1.5 also depicts the core components within the context-aware middleware design. Context manager is responsible for collecting, processing, and maintaining low-level context information (i.e., physical context) acquired through context sources. Basically, it converts low-level information to a high-level event (i.e., sensed context), handles context dissemination and inconsistency detection, and notifies the adaption manager of the high-level event. Adaptation manager queries, processes, and regulates all contextual information/objects (i.e., inferred context) actively being used by each application and also automatically receives a context change in case where a different context is observed due to the heterogeneity of context sources. In addition, it filters unnecessary information to have an optimal and effective result based on a current context together with the inclination or preference of user activity. Application controller has the highest-level context (i.e., presumed context) obtained through interworking with the adaptation manager. It processes the final context and sends attribute information back to the context manager. Most importantly, the application controller does not have to interact with context sources, and even it does not know what context coming from which context sources at any time.

It is also worth noting that semantic metadata plays an important role in context-aware middleware, since it is defined at a high level of abstraction to represent

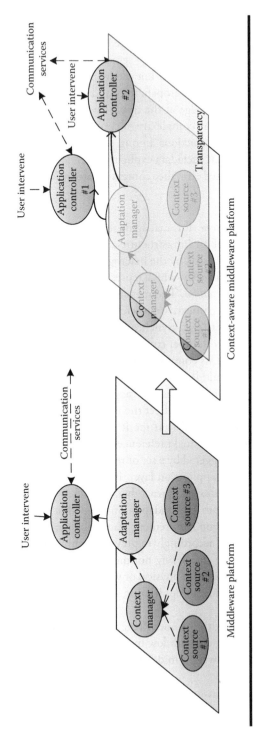

Figure 1.5 Context-aware middleware is capable of wrapping, analyzing, and delivering the physical world information to the application services in a transparent way.

contexts as the structure and meaning of entities and also to present context-related adaptation strategies, which allow the middleware be suitable to behave dynamically with a minimal human intervention. Having semantic metadata allows unambiguous specification of context models and knowledge share among entities without the loss of meaning. Thanks to its interoperability and openness, it also allows inferring some other complex knowledge at the upper layers in the presence of variant semantic metadata. However, the complexity of context resources in heterogeneous physical world and also the interactions among diverse context resources make it difficult to describe the relevant metadata explicitly.

Other properties supported by the context-aware middleware include the following:

- It either runs *stand-alone* for managing entire physical environments or accepts the existence of an infrastructure that can deliver required services. This differentiation is caused by the heterogeneous sensing environment.
- It can have a *reflective* property, which represents the obtained entities through context as semantic *metadata*. The metadata may belong to the application, the middleware itself, context, or interconnected (i.e., *composition*). Note that a context can differ (e.g., asynchronously obtainable over different sensors) and interoperate with other contexts. This reflection property allows the middleware to monitor its computation and possible change in the semantic world, allowing the middleware model itself self-represented. For example, the manipulation of its behavior may be changed. Hence, any change occurring at the meta-level can affect the underlying base level, or vice versa.
- *Adaptation* is an important design merit that empowers users to *customize* systems according to individual preferences. This adaptation is defined by an autonomous process triggered by a set of requirements to improve the quality of service (QoS) at the application layer. It aims to sense the physical world, reason the obtained context, and react dynamically toward the changing context. It also supports proactive adaptations that describe the capability to envision future application requirements caused by the context change and to adjust the functionality accordingly to prevent or minimize direct application interaction with neither interfering nor modifying the application logic.
- It may constitute entities from physical or virtual context for all types of applications, or it can provide an application-specific information delivery (i.e., service provider).
- It must run smoothly with the underlying OS. Since mobile applications run on resource-limited devices with low memory size, slow CPU frequency, and low power supply, lightweight middleware systems need to be designed.

A middleware for context awareness supports the application development task by enhancing the level of abstraction and providing services in dealing with context.

By this means, there are many middleware studies in the literature. The notable ones are listed in the following and compared in Table 1.2:

- Context toolkit [192] is one of the earliest efforts in this domain. It delivers a combination of features and abstractions to capture and manage context source and also to aggregate and share them among applications.
- Aura [81] is an architectural ubiquitous sensing framework. It provides context, application, and task management. Tasks are abstract representations of a collection of services. The framework detects environment changes and migrates task operations into available service providers in the new environment. It is capable of adapting in the presence of dynamic resource variability, thereby supporting the continuity of service for applications.
- CARISMA [36] provides a reflective middleware for mobile systems. It is also adaptive to dynamic environment changes. The tasks in context providing services are prioritized and resolved depending on importance ruled by applications, policies, and configurations under different environmental and user conditions.
- Gaia [189] is a distributed probabilistic-based context-aware middleware that coordinates ontology-based software entities and heterogeneous physical networking devices. It provides context management, detection of events, workload partitioning work event handling, and virtual context file management.
- SOCAM [86] is a service-oriented ontology-based context-aware middleware. It supports the semantic representation and reasoning of context. It also divides context into upper- and lower-level ontologies such as interpreted context through physical world, and memory and battery status, respectively. It allows adaptability by listening, detecting, and invoking events for application services.
- COSMOS [21] is a context-aware middleware that accepts contextual information as a context node and organizes many context nodes in a hierarchical structure. Each context node runs independently while collecting, processing, and reasoning context. The middleware follows this distributed architectural model to create scability by supporting many heterogeneous contextual sources and their relations to each other.
- CoBrA [41] is a centralized middleware architecture that connects various context brokers. Each context broker runs independently, but the middleware creates a knowledgeable context network share. The middleware also addresses resource limitation and privacy issues in mobile computing.
- Hydra [12] is an IoT-based middleware design to deliver solutions to wireless devices and sensor used in ambient awareness. It contains powerful reasoning toward various context sources, including physical device based, semantic based, and abstract layer based. Therefore, it uses a hybrid modeling scheme

Table 1.2 Notable Context-Aware Middleware Studies

Reference	Middleware	Architecture	Context Management	Context Source	Context Level	Reflection	Adaptation	Security and Privacy
[192]	Context toolkit	Centralized	Key value	Any type	High	—	Application based	✓
[81]	Aura	Distributed	Mark-up	Any type	High	✓	Middleware based	—
[36]	CARISMA	Distributed	Mark-up	Mobile	High	✓	Middleware based	—
[189]	Gaia	Distributed	Logic and ontology	Any type	High	—	Application based	✓
[86]	SOCAM	Distributed	Ontology	Any type	High	—	Application based	✓
[21]	COSMOS	Distributed	Object oriented	Physical	High	✓	Middleware based	—
[41]	CoBrA	Component	Ontology	Any type	High	—	Application based	✓
[12]	Hydra	Distributed	Ontology and object	Physical	High	—	Application based	✓
[186]	COSAR	Stand-alone	Ontology	Mobile	Low	—	Application based	✓
[118]	Ubiware	Stand-alone	Ontology	Any type	High	✓	Middleware based	✓
[72]	CASS	Centralized	Logic and object oriented	Mobile	High	—	Application based	✓
[56]	QoSDREAM	Component	Logic and object oriented	Mobile	Low	✓	Middleware based	—
[141]	TinyRest	Centralized	Mark-up	Any type	High	—	Application based	—

to represent low-level context by object-oriented modeling with a key-based approach, and high-level context by ontologies.

- CASS [72] is a centralized middleware for context-aware mobile applications. Mobile clients connect to the middleware service through wireless network, and the middleware listens sensors on mobile clients and gathers information.
- COSAR [186] is a context sharing architecture for mobile network services. It reasons human activity–based context awareness.
- QoSDREAM [56] is a component-based middleware framework for the construction and management of context-aware multimedia applications. It also provides handling of location data derived from a variety of location-sensing technologies.
- Ubiware [118] is a self-managed middleware platform that utilizes different context agents in a decentralized manner to manage mobility and scalability, enable autonomous context discovery, and configure complex functionalities such as composition and interoperability of relations among agents. Therefore, the middleware plans to create a collaboration among heterogeneous sources through semantic communication services.
- SALES [51] and CoMiHoc [225] are mobile environment–based middleware platforms that support context management and situation reasoning through interconnection of various mobile devices.
- TinyRest [141] and Feel@Home [87] create an IoT-based smart offices or homes by actuating wireless sensor networks through Internet connection. They act like a gateway to access different types of sensors and actuators and fuse them to be able to support diverse application domains.

As noted in Table 1.2, the middleware design can accept different architectural structures. Centralized architecture, that is, context server, offers a complete middleware design and allows applications to be developed on top of it. The architecture connects to sensors and devices to provide rich resources and computational power. Communications among devices are handled by queries on the context server. The drawback of this type of middleware is the congestion of received queries. Stand-alone, or self-contained, architecture offers a direct access to sensors, but it does not allow context sharing of devices, connection to external services, or any type of device collaboration. It is ideally designed for small-scale solutions. Distributed architecture creates a hierarchical topology of many connected devices running independently and is also capable of their own context management services. It does not require the existence of a context server. Physical devices are connected through ad hoc communication for information sharing, but the architecture lacks processing computationally intensive resources. Component-based architecture partitions entire middleware solutions on a few major components that interact with each other. Also, there are some other design types available for middleware architecture such as node- or client–server-based one.

1.2.5 Context Inference

As one of the most important properties of context-aware middleware, context inference has drawn much interest in the research area. The middleware provides basic functionalities such as sensory data acquisition, processing, and context recognition. The applied methodology may show differences in context modeling or reasoning. The context initially is called low-level (i.e., atomic) context since all required operations are carried out directly from the data obtained by physical sensors. On the other hand, *high-level context* is obtained later through the combination of low-level and/or high-level contexts, which is called composition. Some mobile context classifier tools such as *Kobe* [46], *WEKA* [89], and *the Context Toolkit*, [192] can deal with low-level context acquisition from raw sensory data and to infer high-level semantic outcomes while exhibiting efficient utilization of available resources and achieving an optimal balance among energy, latency, and accuracy trade-offs. Figure 1.6 shows the stages of context inference problem during the low-level process.

Accordingly, sensory readings are collected by a sliding window with a specific time interval and an overlap value. The length of windowing is an important design merit. The shorter windowing cannot seize the context properly, whereas the wider windowing would create a latency in detections and puts additional workload in computations. Thus, obtained data segments by optimal windowing would provide more relevant information for context classification. In addition, the overlap value is important as well to detect any change in the context.

Preprocessing (e.g., context filtering or fusion) could be applied if raw sensory data are too coarse grained. It may also offer necessary modifications to correct deficiencies in the data due to possible limitations on sensory operations (e.g., power concern).

It is generally very challenging to analyze and build a classification model and infer any context from raw sensory data since it may consist of a large number of variant attributes, irrelevant information, and additive noise distortion. Therefore, feature extraction is applied to exploit hidden information in the sensory data set and remove the direct effect of additive noise distortion. It also enables separability in the context classification algorithm, while extracting and analyzing the spatial characteristics of sensory data in each window and assisting in the identification of different context classes. A feature vector, as a representation of statistical characteristics in the contextual data, is then constructed by using diverse signal processing primitives, ranging from time–space-based features such as mean, standard deviation, and correlation to frequency spectrum-based features such as entropy, fast

Figure 1.6   The processing stages of context inference.

Table 1.3   Feature Selections

Feature Space	Features
Time domain	Mean, standard deviation, variance, magnitude, derivative, min–max, amplitude, histogram, interquartile range, mean absolute deviation, correlation between axes, peak counting, rms, sign, kurtosis, and zero-crossing rate
Frequency domain	Fourier transform (FT), discrete cosine transform, entropy, centroid, maximum frequency, FFT energy, FFT mean, and standard deviation
Others	Autoregressive coefficients and wavelet transforms

Fourier transform (FFT) coefficients, power density etc., and also to wavelet transforms. Table 1.3 summarizes the elements of a feature vector in time and frequency domains. Time-domain feature extraction is the most popular one in many practical real-time applications since sensory samplings are already obtained in a time series way, whereas the frequency-domain features such as FFT coefficients require much computational power to discriminate such features as periodicity of signals. On the other hand, sensors such as accelerometers generate random signals in their nature; therefore, using time-domain features could be successful up to some limit since it is assumed that signals are mostly deterministic in time-domain analysis to make such a differentiation. As a result, it would be better to apply stochastic analysis in these cases in order to describe a suitable feature space. The purpose of the elements being used in the construction of feature vectors is as follows:

■ *Mean* represents the DC component of a signal.
■ *Variance* shows the dynamics of a signal activity. For instance, low dynamic activity, or a stationary signal, will have a low value of variance.
■ *Standard deviation* basically shows the same information as variance does. It also notifies how far signal samples are spread out from its mean value.
■ *Energy or root mean square (RMS)* captures the intensity of a signal.
■ *Correlation among signals* helps distinguish a similar activity occurring through a single dimension or multiple dimensions.
■ *Zero-crossing rate* captures the cyclic pattern of a signal. It could be seen as an approximation of frequency. Thereby, it requires less computation in time domain rather than having frequency value in spectrum analysis.
■ *Spectral peak* shows the dominant frequency of a signal activity.
■ *Spectral entropy* allows specifying whether the energy is evenly distributed through different frequencies. For stationary signals, the entropy increases, whereas nondeterministic signals give out less entropy by having peaky look in the spectrum.

- *Interquartile range* is used where different signals have a similar mean value. It represents the dispersion of signal data except for taking the extreme values into account.
- *Mean absolute deviation* gives the averaged dispersion of signal data with respect to its mean value.
- *Spectral centroid* is the balanced point of the spectral power distribution of a signal.
- *Bandwidth* is the range of frequencies that occupy signal spectrum.
- *Normalized phase deviation* notifies the phase deviations of spectral frequency peaks, which are weighted by their magnitude.
- *Derivative* clears the DC offset of a signal and shows the intensity of variations in signal data.
- *Histogram* captures the density of a signal.
- *Kurtosis* gives the peakedness (width of peak) of the density of a signal.
- *Discrete cosine transform* is similar to FFT, which enables to have spectrum-based analysis, but only using real numbers.
- *Autoregressive coefficients* are used for filters to estimate the characteristics of a signal.
- *Wavelet transform* is essential to time versus frequency analysis. It allows only changes in time extension in correspondence to frequency analysis.
- *Cepstral coefficients* gives information about the rate of change in different spectrum bands.

The diverse characteristics of feature vectors enable to have training data classes (i.e., structural features) for classification algorithms. Thus, a training data class is employed by classifiers to build a classification model, which will allow an unknown feature vector to test for its membership to any class dependency. A confusion matrix can be used to measure the performance of a classifier. The process is basically to test one of the classifiers to map a feature vector into a training contextual data class, called supervised classification.

In this regard, various classification algorithms can be used as a classifier to implement a context recognition system. Techniques include, but are not limited to, naive Bayesian approaches and decision trees (DTs), pattern recognition techniques such as k-Gaussian mixture model (k-GMM), k-means, k-nearest neighbors (k-NN) search, support vector machines (SVMs), and multilayer neural or fuzzy logic networks. In addition, a statistical tool–based classification such as hidden Markov models (HMMs) or AutoRegressive (AR) models is also widely applied, and pattern recognition toolkits such as WEKA provide powerful solutions to the context clustering problem. Table 1.4 classifies studies according to the applied classification methods. The followings are listed for widely used classification algorithms and for their roles in context awareness:

Table 1.4 Classification Algorithms

Classification Algorithm	References
Decision tree (DT), Bayesian network (BN), naive Bayesian (NB)	[68,109,116,149,173,176,221]
Multilayer neural networks (MNN)/meta classifier fusion	[24,43,145,238,244]
Fuzzy logic	[24,43,117]
Gaussian mixture model (GMM)	[147]
k-Means/k-nearest neighbor (k-NN)	[164,202]
Hidden Markov models (HMM)	[132,173,215,244]
Auto-regressive models (AR-M)	[93,187]
Support vector machine (SVM)	[93,94,149,208]
Principal component analysis (PCA)	[43,94]
Linear/quadratic discriminant analysis (LDA/QDA)	[43,145,202]
HAAR wavelet models	[92]
Classifier ensembles: boosting and bagging	[150]
Toolkits: WEKA	[16,92,128,211]

■ Naive Bayesian approach [158] assumes that each feature is conditionally independent in a given class definition and estimates inter-class-conditional probability. Therefore, a naive Bayes classifier fuses individual classification results to improve classification accuracy and robustness. This method uses the probability information residing in training data in order to find the maximum probability of given hypothesis using the Bayes rule. On the other hand, DTs [172] partition the feature space according to a tree structure. These structures fit the purpose of induction and being fast to build and process the implementation of context inference on mobile devices.

■ k-GMM [82] is a maximum likelihood classifier based on mean vector and covariance matrix estimated from each class. Any feature vector (i.e., tested data set) can be drawn from this model to check for which data class encapsulates a given specific feature vector (i.e., training data set), *clustering problem*. This is also called density problem, in which each class represents a cluster that is assigned as a Gaussian model with its mean approximately in the middle of the cluster, and also with a standard deviation showing a measure of how far the cluster spreads out.

- *k*-NN search algorithm [222] assigns the nearest class set for the input feature vector by defining a dissimilarity function that measures the nearness between training data set and new data points in the feature vector. The dissimilarity function is generally defined by the squared Euclidean distance. However, the Euclidean distance does not consider how the data are spread out and also may let the largest length scale between data points dominate the dissimilarity function. Therefore, the Mahalanobis distance is used where the covariance matrix rescales all length of scales to make them essentially equal.

- SVM [95] differentiates two classes from each other by using linear discrimination. SVM denotes each class as a binary data by labeling them $+1/-1$. The objective is to create a hyperplane that sets a rigid margin among data classes to achieve an optimal linear distance separation. Unfortunately, SVM cannot deal with multiclass classification directly. The multiclass classification problem is usually solved by the decomposition of the problem into several two-class problems.

- Multilayer neural or fuzzy logic networks [102,237] create multidimensional Gaussian memberships. They can also be decomposed into a number of one-dimensional Gaussian membership functions in order to correlate with the number of input feature data. Each class in a multidimensional feature space represents a member of the classification network. The output is obtained by checking for Gaussian memberships of each input according to majority vote in the network classifiers.

- *k*-Means clustering algorithm [218] is associated with a specific case of a Gaussian mixture model that stems from the limitation of covariance matrices such as them being equal, diagonal, or small for each user state class. *k*-Means algorithm finds the members of each class from a given data, where the classes are represented by their centers, which also represent the reupdated/reconstructed mean values.

- A statistical tool shows dependencies of states at discrete time *t* that are influenced directly by a state at prior discrete times. Discrete time is used to specify periodic sensor readings. Therefore, HMM [64] is a mostly applied statistical tool that models time series with spatial and temporal variability. In such statistical classifiers, sensor readings (i.e., extracted user contexts through mobile device–based sensors) are seen as inputs. These readings undergo a series of signal processing operations and eventually end up with a classification algorithm in order to provide desirable inferences. A required classification algorithm differs in terms of the explanation of extracted context through a specific sensor. The outcomes of the algorithm are represented in a matrix whose elements show probability weights for possible context selections. Classification algorithms produce observations (i.e., *visible states*) of HMM. Among observations, only one observation is expected to provide the most likely differentiation in the selection of final context inference. On the other hand, desirable context inferences are defined as *hidden states* of HMM since they are not directly observable but only reachable over visible states. Therefore, each observation has cross probabilities to point any context inference. These cross probabilities build an emission matrix, which basically defines decision probabilities of picking context from available observations.

■ AR models [57] are used to show the correlation among various feature parameters for each context inference. AR models apply time series analysis in which a multidimensional vector is transformed into a number of coefficients to make the analysis much easier. By doing that, AR captures the evolution and interdependencies among time series.

■ The feature vector constructed by any classification algorithm requires much computation. There is also no necessity to compute such features that are irrelevant or redundant to infer the context by providing insignificant improvement in accuracy. Hence, it is desirable to reduce the complexity and dimension of the feature set by retaining the core probability distribution spanned through feature vector spaces. In such cases, the dimension of feature vector can be reduced by using PCA [111] or LDA/QDA [76,104]. They help obtain sufficient statistics to model the context and allow lower computational complexity. Both methods seek a projection vector that transforms the original features into a lower-dimensional space by preserving the content of separability. Unlike the PCA, the LDA performs well in seeking a suitable projection for data discrimination by applying an effective separation in data transform into different classes.

The output of classifiers sometimes cannot resolve consistent discrimination in a time sequence of adjacent context inferences. In this case, a basic smoothing technique takes a majority voting scheme with a sliding window of a specific history length of context inferences. Hence, any inconsistency (i.e., false truthfulness) can be eliminated.

On the other hand, a desired approach to implement the context recognition process should provide context inference without considering a priori information, fixed thresholds, and initial training data classes. It also needs to show robustness in terms of any change in the orientation of the device and dynamic profile in the user context and employ sufficient signal processing by causing nonredundant computational workload. Since supervised classifiers need extensive computations to generate models for training contextual data classes, and testing for unknown patterns, unsupervised learning is an active research area due to its nature of focusing on clustering or pattern discovery rather than classification. Therefore, the definition of self- or co-learning-based semi- or unsupervised classifiers to actualize proactive context inferences without knowing a prior data class has been actively investigated [245]. Table 1.5 delivers a comparison table among classification algorithms used in context awareness.

Table 1.5 Classification Algorithms

Algorithm Name	Pros	Cons
Naive Bayesian	■ Uncertainty handling ■ Allows combinational reasoning	■ Probability bounded ■ Numerical outcomes
Supervised (e.g., *SVM, k-NN, ensembles*)	■ Many techniques available ■ Discriminates morphologically interconnected patterns ■ Provides more accurate inference	■ Computationally expensive ■ Requires huge data set to have more accurate assumptions ■ Training data set required to matching ■ Challenging to find optimum feature set ■ Mostly user intervention needed to specify training data
Unsupervised (e.g., *k-means*)	■ No training data set needed ■ More machine learning included ■ Robust and adaptive	■ Computationally expensive ■ Complex system design ■ Difficulty in validation
Fuzzy logic	■ Simple and easily applicable ■ Provides more understandable reasoning ■ Uncertainty handling	■ Manually defined ■ Prone to have false truthfulness ■ No quality check
Decision tree	■ Simple and easily applicable ■ Requires less computations ■ Expandable	■ Manually defined threshold based ■ Prone to have false truthfulness ■ No quality check
Stochastic	■ Provides accurate inference ■ Allows combinational reasoning ■ Quantitative features ■ Uncertainty handling	■ Predefined expected probabilities ■ Training data sets for coefficients ■ Difficult to discriminate morphological patterns ■ Probability bounded, ignoring feature relationships

1.2.6 Context-Aware Framework Designs

The pervasive mobile computing, which captures and evaluates sensory contextual information in order to infer user-relevant actions/activities/behaviors, is becoming a well-established research domain. Most of the studies rely on the recognition of user activities (especially posture detection) and definition of common user behaviors by proposing and implementing numerous context modeling systems. In addition, researchers have been aware of the need for computational power while trying to accurately infer sensory context. However, most of the studies provide partial answers to the trade-off between context accuracy and battery power consumption. It is hard to say that power saver considerations have been significantly taken at low-level physical sensory operations. Especially, there is not a generic framework that applies *adaptively changing* dynamic sensor management strategies. In contrast, most studies for creating a context-aware application emphasize either to set a minimum number of sensors when they are needed or to maximize power efficiency by solely applying less complexity in computations and/or changing transferring methods of obtained context to the outer network services.

From the standpoint of the creation of a generic framework design for context-aware middleware services, it would be notable to mention the following studies:

- *EEMSS* in [221] uses hierarchical sensor management strategy by powering a minimum number of sensors and applying appropriate sensor duty cycles so that the proposed framework could recognize user states through smartphone sensors while improving the device's battery lifetime. Unfortunately, sensors employ fixed duty cycles whenever they are utilized, and also they are not adjustable to respond differently to variant user behaviors. Energy consumption is reduced by shutting down unnecessary sensors at any particular time. On the other hand, classification of sensory data is based on predefined test classification algorithms.
- The hierarchical sensor management system is also studied by introducing *SeeMon* system in [116], which achieves energy efficiency and less computational complexity by only performing continuous detection of context recognitions when changes occur during the context monitoring. The framework also employs a bidirectional feedback system in computations to detect similar context recognitions in order to prevent from redundant power consumptions.
- Similarly, *Sensay* in [201] is a context-aware mobile phone but is in the form of an external sensor box, which is mounted on the user's hip area. It receives many different sensory data and eventually determines to dynamically change cell phone ring tone, alert type, and uninterruptible user states. However, it classifies user state off-line, and the system does not have energy efficiency.
- *Darwin* studied in [147] proposes a system that combines classifier evolution, model pooling, and collaborative inference for mobile sensing applications.

It is implemented for a speaker recognition application by using efficient but sophisticated machine-learning techniques; however, there is no power consideration applied.

- "Jigsaw" presented in [140], a continuous sensing engine for mobile phone applications, balances the performance needs of an application and resource demands. The engine employs each sensor under a processing pipeline. It performs all the sensing and classification processing exclusively on the mobile phone. It also uses sensor-specific pipelines that have been designed to cope with the individual challenges experienced by each sensor. Duty cycling techniques are attached to adaptive pipeline process if applicable to conserve battery life.

- The study in [246] creates a general framework problem under an energy-efficient location-based sensing application. It is noted that there are four critical factors that affect energy efficiency in location sensing through GPS. These factors are static use of location sensing mechanisms, absence of use of power-efficient sensors to optimize location sensing, lack of sensing cooperation among multiple similar applications, and unawareness of battery level. The middleware solution is given by introducing *substitution* to find an alternative less power-consuming location-sensing mechanism, *suppression* to use less power-consuming sensor instead of GPS when user location is static, *piggybacking* to synchronize with other location-based applications to infer a collaborative location info, and *adaptation* to adjust system parameters such as time and distance longer when battery level is low.

There are also some other studies proposed in [187,200,244] in order to provide comprehensive solutions in creating a base framework for context-aware applications. Table 1.6 analyzes some important frameworks by breaking down each study and comparing them in terms of learning paradigm, applied algorithm, power efficiency, processing method, interested context, input sensor, platform where implementation is carried out, and accuracy of framework outcome.

1.3 Context-Aware Applications

Mobile phones are equipped with sophisticated sensors. Most sensors currently available on smart devices are designed to perform some specific applications, such as accelerometers for detecting screen orientation, a microphone for voice conversations, a camera for capturing images, and a GPS for displaying location. However, by introducing intelligence, situational awareness, and context recognition into these devices, and given the right architecture within the context of ubiquitous sensing by enhancing and systematizing the existing methodologies, built-in sensors could be repurposed and act as sensor nodes to proactively assist users in their daily activities by increasing the quantity, quality, and credibility of community-gathered

Table 1.6 Analysis of Some Notable Framework Designs

Reference	Learning Paradigm	Algorithms	Power Efficiency	Processing	Interested Context	Input Device	Platform	Results Accuracy
[16]	Supervised	k-NN, DT and NB	N/A	Off-line	Activities	ACC		50%–80%
[39]	Supervised	NB and HMM	N/A	Off-line	Activities	ACC	Development board	90%
[107]	Unsupervised	k-means	N/A	Off-line	Activities	ACC	Wearable	77%
[140]	Supervised	DT, GMM, SVM, and NB	MDP-based DSS	Online	Activities and ambient sound	ACC, MIC, and GPS	Smartphone	94% for act. 84% for sound
[206]	Semi-supervised	Multiple SVMs	N/A	Off-line	Activities	ACC	Wearable	70%–80%
[229]	Supervised	DT, SVM, NB, AdaBoost	N/A	Off-line	Activities	ACC	Wearable	77%
[221]	Supervised	DT and FE	DSS and DC	Online	Activities and ambient sound	GPS, MIC, Wi-Fi, and ACC	Smartphone	73%–100% for act. 70%–94% for sound

(Continued)

Table 1.6 (Continued) Analysis of Some Notable Framework Designs

Reference	Learning Paradigm	Algorithms	Power Efficiency	Processing	Interested Context	Input Device	Platform	Results Accuracy
[238]	Supervised	FE, HMM, NB, and NN	DSS	Off-line	Activities	ACCs	Wearable sensors	80%–90%
[173]	Supervised	FE, HMM, and NB	N/A	Off-line	Activities	ACC and proximity	Wearable sensors	88%–94%
[176]	Supervised	FE and NB	AS	Online	Activities	ACC, BT, and MIC	Smartphone	70%–90%
[93]	Supervised	FE, AR, and SVM	N/A	Off-line	Activities	ACC	Development board	92.25%
[208]	Supervised	FE and SVM	N/A	Off-line	Activities	ACC	Smartphone	91%–95%
[164]	Semisupervised	FE, k-means, PCA, and AdaBoost	N/A	Off-line	Location	MIC	Smartphone	88.7%
[43,145]	Supervised	FE, LDA, and FBF	N/A	Off-line	Activities	ACC	PC	93%
[128,211]	Supervised	FE and WEKA Toolkit	N/A	Off-line	Activities	ACC and HR	PC	80%–94%

[68]	Supervised	FE	N/A	Online	Activities	ACC	Wearable	82%–97%
[109]	Supervised	FE, NB, k-NN	N/A	Off-line	Activities	ACC and HR	Development board	75%–95%
[139]	Semisupervised	DT and FE	N/A	Online	Ambient sound	MIC	Smartphone	78%–93%
[92]	Supervised	FE, HAAR, and WEKA	N/A	Off-line	Activities	ACC	Development board	90%–94%
[161]	Unsupervised	DT	N/A	Online	Activities	GPS, Wi-Fi, and GSM	Smartphone	90%
[244]	Supervised	FE, HMM, and NN	N/A	Off-line	Activities	ACC	Smartphone	87%–90%
[45]	Unsupervised	FE and DT	N/A	Online	Activities and location	ACC, GPS, and WiFi	Smartphone	90%
[132]	Supervised	FE and HMM	N/A	Off-line	Activities	ACC and MIC	Development board	77%–85%
[202]	Supervised	FE, QDA, and k-NN	N/A	Off-line	Activities	ACC	Smartphone	90%

(Continued)

Table 1.6 (*Continued*) Analysis of Some Notable Framework Designs

Reference	Learning Paradigm	Algorithms	Power Efficiency	Processing	Interested Context	Input Device	Platform	Results Accuracy
[24]	Supervised	FE and FN	N/A	Off-line	Activities	ACC	Smartphone	97%
[147]	Semisupervised	FE and GMM	N/A	Online	Location	MIC	Smartphone	80%–90%
[149]	Supervised	FE, DT, and SVM	DC	Online	Activities and social context	ACC, MIC, and GPS	Smartphone	90%
[174]	Semisupervised	FE, AR, and estimation	RO	Online	Location	WiFi and GSM	Smartphone	90%

Note: DT, decision tree; FE, feature extraction; HMM, hidden Markov model; NB, naive Bayesian; BN, Bayesian network; SVM, support vector machine; AR, auto-regressive model; PCA, principal component analysis; LDA, linear discriminant analysis; FN, fuzzy networks; *k*-NN, *k*-nearest neighbor; GMM, Gaussian Markov model; SVM, support vector machine; NN, neural networks; DSS, dynamic sensor selection; DC, duty cycling; AS, adaptive sampling; MDP, Markov decision process; RO, radio optimization; ACC, accelerometer; BT, bluetooth; MIC, microphone; HR, heart rate monitor; POMDP, partially observable Markov decision process.

data. Hence, these smart devices could be used as instruments, recall Figure 1.1, to collect data and provide meaningful observations belonging to user behaviors and surrounded environments. Some applied examples are activity measurement by accelerometer, ambient sound environment by microphone, and also the estimation of time and location a user spends indoors and outdoors by GPS. In addition, external sensors, such as biomedical sensors (e.g., ECG, BVP, GSR, and EMG*), can also be deployed with a wearable strap on human bodies. Hence, more than one sensor (multiple sensory system) would be available in ubiquitous sensing for health. Information obtained from different sensors can be cross-linked and presented as a new valuable input. For instance, GPS and accelerometer actualize geographic information systems (GIS) with potentially providing insight into how the proximity of recreational facilities affects physical activity levels or how the relative accessibility of grocery stores and fast-food restaurants influences a diet program. Wi-Fi can be leveraged to determine the relative proximity of individuals to each other or fixed locations; it could be used for a study to examine the spread of an infectious disease. Bluetooth, as well as ZigBee, can also be used for ambulatory data collection of more traditional signals, such as blood pressure, heart rate (HR), respiration, and blood glucose level.

In this section, context-aware applications are categorized in terms of the application design field that they intend to make an impact of. The categorization, as shown in Figure 1.7, introduces different application fields that researchers have been studying extensively.

1.3.1 Health Care and Well-Being Based

Previously, the use of mobile devices within the context of ubiquitous sensing has been successfully integrated in zoology and veterinary medicine to study the feeding habits and social behaviors of some types of animals from zebra to whales, and the adaptation of this technology to human health has also been paid attention recently.

With the advancement and increasing deployment of microsensors and low-power wireless communication technologies within the personal/body area network (PAN/BAN), the studies conducted under ubiquitous computing have grown interest in health-care domain. Besides the high demands for applying and understanding human activity recognition (HAR)–based systems, the integration of monitoring and analyzing vital sign data (e.g., HR, blood sugar level and pressure level, respiration rate, and skin temperature) through sensors also more likely enables to change assessment, treatment, and diagnostic methodologies in health-care domain

---

* Electrocardiography (ECG), blood volume pulse (BVP), galvanic skin response (GSR), and electromyography (EMG).

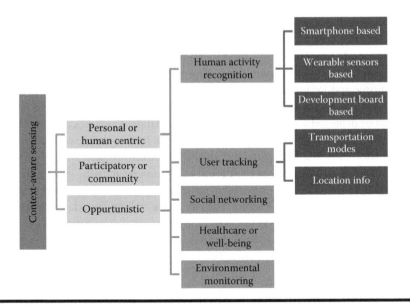

Figure 1.7 The categories of context-aware sensing.

since the traditional methodologies have been based on self-reports, clinic visits, and regular doctor inspections [153].

The sensor-enabled autonomous mobile devices can help caretakers continuously monitor patients, record their well-being process, and report any acute situation when abnormal behavior is detected. Thereby, it would be more easier and efficient to monitor and manage the lifestyle and well-being of the patients with chronic diseases, the elderly people, the rehab patients, the patients dealing with the obesity, the patients with cognitive disorders, and children and even more significantly to monitor and rescue the emergent vitals and status notifying soldiers in the combat zone.

The home-based health-care monitoring by mobile-based devices is defined under smart home applications. The studies in [53,71,203] are carried out to create a smart home environment for treatment procedures of patients (e.g., having cardiac problem [103] or diabetics) based on collecting data through different wearable physiological sensors (e.g., body temperature, HR, blood pressure, blood oxygen values, respiration level, and ECGs) and also reporting feedbacks remotely to the health-care givers. Wearable sensors (including accelerometers, HR monitors, and many others) have also been studied in [3,137,160,185] in order to recognize activity patterns in order for measuring fitness level, discovering frequentness of body movement against obesity and weight loss programs [136], diagnosing insidious diseases [108] (e.g., hypotension), and understanding emotional states [113,166] (e.g., stress level). Besides, smartphones can be used as a reminding system [53] for aging-related cognitive disorders such as Alzheimer's treatment. Also, as studied in a well-known example, UbiFit [50], smartphones can capture user-relevant physical activity level and correspond the obtained information to personal fitness goals by presenting feedback reports to the user.

There are many commercial products available at the market to give ubiquitous computing solutions in the health-care domain. These products are mostly focused on assisting people in controlling dietary programs/weight management, discovering fitness level, measuring burnt calorie or energy level, counting step numbers, and recognizing activities. Philips Directlife, FitBit Zip, and BodyMedia GoWear are some device examples produced for tracking activity patterns, counting steps, measuring calories burnt, and calculating distance traveled. In addition, Impact Sports ePulse proposes heart pulse monitoring system. Many other products can also be found for measuring heat flux, galvanic skin response, and skin temperature.

1.3.2 Human Activity Recognition Based

Recognizing human-centric activities and behaviors has been an important topic in pervasive mobile computing. HAR intends to observe human-related actions in order to obtain an understanding of what type of activities/routines that individuals perform within a time interval. By providing accurate information about HAR relevant data history could assist individuals in having better well-being, fitness level, and situational awareness [25,114,228]. For example, patients with diabetes, obesity, or heart disease are suggested to follow a predefined fitness program as part of their treatment [28,205]. In this case, information corresponding to human postures (e.g., lying, sitting, and standing) and movements (e.g., walking and running) can be inferred by an HAR system in order to provide useful feedbacks to the caregiver about a patient's behavior analysis. In addition, with external sensor devices, for example, HR monitor, attached, patients with abnormal heartbeats can be tracked easily and notified to caregivers in case of emergency in order to prevent undesirable consequences [130]. In practical, HAR has only interest in single-person activity detection; however, it can be extended to multiple-person recognition, which is called activity of daily living (ADL). ADL is a way to describe the functional status of a person, and his/her interaction with others. Hence, ADL becomes an essential part of community sensing especially for community health-care concerns (e.g., finding stress level in a group of people [44]).

Studies for HAR, as shown in Table 1.7, can be divided into subcategories based on the platform that a context-aware system is built on:

- *Smartphone based*: Activity recognition basically concerns about human beings and/or their surrounding environment. The constant monitoring of activity recognition was carried out by deployment of cameras with high-cost or personal companion devices with no easy use. In addition, the aggregation

Table 1.7   HAR in Mobile Devices

Platform	Reference	Sensors
Smartphone	[24,92,96,202,208]	ACC
	[164]	MIC
	[187]	ACC, GPS
	[176]	ACC, MIC, BT
	[22,174]	WiFi, GPS
	[140]	ACC, MIC, GPS
	[147,149,221]	ACC, MIC, WiFi, GPS
Wearable devices	[16,93,238,244]	ACC
	[173]	ACC, proximity
	[211]	ACC, HR
	[68,109]	ACC, BT
Mobile development boards	[43,93,128,180]	ACC
	[92]	ACC, BT
	[116,145,201]	ACC, temperature, light
	[68,132]	ACC, MIC, compass, temperature, light

Note: ACC, accelerometer; BT, bluetooth; MIC, microphone; HR, heart rate monitor.

of monitored data was very complicated and impractical. However, since mobile devices are carried by people throughout the day, it makes them appear to be an ideal platform for human-centric sensing. Especially, the accelerometer sensor, which can return a real-time measurement of acceleration through all coordinate spaces, is commonly used for HAR. It is employed either as a pedometer to measure step counts and calorie consumption or as a monitor to recognize the user's physical activities such as postures and movements. Most measured events/actions/attributes are related to human posture or movement (e.g., using accelerometers or GPS/Wi-Fi/Cell Tower), environmental variables (e.g., using temperature and humidity sensors, microphone, and cameras), or physiological signals (e.g., attachment of external devices such as HR or electrocardiogram and finger pulse). In this aspect, many studies [208] propose to use smartphones to monitor users' daily physical activities according to their lifestyle.

■ *Wearable sensors based*: Wearable sensors, that is, multiple-sensor multiple-position solutions, have been put forward to recognize complex activities and gestures within the HAR concept. It basically introduces multiple-sensor placement on multiple location of human body to well capture some specific target activities (e.g., brushing teeth and arm and wrist movements while folding laundry) that a smartphone cannot detect by itself. With the use of wearable sensors, sensory context is extracted from miniature sensors integrated into garments, accessories, or straps. Especially, traditional accelerometer-based HAR solutions cannot provide recognition at finer granularities for the differentiation of some postures such as sitting and lying down since there are some drawbacks observed such as misadjustment of device orientation and position or an insufficient number of sensors to have enough spatial information. Hence, wearable sensors with the utilization of heterogeneous sensor deployment have been an active research area to respond to a growing demand for HAR systems in the health-care domain, especially elder care support, assisting cognitive disorders, and fitness/well-being management [16,128,173,211].

Heterogeneous sensors are connected to each other with wired/wireless communication (mostly Bluetooth). Smartphones can be used as a center position for external sensor attachments. Proximity sensors determine the distance between sensor nodes (i.e., topology of sensor placement) by measuring the received signal strength indication (RSSI) of radio frequency in dBm. On the other hand, the deployment of heterogeneous sensors entail high cost as well as bringing computational constraints since it requires intensive supervised classification algorithms. These algorithms are mostly carried out in off-line analysis, which also makes the solution impractical. The constraints may also stem from sensor degradation, interconnection failures, and jitter in the sensor placement. Hence, the reduction of sensor dimension is highly important for node interconnection and making the system stay unobtrusive.

■ *Embedded platform based*: In an HAR-based system, higher classification accuracy is always desired. Especially, this implies a large number of sensor placements over the body in wearable sensor-based applications. Variations in sensors and center device placements must let the system act robust to diverse feature extractions and set specific classification models to make a context differentiation in any condition. Compared with multiple-sensor multiple-position solutions, creating a development platform consisting of multiple sensors could be a more practical way for HAR-based applications since attaching sensors on specific body locations could return in similar reflection of feature signal characteristics on different activities, and it could lack of distinguishing diverse contexts. Therefore, like using smartphones, researchers have been studying mounting one-board-based embedded hardware platforms with a predefined device position and orientation in order to investigate the effect of sensor placement on activity recognition performance and make a better differentiation in context by fusing multiple sensor information with a priori experiment setups and unchanging conditions of training contextual data.

1.3.3 Transportation and Location Based

Location-based sensing [59] aims at tracking people over a period of time by recognizing their activities in terms of specifying transportation modes (e.g., walking, running, and biking when the user is outside). Especially, since GPS receivers have been an integral hardware component in smartphones, data collected by GPS become handy to be used for network-connected applications. Thereby, GPS is employed as an instrument for location-based sensing to inspect the habits and general behaviors of individuals and communities [135,233,241].

The localization is inferred with the help of GPS, which delivers speed and location information as well as a large amount of a priori data (e.g., street maps). GPS provides 2D data by setting a resolution value (e.g., generally 10 m) at a certain distance within two successive data points (i.e., unit difference). Hence, consecutive GPS readings are grouped based on their spatial relationships to create distinctive segmentations among GPS traces. Then, GPS traces are associated with available street maps, which are represented as directed graphs where an edge represents a street and a vertex represents the intersection of streets.

GPS cannot penetrate through walls, and therefore, the received data get degraded. Thus, the usage of GPS for location-based sensing is valid for outdoors. Once GPS times out because of the loss of satellite signals, Wi-Fi scan can be performed for indoors by checking for surrounding wireless access points. Wi-Fi could be used for outdoors either since it covers a range of 20–30 m as radius. Indeed, smartphones apply a hybrid localization scheme by using GPS with network-based triangulation by leveraging wireless access points for achieving coarse positioning [121]. The network-based triangulation collects information from RF signal beacons around reachable wireless cell towers or Wi-Fi access points or even Bluetooth (which is not effective but could be used indoor in the presence of multiple users around), and then it uses the received RF signal strength to measure the relative distance through the physics of signal propagation among network nodes (e.g., utilization of local and mobile base stations). Hence, by measuring sequential RSSI data, the transportation modes for users can be identified. In addition, during the Wi-Fi scan, MAC address (i.e., BSSID) of wireless access points might have already been tagged as a point of interest, which yields to retrieve automatically that user is in a familiar environment (e.g., office, home, and gym). Although GPS could detect some postures such as sitting or standing, the accelerometer sensor is rather used for such static activities as GPS may not provide a concise solution for the differentiation of user state classes at a similar speed. Besides, the efficiency in power consumptions would be increased in cases where the accelerometer sensor is used.

The investigation of mobility patterns to extract places and activities from GPS traces is generally implemented in a hierarchical structure [14,135,241]. According to the structure, the lower level begins with the association of GPS traces with street maps, and the structure rises up by inferring activity sequences; and eventually, the structure ends up with discovering significant places from activity pattern with the help of spent time within each activity. By taking a log of recent history of transportation modes belonging to individuals throughout their daily activities as well as mapping their location history, a general physical activity report can be documented and also the goals of future activity plan can be reconfigured for the purpose of health and fitness monitoring. For instance, from physiological perspective, driving behaviors are investigated in [126] by taking trip destinations, trip times, and driving efficiency into consideration.

By actuating community sensing, it could be possible to monitor highways for real-time traffic conditions, to forecast probabilistic traffic congestions, and to reroute the traffic flow [14,99,151,212]. This scenario can also be applied to biking [65,184]: bikers can share their routes to give participation level away to infer noisiness of the bike trails and also to take ride statistics for fitness documentation. Besides, most significantly, crowdedness level of metropolitan areas can be investigated in terms of daily visitor density [6,106]. Meanwhile, the existence of multiple users in a specific area could also help to track and notify air pollution level for environmental monitoring.

1.3.4 Social Networking Based

The ubiquity of Internet usage has enabled people to exchange innumerable different forms of information at a global scale. This has led to explosive growth in the creation of social network platforms (e.g., Facebook and Twitter), where people can describe and share their personal interests, preferences, and information. With the emergence of smartphones equipped with sophisticated sensors, the integration of smartphones and social networks has leveraged data collection capability resulted in the birth of exciting context-aware applications as well as the evolution of the IoT. However, the question of how the inference of a human-relevant context can be incorporated into social network platforms in an autonomous way is still the most exciting research topic. In this sense, researchers have been trying to create context-aware systems where diverse and large data streams (e.g., image, video, user location, and user transportation mode) are automatically sensed and logically fused together for social interaction of individuals or groups of people, which is sometimes called *crowdsensing* or *crowdsourcing*. CenceMe [148] is the foremost study that enables to infer user-relevant activities, dispositions, habits, and surroundings and then to incorporate this information into social network platforms. The fusing of social, sensor, and software (virtual) data for context-aware computing is also studied in [20]. A detailed study of the current state and future challenges of the crowdsensing is given in [40,80]. In addition, some exciting futuristic project ideas can be obtained through *www.funf.org.*

On the other hand, privacy, security, and resource considerations unfortunately limit the expansion of community-based sensing applications since cyberstalking [199] by tracing the revealed user information could harm mobile users economically, physically, and legally. In the absence of relevant concerns, some websites/applications such as [214] can be used for reducing the risks of community sensing.

1.3.5 Environmental Based

Environmental monitoring, on one hand, aims at sensing and collecting information about the surrounding environment by basically providing a personalized environmental scorecards at the human level; on the other hand, it creates an impact toward environmental exposure by contributing environmental solutions at the community level. The surrounding environment is either a small area (e.g., indoor) or a large one (e.g., outdoor). For indoor environments, applications to monitor heat and air conditioning systems and building maintenance can be considered [85,169]. For instance, one can use a smartphone to measure the temperature inside a room, and then smartphones can adjust heater or ventilator automatically to change air balance in a smart home environment. Moreover, it would be more reasonable to apply environmental monitoring in the context of community sensing. The studies in [2,77,79,101,105,154,157] provide applications for environmental monitoring to track and notify the hazard exposure such as carbon emission level, air pollution, waste accumulation, and water intoxication level. In addition, noise pollution and ambience fingerprinting (fusion of sound, light, and color) are other topics that have been studied in this content [11,142].

1.4 Challenges and Future Trends

Mobile, smart devices supporting emerging pervasive applications will constitute a significant part of future mobile technologies by providing highly proactive services requiring continuous monitoring of user-related contexts. However, a major challenge standing up to these sensor-rich smart devices is the limited computational, storage, and energy resources. Table 1.8 summarizes forthcoming challenges in the design process of context awareness in mobile sensing.

In the following, we identify some interesting research opportunities for future context-aware development.

1.4.1 Energy Awareness

Because mobile devices operate on a finite supply of energy contained in their batteries, energy awareness is one of the key resource management issues in mobile

Table 1.8 Awaiting Challenges in Design of Context Awareness in Mobile Sensing

Research Area	*Challenges*	
Energy awareness	■ Creation of energy profiles ■ Radio optimization ■ Energy-efficient routing ■ Battery characterization	■ Energy estimation ■ Data reduction ■ Sensing scheduling
Sensing management	■ Dynamic sensor selection ■ Opportunistic workload division	■ Adaptive sampling ■ Optimal sensing
Battery behavior	■ Nonlinearity ■ Effects of usage patterns	■ Estimation of energy delivery ■ Battery discharge profiles
Data acquisition	■ Data calibration ■ Distortion, noise	■ Orientation change in device ■ Device placement
Context inference	■ Learning paradigm ■ Online processing	■ Computational complexity ■ Redundancy check
Framework design	■ Generalization ■ Adaptability ■ Estimation/prediction ■ Robust processing	■ Inhomogeneous physical world ■ Trade-off handling ■ Time-variant sensing ■ Optimization in sensor sensing
Middleware design	■ Collection of async. heterogeneous context ■ Interoperability ■ Creation of an abstract layer ■ Generic infrastructure, standardization ■ Fault tolerance	■ Full transparency ■ Scalability ■ Decentralization ■ Dynamic adaption, auto/self-configuration ■ Smartness

(Continued)

Table 1.8 *(Continued)* **Awaiting Challenges in Design of Context Awareness in Mobile Sensing**

Research Area	Challenges	
Mobile cloud	■ Transparently partitioning data, off-loading ■ Adaptability, self-awareness ■ Scalability ■ Frequent network disconnections ■ Augmentation process	■ Reconfigurability ■ Resource scarcity ■ Mobility ■ Fault tolerance ■ Resource optimization, intercontext relations
General	■ Limited power, bandwidth, and storage ■ Complex device architectures	■ Richness in context sources ■ Security, privacy, and trust issues

sensing. Specifically, continuously capturing user context through sensors imposes heavy workload in physical and computational capacity aspects of the device working process, and it drains the battery power rapidly.

To understand this issue better, an application example [168] can be examined. Accordingly, the accelerometer sensor built-in HTC Touch Pro is employed at a fixed sampling frequency. When the phone samples the accelerometer, overall power consumption on device increases by 370 mW, whereas according to the data sheet of the accelerometer, it should consume less than 1 mW when active. Even if the accelerometer itself wastes very little power to operate its functionality, the phone with its main processor and other hardware components causes much more power consumption during the operation to accomplish a contextual sensory data extraction. Another example provided in [37] reports that today's smart devices are not durable to employ all sensors at the same time by giving an example of Samsung Galaxy SIII smartphone with a fully charged battery. It is experimentally examined that the smartphone consumes 805 mW in idle mode, whereas the same device consumes extra 573 mW power employing GPS connectivity. The experiment shows that constant sensor usage reduces battery life by half. Given examples conclude that any sensor employment in mobile devices draws more current from the device's battery than during a regular device use. Therefore, the mobile device's battery will not last a long time to support service.

Energy awareness can be integrated by creating energy profiles and energy estimation to present maps of power usage, allowing the analysis of power draining caused by physical sensor hardware, computations in coding, and transmission of data. Using this analysis and having more statistics on behavioral characterization of mobile device infrastructure, context-aware applications can benefit more efficient process environment.

On the other hand, increasing usage of mobile device application features along with network connectivity all the time will force the need for enhancing energy efficiency. Especially, energy cost of operations in wireless networking addition to the expectations of future context-aware applications requiring more use of multimedia, image and video rendering, data compressions/decompressions, complex web service connections will be extremely high. Therefore, there are some actions needed to be taken to decrease energy consumption and to prolong battery lifetime as in the following:

- *Radio optimization* could reduce energy dissipation due to wireless communications by enhancing some radio parameters such as coding, modulation schemes, power transmission, and antenna direction.
- *Data reduction* could be a solution to reduce the amount of data to be processed or transfered. Methods such as adaptive sampling, network coding, and data compression could help remove unnecessary information in sensing task.
- *Energy-efficient routing* aims at ensuring connectivity and coverage, and exploiting redundancy in topology control protocols by dynamically adapting network settings with respect to application needs.
- *Sensing scheduling and battery characterization* are examined in detail in the following section.

1.4.2 Adaptive and Opportunistic Sensory Sampling

To address power efficiency in context awareness, efficient sensor management systems infusing low-level sensory operations need to be created. An example method could be illustrated in Figure 1.8. The first stage starts with dynamically selecting a sufficient number of sensors [116,221], called *dynamic sensor selection*, while a context-aware application is running. Thereby, sensors can be put in an order according to their power consumption level and application relevance depending on an interested context. In addition, the best energy saving algorithm would be the one that manipulates the frequentness of sensory sampling intervals. In this regard, different duty cycling approaches would be the next stage of the ladder by tuning the wave form to power a sensor for a desired power efficiency. Besides that, adaptively changing sensor sampling periods can also be the final stage to achieve a certain level of power efficiency [176]. By adjusting sampling periods in sensory operations as needed, the total number of sampling occurrences either increases or decreases. As a result, relevant power consumption will adjust accordingly.

Above all, an adaptive sensor management mechanism/system to assign a mixture pair of duty cycles and sampling periods simultaneously would be a cure of

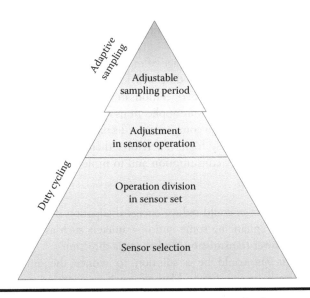

Figure 1.8 A power-efficient sensor management system for future context-aware applications.

consuming less power while running context-aware applications accurately enough [235]. However, intervening sensory operations to achieve power efficiency may jeopardize the accuracy of context-aware services, and thereby, it creates a trade-off between power consumption caused and accuracy provided by these services.

In this sense, optimization of physical sensor hardware operations during data acquisition needs to be created in a collective way by employing a sufficient number of sensor sets to characterize contextual information, creating work division among chosen sensors, scheduling time-variant duty cycles, and setting adaptively changing sampling periods.

1.4.3 Modeling the Smart Device Battery Behavior for Energy Optimizations

The use of smart devices is constrained by limited battery. The slow growth in energy densities of battery technologies compared with the increasing computing power requirement and hardware capabilities is now driving the need for accurately modeling power consumption profiles. To do this, we need to explicitly consider the impact of different usage patterns and its relationship with the projected effect on power consumption. The modeling of battery's nonlinearities [48,182] and understanding the correlation between usage patterns and battery depletion will lead to successful discovery of optimal energy reduction strategies that will eventually help maximize the wasted energy consumption to improve the QoS of context-aware applications.

In this regard, the topics such as the extension of battery lifetimes, estimation of energy delivery or battery discharge, and optimal energy management have drawn much research interest in mobile computing. The examination of nonlinear battery behaviors becomes crucial in terms of creating optimal sensor management systems. Correspondingly, battery lifetime mostly depends on energy consumption rate, discharge profile, that is, usage pattern, and battery nonlinearities. At high energy consumption rate, the effective residual battery capacity degrades and results in having a shorter battery lifetime. However, any precautionary change in the usage pattern could extend the battery lifetime. More importantly, physical nonlinearities in the batteries could recover the lost capacity while energy consumption decreases.

The future research should investigate mobile device–based battery behavior with respect to variant sensory operations in smart devices. Thereby, the linkage between battery discharge and power consumption caused by the sensors can be analyzed, and most importantly, a fine power efficiency can be objected to achieve while satisfying the continuity of mobile device–based context-aware services.

1.4.4 Data Calibration and Robustness

A constant sensor displacement in a motion-based activity recognition system is a serious disadvantage that causes a decrease in application accuracy. More significantly, a change in orientation of the mobile device, such as rotation, is an important design drawback for the most of the classification algorithms, especially for those that solely rely on exploiting feature vectors through specific axis information. In case where the sensor is not placed fixed, suppose an accelerometer is used in an HAR based application, it would produce some distortion over acceleration axises. The upward or downward position change of the device causes x-axis flipped to y-axis or vice versa. Therefore, an adaptive context inference scheme needs to be employed to detect the sensor position or orientation in order to satisfy the robustness toward various practical usage conditions. This scheme also should select the most relevant context inference strategy dynamically. In addition, orientation-independent features should be considered during the context inference process. Finally, to be able to obtain correct sensing samplings and later context inference, a calibration and normalization process needs to be applied on sensory sampling operations by setting proper sampling offsets and scaling factors.

1.4.5 Efficient Context Inference Algorithms

Besides the power consumption and battery density considerations, the analysis and inference process of contextual sensory data has many drawbacks. Many studies can be found in which a framework is proposed to capture and evaluate sensory data. Most studies rely on the recognition of user activities and definition of common user behaviors. The applied methods in relevant studies are based on using statistical models, predefined feature extraction, and classification algorithms. However, none of these studies engage themselves to model a common framework in order to construct a base structure for future context-aware applications. They would rather have canalized solutions to solve their own unique applications instead of a generalized approach. Therefore, these studies mostly focus on a specific sensor to discover possible target applications in order to exploit the contextual data.

Another important system attribute to consider is to prevent the use of supervised learning strategy. Most systems take predefined models or classifiers where training data are obtained through several repetitions of a similar experiment setup. However, it yields to have a large amount of data in return to process and makes the subsequent analysis to be carried out off-line. Especially, obtaining training data classes to feed statistical models, classification or machine-learning algorithms in a supervised learning strategy is an expensive real-time operation for smart devices, and it is impractical when considering the computational manner, that is, acquisition and analysis of data, resource management by storing training samples, scalability problem by labeling data, and bandwidth problem by exchanging a large amount of information. Therefore, the utilization of sensors must be lightweight and unobtrusive, and also the applied classification/clustering and machine-learning algorithms must be applied without computationally expensive, human-intervening off-line methods. For example, future studies should provide a lightweight, unsupervised, and online classification method while detecting user context by collecting data from smartphone sensors. The required solutions should apply a sufficient number of signal processing and statistical techniques (*light weightiness*) without receiving any a priori information related to user state classes and setting any predefined/fixed thresholds over any sensor signal (*unsupervised learning*) in order to differentiate user activities. As a result, a similar type of implementation mentality needs to be applied to context-aware applications in order to meet requirements set by resource-constrained mobile platforms.

1.4.6 Generic Context-Aware Framework Designs

A generic framework that fulfills requirements set by all types of context-aware applications has not yet been clearly identified. The problem often comes from the difficulty in building a reliable data set to represent a specific context interest, since the obtained sensory data can vary significantly under different circumstances (e.g., human speech with a variant background noise or placement of the mobile device). As a result, classifiers would not be practical toward varying sensing conditions, and eventually it would perform poorly. Hence, the adaptation becomes an important system attribute to consider. This issue even turns into a severe problem in case of resulting in different inference assumptions by multiple co-located mobile devices on a similar sensing event where a participatory sensing application takes place. One solution is to take advantage of cloud computing technologies, enabling to share information and ensemble situational resources among co-located mobile devices.

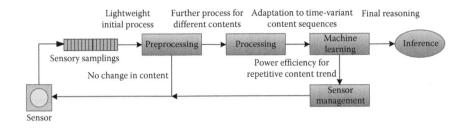

Figure 1.9 **The futuristic context-aware framework designs seek to find a fine balance between power efficiency and application accuracy, to manage adaptability to time-variant user preferences and behaviors, and apply lesser computational processing workload.**

A futuristic context-aware framework design, as illustrated in Figure 1.9, must provide a generic solution that aims at achieving a fine balance between power efficiency and application accuracy. Accordingly, the framework initially acquires sensory observations and makes them undergone into a preprocessing structure. This structure basically filters out the required information from raw sensory data and applies basic signal processing so that it may help decrease redundant computational operations by not letting go further processing in the case where there is not much change in desired context in the sensory data. Processing structure is reserved for context inference. A required context inference algorithm could differ according to the interested context through a specific sensor. Machine learning is applied later to obtain a better realization in context awareness in order to create adaptability to time-variant user preferences and behaviors, estimate missing context inferences in the presence of idle sensory operations, and also preserve the functionality against aperiodically received sensory observations. Most importantly, machine-learning structure regulates sensor management by estimating user preference trends, and opportunistically finding out stable moments. Thereby, sensor management structure could use this information to figure optimal sensing policies, and change sensor sampling settings so as to power efficiency could be achieved while satisfying the accuracy of context-aware application services.

1.4.7 Standard Context-Aware Middleware Solutions

A standard contex-aware middleware needs to cover all types of application settings, provide an adaptation toward changing context, and acquire a collection of asynchronous heterogeneous contexts to create different abstract entities. It also needs to succeed to have a full transparency, which eliminates direct involvement of an application in context modeling process. In this direction, gathering diverse and asynchronous information and presenting it to the application would be the future work in mobile computing middleware research.

Futuristic context-aware middleware also must deal with

- *Interoperability* challenge that expects to collaborate among heterogeneous context providing devices.
- An increasing number of context providers, for example, today's built-in sensors or future intelligent products, which bring about *scalability* problem. This results in many devices interacting in a small space. Therefore, efficient information management and exchange are required.
- Creation of an *abstraction layer*, not a centralized coordination, because context-aware middleware handles operations through various levels of heterogeneous input and output hardware devices, software interfaces and protocols, data streams, and transfer. A central entity cannot guarantee managing all various system-level activities, especially while having spontaneous interoperation and decoupled coordination among connecting devices.
- *Generic infrastructure* where any context resources can be manageable and sudden interactions of context providers are handled, such as plug and play of physical sensors.
- *Standardization* for different types of domains and applications to address common requirements. This might be impossible to have, but at least standardization needs to be specified for a certain domain.
- *Dynamic adaptation* and *autoconfiguration* support to context changes or context lost due to the underlying network is transient and fragile to have disconnections, as well as due to physical hardware that frequently join and leave context inference process.
- *Fault tolerance* that determines the reliability and safety of ongoing processes. It is triggered by incomplete, interrupted, or delayed tasks, for example, a sensor operation to infer a context.
- *Smartness* that helps act as an autonomous and intelligent delegate by being robust to mobility and context prediction while reasoning context.

1.4.8 Mobile Cloud Computing

Cloud computing, that is, on-demand computing, refers to the applications delivered as services through the Internet, and the aggregation of computing as a utility together with the required hardware and software provides those services [9]. Enabling cloud computing within resource constraint mobile devices along with context-aware sensing has led to the creation of a new paradigm called mobile cloud computing. Thereby, it is intended that computationally expensive and more resource-demanding jobs are transparently partitioned and off-loaded to the cloud in order to remove the obstacle that mobile devices encounter in terms of limited battery and processing power, limited connectivity, and low memory storage. In addition, another significant merit in the creation of a mobile cloud is that mobile devices themselves are not only contextual resource providers to the cloud but also could connect a mobile peer-to-peer network by collecting resources of the various providers in a local vicinity. The idea of building a shared pool of configurable computing resources benefits from provisioned services with a minimal management effort and redeeming the disadvantages of having limited connectivity to remote servers and limited power to burst long-range communications.

Despite increasing trend toward mobile cloud computing, there are certain requirements such as adaptability, resource scarcity, scalability, mobility, frequent network disconnections, and self-awareness need to be met. Therefore, a mobile computing cloud has to be aware of resource scarcity, availability, and quality of its service to enable diverse mobile computing entities located in an efficient scale by considering some aspects of mobility, low connectivity, and finite power source, and finally dynamically engage with these entities depending on their requirements and workloads. In addition, fault tolerance becomes very important due to mobility and its effects on network signal losses. Most importantly, adaptability while employing mobile cloud–based computing resource is not an easy task. Especially, augmentation process [4] and optimum selection of resource types stand as a big challenge to enhance and optimize computing capabilities of mobile devices that perform context-aware applications on a resource constraint platform.

1.4.9 Security, Privacy, and Trust

Autonomous operation of real-life-related ubiquitous objects creates a huge potential to interfere people's trust, security, and privacy. Especially, context-aware-based applications could give a feeling that users are being monitored all the time. This type of surveillance needs to be addressed as one of main functions during the design process of context-aware middleware to manage and protect security and confidentiality. Together with the deployment of IoT and mobile cloud, the scale of interactions, complexity, mobility, and heterogeneity will grow drastically, which make the cloud of things hard to be controlled and open to security threats such as application-, web-, network-based or physical attacks. For this purpose, innovative encryption, cryptography, and enforcement on data stream access control technologies need to be used for securing off-loading data management and exchange. However, this will necessitate utilizing computational expensive and energy harvesting algorithms. On the other hand, for privacy protection, perception of the general public is still immature. Since mobile environments are dynamic and unpredictable, it is important for mobile users to have transparency and choices in order to control their personal information and also to have knowledge of data collection being operated by authorized services by authorized service providers. Moreover, privacy-preserving context-aware technologies are still an open subject for resource-restricted devices on identifying what measures that privacy is secured. In this sense, the issue with contextual data ownership in a collaborative cloud networks along with data anonymity suffers from privacy of user and needs to establish trust and authentication. Trust can be established only if security policies are modeled to regulate the access to resources and credentials.

In summary, this chapter provides an overview of the context awareness in ubiquitous/mobile sensing. It provides a comprehensive introduction to the definition, representation, and inference of context. It also points out the importance of a context-aware middleware design and the challenges faced during design process and system integration. Moreover, the chapter categorizes and gives an inside-out look into context-aware applications depending on the interested context and identifies opportunities in this research area. Looking into the future, we tend to believe that with the evolution of smartphones, software developers have empowered to create context-aware applications for recognizing human-centric or community-based innovative social and cognitive activities in any situation and at any location. This leads to the exciting vision of forming a society of *IoT*. With the highlights of this chapter, we intend to enlighten future directions to enhance the existing trade-offs and drawbacks in mobile sensing while context is being inferred under the intrinsic constraints of mobile devices and around the emerging concepts in context-aware framework technologies.

Chapter 2

Context Inference: Posture Detection

The understanding of human activity is based on the discovery of the activity pattern and accurate recognition of the activity itself. Therefore, researchers have focused on implementing pervasive computing systems to infer activities from unknown activity patterns, which are defined as the extracted context by mobile device–based sensors. The evolution of ubiquitous sensing has enabled smartphones to be repurposed in order to recognize daily-occurring human-based actions, activities, and interactions that mobile device users encounter with the surrounding environment. It is believed that recognizing human-related event patterns, called user states in this chapter, accurately enough could give a better understanding of human behaviors. Therefore, recognizing human-centric activities and behaviors has been an important topic in pervasive mobile computing. Human activity recognition (HAR) [42] intends to observe human-related actions in order to obtain an understanding of what type of activities/routines that individuals perform within a time interval. Providing accurate information about HAR-relevant data history could assist individuals to enhance the quality of life such as having better well-being, fitness level, and situational awareness [25,114]. For example, patients with diabetes, obesity, or heart disease are suggested to follow a predefined fitness program as part of their treatment [205]. In this case, information corresponding to human postures and movements can be inferred by HAR system in order for providing useful feedback to the caregiver about a patient's behavior analysis.

2.1 Discussions

Many studies have been conducted to detect user-centric postural actions within the concept of HAR [34,43,73,109,110,173,183] using accelerometers, Wi-Fi, GPS, or other smartphone sensors. In this chapter, we only study the smartphone accelerometer in an HAR-based analysis, which makes the analysis more challenging due to lack of data fusion of multiple sensors and also due to difficulty in data calibration rooted from signal distortion caused by frequent changes in smartphone orientation.

A statistical tool–based classification, mostly using hidden Markov models (HMMs) [120,198,243] or using AutoRegressive (AR) models [93], is one of the foremost methods to detect user-related physical activities by exploiting the context obtained via wearable or built-in mobile device sensors. However, these studies mostly apply predefined and user-manipulated system parameter settings, such as pretrained state transition matrix in HMMs or filtering coefficients in ARs, which is not suitable for online processing due to the increasing computational workload while enlarging data size. Also, fixed system parameters do not provide robustness in adaptability to time-variant nature of user activity behaviors.

On the other hand, other studies rely on creating feature vectors as the first step to exploit signal characteristics of sensory data. A feature vector consists of many signal processing functions starting from mean, standard deviation, correlation to frequency and wavelet transform models [68,128,162,211]. Then, the studies attempt to classify feature vectors according to predefined specific data classes. Accordingly, after creating a high-dimensional feature vector, pattern recognition algorithms are applied to find out the hidden context inside the feature vector. The major drawback of these algorithms stems from an *off-line* decision process, which is carried out as follows: First, all sensory observations are recorded; second, feature vectors are constructed by partitioning data records with a predefined window length; third, the selection of default feature vector for specifying a *training* data class is *user manipulated*, which means the feature vector is extracted from a specific (e.g., visually observed) window of fully recorded data; the final step, called *testing*, is to use a template matching algorithm by mapping instantly constructed feature vectors into default feature vectors. Pattern recognition techniques for clustering diverse data classes, such as k-means [164], k-nearest neighbors (k-NN) search [202], support vector machines (SVMs) [93], are involved in this final step in order to infer the context. Unfortunately, the given clustering techniques are not efficient while processing large data clusters, and also SVMs cannot deal with multiclass classification directly. The multiclass classification problem is usually solved by the decomposition of the problem into several two-class problems [208]. Furthermore, pattern recognition toolkits such as WEKA [89] are also used to obtain off-line running classification results [231,232].

Toward this end, this chapter proposes an online solution that perfectly exploits acceleration signals within the fast decision tree (DT) classifiers without setting any predefined/fixed thresholds over any specific acceleration spaces in order to differentiate user activities. DT-based classification is used in almost every other studies, whereas our proposed classification method provides the following properties, which also make findings in this chapter differ from other studies such as [43,73,93,128,183,208] under a similar name:

- *Unsupervised learning*: no a priori information, no fixed thresholds, no initial training data classes
- *Adaptive*: robust solution to a changing orientation of the device
- *Lightweight*: efficient tree-based classification by applying sufficient signal processing toolbox: no redundant computational workload
- *Online*: instant context inference
- *Assisting*: working standalone and/or assisting other classification algorithms by creating training data classes or input matrices
- *Updating*: computational efficient update/add/delete process on training data classes

Our proposed solution also enhances some widely used supervised classification methods such as Gaussian mixture models (GMM), *k*-NN, and linear discriminant analysis (LDA) for online processing by providing training data classes *without a prior off-line process* as well as *supporting the observation analysis* defined in statistical-based tools such as HMMs. The reason is fourfold: first, the construction of a feature vector generally employs a huge number of signal processing primitives (e.g., usually including around 40 features), and these features are mostly randomly chosen without analyzing processed signal characteristics in detail, whereas our solution only offers 15 features. Second, we do not use an off-line process to specify which signal time frame belongs to which activity. Our solution recognizes activity and creates related training data classes on the fly. Third, we set the transition probability matrix in HMM analysis with equal probabilities among state transitions; however, observations collected by our solution route the evolution of HMM chain. Fourth, there are two important issues in mobile online processing. One is less complexity in computations to have energy efficiency, and the other one is being adaptive to heterogeneous sensor readings. Therefore, whenever our solution predicts a high accuracy in activity recognition, it updates training data classes, which will allow us to collect dynamic information of activity patterns. Also, we use computationally efficient algorithms to update existing training data classes instead of regenerating them over and over.

2.2 Proposed Classification Method

The complete system architecture is given in Figure 2.1. Accordingly, a sequence of sensory data is collected by a sliding window. To be able to infer the hidden context (i.e., user states: sitting, standing, walking, and running), there are two modes suggested: standalone and assisting modes. Standalone mode uses a proposed

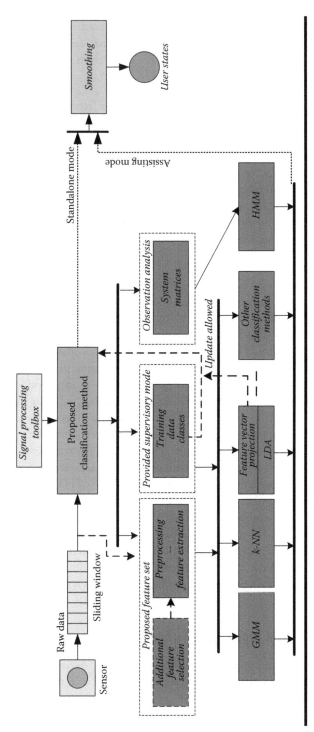

Figure 2.1 The proposed structure for lightweight, online, and unsupervised user state classification: standalone or assisting mode.

classification algorithm in this chapter. The proposed classification method provides a lightweight, online, and unsupervised context inference solution by using a sufficient number of statistical/signal processing techniques. It not only produces training data classes or system matrices to represent user states, but also decides feature selections to be used in assisting mode.

Assisting mode receives sensory data sequences as input along with having *a priori information* provided by standalone mode. The input undergoes a feature extraction process, whose functions are already defined by standalone mode, to build a corresponding feature vector. Note that additional features could be added to this process to have more accurate results, but we only use what standalone mode produces. Then, context inference is made in assisting mode by using diverse classification methods such as GMM, *k*-NN, LDA, or HMM. In addition, another powerful property provided in this mode is to be able to update data sets dynamically in a computational efficient way for online processing. The update occurs whenever standalone mode makes a solid differentiation in user states; thereby, adaptability can be achieved toward changing user behavior profiles or time-variant sensor signal characteristics.

The rest of the chapter is organized as follows: Section 2.3 describes a novel DT-based classification method designed for posture detection, which is used in standalone mode. The introduction of widely used classification methods and their integrations with the proposed classification algorithm, which is used in assisting mode, are explained in Section 2.4. This section also provides updating procedures in online processing for each classification method to achieve less computational overhead. Performance analysis among classification methods is carried out in Section 2.5. In addition, Table 2.1 summarizes important symbol notations used in this chapter.

2.3 Standalone Mode

Accelerometer sensor retrieves three-axial acceleration data $\{x, y, z\}$ at each sampling time. Sensory readings are collected by a sliding window with a length of L and an overlap value of 50%. The length of windowing is an important design merit. The shorter windowing cannot seize the activity pattern properly, whereas the wider windowing would create a latency in detections and put additional workload in computations. In addition, the overlap value is important as well to detect user state transitions in activity pattern.

The window at the current time is called active frame, and it is denoted by $f_{\{x,y,z\}}(\tau)$ where $\tau \in [t - L + 1, t]$ and t are the time indexes, and L is the total number of samples for each axis window. Hence, in the case where $L/2$ number of new samples are inserted into the active frame due to the overlapping, the proposed classification method begins to operate by receiving inputs as shown in Figure 2.2.

Table 2.1   Summary of Important Symbols Used in This Chapter

Symbol	Definition (Section Where the Symbol Is First Used)
$\{x, y, z\}$	Accelerometer sensor readings (i.e., three-axial info) (2.3)
i, j	Indexes for the accelerometer axes (2.3)
u, t	Time indexes (2.3)
L	Length of sliding window (2.3)
f	Active sliding window at current time (2.3)
f^p	Previously active sliding window (i.e., $L/2$ samples earlier) (2.3)
x	Feature vector (2.4.1)
$s, s^*, \acute{s}$	Indexes for user state classes (2.4.2)
n, m	Indexes for a data point in a class/feature vector (2.4.2)
W	Feature projection matrix (2.4.2)
y	Feature projection vector (2.4.2)
μ, m	Mean values (2.3)
σ	Standard deviation (2.3)
Λ, S	Covariance matrices (2.4.2)
A, B	Between and within class scatter matrices (2.4.2)
a, b	User state transition and observation matrices (2.4.4)
$n, \acute{n}$	The number of samples (2.4.2)

The inputs are considered as two data sets: the active frame and the previously active frame, which is denoted $f^p_{\{x,y,z\}}(\tau)$ where $\tau \in [t-3L/2+1, t-L/2]$ and superscript p represents *previous time frame*.

For the preprocessing, a noise cancellation filter, for example, an LMS filter, could be used before any signal processing technique is applied in order to reduce possible distortion over sensory readings. However, the proposed method would show that it can still produce valid results with/without the noise affect.

The applied method begins with normalizing each axis into unit power $\left(\text{e.g.,} \hat{f}_x = f_x(t) \middle/ \left(\sqrt{\sum_{\tau=t-L+1}^{t} f_x^2(\tau)}\right)\right)$ and then takes cross-correlations among acceleration axis pairs in the active frame,

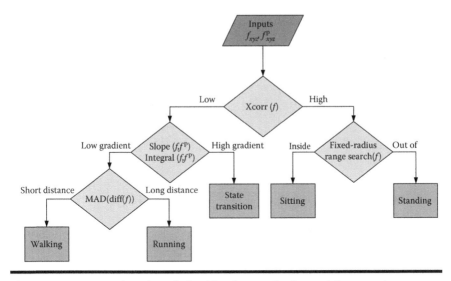

Figure 2.2   Proposed DT-based classification method: standalone mode.

$$R_{ij}(u) = \begin{cases} \sum_{\tau=0}^{L-u-1} \hat{f}_i(\tau+u)\hat{f}_j(\tau), & u \geq 0 \\ R_{ij}(-u), & u < 0, \end{cases} \qquad (2.1)$$

where u and τ time indexes, $i, j \in \{x, y, z\}$ and $i \neq j$.

If high correlations are obtained among axis pairs, $\max\{|R_{ij}|\} > \varepsilon$ where $\varepsilon \in$ [0.75, 1], user state is identified as either *sitting* or *standing*. Otherwise, it is notified that user state could be either *walking/running* or be in transition. Note that the applied method seeks the highest correlations at first for specifying a starting reference point, which also defines a *training data frame* for the corresponding user activity so that the learning from future sensory samplings will be more accurate. Generally speaking, experiments show that $|R_{xy}|$ mostly satisfies the highest correlation, whereas $|R_{xz}|$ and $|R_{yz}|$ do not. Also, the training data frame of each user activity can be updated whenever a clear classification result is obtained for the classification of the corresponding user state.

Figure 2.3 gives the information of how user states occupy the Euclidean space. According to Figure 2.3, user state *sitting* can be differentiated from other user states easily over the Euclidian space by assigning a data set of user state *sitting* as the reference point. However, the similar conclusion cannot be made that easy for user states *standing*, *walking*, and *running*. In other words, these three user states can be put in a same group in comparison with user state *sitting*.

The differentiation between *sitting* and *standing* relies on Euclidean distance analysis among three-axial accelerations. The reason is relevant data samples for these two user states are scattered distinctively over the coordinate spaces. Remember that the

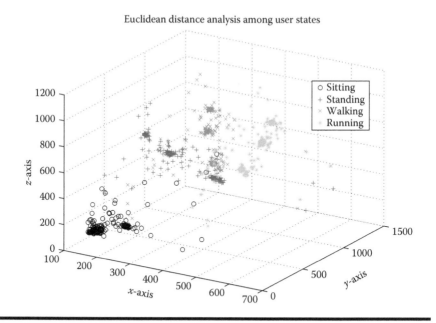

Euclidean distance analysis among user states

Figure 2.3 Euclidean distance analysis: user state *sitting* is the reference point.

Euclidean distance between two random points h and q on a coordinate space is given by $|hq| = \sqrt{(h_i - q_i)^2 + (h_j - q_j)^2}$ where $i \neq j$. Hence, pairwise Euclidean distance vectors between the active frame and the training data frame for all three-axial accelerations are calculated.

After that, a radius r is defined for the training data frame that belongs to the recent recognized user state. Since the dispersion in accelerations would be distinctive to select a proper user state, the variance values of accelerations must be taken into account in order to see how far sampling points within the training data frame are spread out from the mean. Thus, the magnitude (i.e., the norm) of a vector containing standard deviation of each axis gives out a required radius, $r = \sqrt{\sum \sigma_x^2 + \sigma_y^2 + \sigma_z^2}$. Note that the geometric mean of standard deviations could also be used for defining the radius, $r = \sqrt[3]{\sigma_x \sigma_y \sigma_z}$.

In order to identify user state *sitting* from *standing* in the presence of Euclidean distances and defined radius, a distance-based learning function is used for clustering user states. Range search algorithm (i.e., fixed-radius near neighbors [23]) is implemented for this purpose. This algorithm finds all points inside the pairwise Euclidean distance vectors within a radius r centered at the mean. By applying a brute-force approach, given the set H and a distance $r > 0$, all pairs of distinct points $h, q \in H$ such that $|hq| \leq r$ are found. In addition, the radius needs to be smoothed whenever a new radius value becomes available, especially at times when a perfect correlation is satisfied among axes. Hence, a better spreading circumference is maintained.

The points that stay in and out of radius r are considered to create a separation in relevant user state detections. However, to this end, the proposed method does not know yet which user state is *sitting* or *standing* due to the placement, that is, orientation, of the smartphone. The absolute decision will be made whenever user state *walking/running* is recognized. User state *standing* lies over almost the same signal level that user state *walking/running* does.

Note that instead of range search algorithm, SVMs could be another choice to differentiate two user states from each other by using linear discrimination. SVM denotes two *user states* as binary data *classes*. The objective is to create a hyperplane that sets a rigid margin among data classes to achieve an optimal linear distance separation. The hyperplane $w^T x + w_0$ is either $\geq$ *class*$\{+1\}$ or $<$ *class*$\{-1\}$ where w and w_0 are defined as weight and bias, respectively. The hyperplane boundary satisfies $w^T x + w_0 = 0$ for a data point x.

On the other hand, in the case where correlations observed among axis pairs by (2.1) are not sufficient, that is, $\max\{|R_{ij}|\} < \varepsilon$ where $\forall i$ and $i \neq j$, integrals of both zero-mean input frames are taken to check if both inputs are on the same signal level. Range search algorithm is applied for this purpose as well by receiving the absolute values of both integral results, $\left| \Sigma_{\tau=t-L+1}^{t} (\tau - (t - L)) \left(f_i(\tau) - \mu_{f_i} \right) \right|$ and $\left| \Sigma_{\tau=t-3L/2+1}^{t-L/2} (\tau - (t - 3L/2)) \left(f_i^p(\tau) - \mu_{f_i^p} \right) \right|$ where $i \in \{x, y, z\}$ and μ is the mean. The required radius is defined by the geometric mean of integral results belonging to f^p, $\sqrt[3]{\prod_{\forall i} \left| \Sigma_{\tau=t-3L/2+1}^{t-L/2} (\tau - (t - 3L/2)) \left(f_i^p(\tau) - \mu_{f_i^p} \right) \right|}$. Finally, if the signal levels are found similar for both inputs, user state becomes either *walking* or *running*. Otherwise, we say user state is in transition; thereby, the previous user state is taken as the current user state.

To differentiate *walking* and *running*, it would be a reasonable start to take the first-order differentiation of acceleration samples to exploit the contextual information better since these predicted user states exhibit more frequently changing variations in acceleration data. For this purpose, the first-order regression coefficient is defined by

$$\dot{f_i}(t) = \frac{\left(f_i(t+1) - f_i(t-1) \right) + 2 \left(f_i(t+2) - f_i(t-2) \right)}{2 \left(1^2 + 2^2 \right)}. \tag{2.2}$$

The given regression coefficient is mostly introduced in speech signal recognition systems [131,213] to provide temporal information about the pitches in speech signals in order for accuracy enhancement.

After taking the first-order differentiation, the next step is to extract the mean absolute deviation (MAD) of the differentiated sensory samplings so as to discern how far the points can reach out. MAD is given by

$$(\text{MAD})_i = \frac{1}{L} \sum_{\tau=t-L+1}^{t} \left| \dot{f}_i(\tau) - \dot{\mu}_i \right|, \tag{2.3}$$

where $\dot{\mu}_i$ is the mean value of the modified acceleration instance (2.2) for any axis. Then, range search algorithm is also applied onto points obtained from (2.3) to differentiate user states *walking* and *running*. When the differentiation completes, the user state that has a bigger geometric mean of all three relevant values as in (2.3) is marked as running; other one becomes *walking*.

It has been already remarked the condition in which user state could be in transition. The recognition process where an user state just goes into or exits from a transition would lead to having a false truthfulness even though the cross-correlation analysis gives the opposite results by showing high correlations. In such cases, the slope of the active frame needs to be calculated. The relevant slope information is given by

$$\Theta_i^{slope} = \arctan \left\{ \frac{\frac{4}{L}\sum_{l=3L/4+1}^{L} f_i(l) - \frac{4}{L}\sum_{l=1}^{L/4} f_i(l)}{2} \right\}, \tag{2.4}$$

that basically takes the first-order difference of the mean values residing at the last and the first 25% portions of the active frame.

According to the retrieved slope information from (2.4), low angles show that user state occurs at a same signal level, whereas high angles show that user state transits into another one. Basically, having low angles shows the evolution of the active frames still lies in the range of $\left| \mu_{f_i^p} \pm \sigma_{f_i^p} \right|$ where $\mu_{f_i^p}$ and $\sigma_{f_i^p}$ denote the mean and the standard deviation of the previously active frame, respectively. Finally, if user transition is detected, the previous user state is taken as the current user state.

In summary, Figure 2.2 organizes the user state differentiation process from the acquired contextual data and diminishes it in the scope of DT-based classification method. This algorithm initially takes the accelerometer data stored inside the sliding window. Then, it applies the cross-correlation function through pairs of coordinate axes in the sensory data to check for the data consistency among axes. If there is a high match observed, then current user state becomes either *sitting* or *standing* after utilizing either range search or SVM, analysis over the Euclidean space. On the other hand, user state could be *walking*, *running*, or in transition in the case where the inconsistency occurs after the cross-correlation checks. The differences from slope and/or integral information of two subsequent sensory data sequences expose whether user state is in transition. Low gradient in the differences reveals that the sensory data have a stable continuity on the previous signal level through axes, that is, user state is not in transition. Finally, the differentiation between *walking* and *running* is determined by the spreading factor of the first-order regression coefficients of the sensory data. Accordingly, a far distance spread within the regression coefficients indicates user state *running*, while the opposite indicates user state *walking*.

Another significant merit provided by this algorithm is that a sufficient number of functions exploited from statistical/signal processing techniques are used for user state classifications. In contrast, existing classification methods do not consider this distinction either by setting simple thresholds over a specific acceleration axis while the phone placement is fixed or by applying a large number of features to differentiate user states.

2.4 Assisting Mode

The proposed method not only provides a standalone online solution but also either assists pattern recognition–based classification methods by generating training data classes or feeds statical tool–based classification methods by delivering input system matrices. In such cases, each user state is represented by a template data class. The properties of each class are defined by signal processing functions and primitives, which is called feature extraction. After that, whenever a new data set comes in, diverse classification algorithms attempt to match, that is, map, this new data set with an existing template data class to identify the hidden user state. This process is called clustering by supervised learning that first allows learning the mixture parameters of the stochastic distribution representing a data set and then assumes that the new sample comes from a known distribution. In this section, the extraction of a feature vector is explained initially. After this, it is examined how our proposed method can assist to other existing classification methods for online processing.

2.4.1 Feature Extraction

Extracting features is an effective way to identify diverse characteristics from a given sensory data set. It also preserves class identity for each user state. In Section 2.2, features such as mean, standard deviation, cross-correlation, slope, first-order differentiation, integral, and MAD have been used. There are also many other features, such as angular velocity, cepstral coefficients, DC gain, energy, frequency-domain entropy, the highest peaks of the power spectrum density, magnitude, peak frequency, rms, variance, and so on, can be found in the literature [68,92,128,162,211]. However, the ultimate goal desired for online processing is to define the dimension of the feature vector $\{\mathbf{x}\}$ as the smallest as possible. Therefore, we plan to construct feature vectors in this section with similar signal processing techniques used while examining our proposed method. Therefore, feature vectors will be constructed as in

$$\{\mathbf{x}\} = \left[\left| \mu_{\{x,y,z\}} \right|, \sigma_{\{x,y,z\}}, \max\left\{ \left| R_{xy} \right| \right\}, \max\left\{ \left| R_{xz} \right| \right\}, \max\left\{ \left| R_{yz} \right| \right\}, \right.$$

$$\left. \Theta^{slope}_{\{x,y,z\}}, (\text{MAD})_{\{x,y,z\}} \right] \qquad (2.5)$$

with a size of $\mathcal{L} = 15$. It is important to note that the proposed method does not use every feature at a decision time. However, existing classification methods use features at every decision time, which burdens computational complexity in online processing.

2.4.2 Pattern Recognition–Based Classification

In this section, we enhance some widely used classification methods for online processing. The introduction of these methods could be seen redundant at a first sight, whereas it is prepared concisely to have a better understanding on how their inference process of given user states takes place and also how their system parameters are updated for online process, studied in Section 2.4.3. In addition, recall that the proposed method provides training data classes for these methods in the form of feature vectors.

2.4.2.1 Gaussian Mixture Model

User state classes can be individually represented in a mixture K-Gaussian model. Any feature vector can be drawn from this model to check for which user state class, that is, training data set, encapsulates it more. This is also called density/clustering problem, which is defined as follows: given a set of N points in $\mathcal{D}$ dimensions, $\mathbf{x} = \{\mathbf{x_1}, \mathbf{x_2}, \ldots, \mathbf{x_N}\} \in \mathcal{R}^{\mathcal{D}}$, find the probability density function, $f(\mathbf{x}) \in \mathcal{F}$ on $\mathcal{R}^{\mathcal{D}}$, which is most likely to have generated the given points.

The relevant GMM is given by

$$f(x; \theta) = \sum_{k=1}^{K} q(k, n) = \sum_{k=1}^{K} p_k \mathcal{N}(x_n; \mu_k, \sigma_k), \tag{2.6}$$

where $n \in N$, $k \in K$, and K-components parameters are defined as $\theta = \{\theta_1, \theta_2, \ldots, \theta_K\} = \{(p_1, \mu_1, \sigma_1), \ldots, (p_K, \mu_K, \sigma_K)\}$ and $\{p_k, \mu_k, \sigma_k\}$ are described as the mixing probability, the mean, and the standard deviation of the model, respectively, and also

$$\mathcal{N}(x_n; \mu_k, \sigma_k) = \frac{1}{(\sqrt{2\pi\sigma_k})^{\mathcal{D}}} e^{-\frac{1}{2}\left(\frac{\|x_n - \mu_k\|}{\sigma_k}\right)^2} \tag{2.7}$$

is given with the properties of $\sum_{k=1}^{K} p_k = 1$, $p_k \geq 0$.

Parameter estimation—Creating training context classes: Each user state class represents a cluster that is assigned as a Gaussian model by (2.6) with a mean approximately in the middle of the cluster and also with a standard deviation showing a measure of how far the cluster spreads out. Therefore, Gaussian parameters θ of each user state class need to be estimated.

The maximum likelihood (ML) parameters $\hat{\theta}$ are estimated iteratively using the expectation–maximization (EM) algorithm [27] in the presence of each user state class specifiying feature vector according to the following steps:

■ E step

$$p^{(l)}(k/n) = \frac{p_k^{(l)}\mathcal{N}(x_n; \mu_k^{(l)}, \sigma_k^{(l)})}{\sum_{k=1}^{K} p_k^{(l)}\mathcal{N}(x_n; \mu_k^{(l)}, \sigma_k^{(l)})}, \tag{2.8}$$

where $p(k/n) = q(k, n)/\sum_{k=1}^{K} q(k, n)$ is defined as the conditional probability of the component k given data point x_n.

■ M step

$$\mu_k^{(l+1)} = \frac{\sum_{n=1}^{N} p^{(l)}(k/n)x_n}{\sum_{n=1}^{N} p^{(l)}(k/n)},$$

$$\sigma_k^{(l+1)} = \sqrt{\left(\frac{1}{D}\right)\frac{\sum_{n=1}^{N} p^{(l)}(k/n)||x_n - \mu_k^{(l+1)}||^2}{\sum_{n=1}^{N} p^{(l)}(k/n)}},$$

$$p_k^{(l+1)} = \frac{1}{N}\sum_{n=1}^{N} p^{(l)}(k/n), \tag{2.9}$$

given initial estimates of $\left\{p_k^{(0)}, \mu_k^{(0)}, \sigma_k^{(0)}\right\}$, where l is the step index,

until the logarithmic likelihood function,

$$\lambda(x; \theta) = \sum_{n=1}^{N} \log \sum_{k=1}^{K} p_k \mathcal{N}(x_n; \mu_k, \sigma_k), \tag{2.10}$$

converges to a local maxima, which is computed by partial differentiations of λ with respect to μ_k, σ_k, and p_k, after η times iterations.

User state inference–Testing a given context class: For all user state classes, the corresponding joint probability of density function (pdf) of the mixture K-Gaussian model is finally given by

$$p(x_n|s) = \sum_{k=1}^{K} p_{sk}\mathcal{N}(x_n; \mu_{sk}, \Lambda_{sk}), \tag{2.11}$$

where $\left\{p_{sk}, \mu_{sk}, \Lambda_{sk}\right\}$ at this time denotes the weight, the mean vector, and the covariance matrix of the kth Gaussian in user state s, respectively.

In the supervised learning case, the number of classes and their parameters are known. Hence, with the help of the delivered training data classes by our proposed system, the GMM parameters are estimated through (5.16), and then (2.11) is derived. Whenever a new feature vector is constructed, the desired user state class s^* is identified by the cluster index satisfying the ML estimation,

$$s^* = \arg \max_s \{p(x_n|s)\}. \tag{2.12}$$

2.4.2.2 k-Nearest Neighbors Search

This algorithm assigns the nearest class set x^m, where $1 \leq m \leq k$, for a given input feature vector by defining a dissimilarity function that measures the nearness between training data set and new data points in the feature vector. The dissimilarity function is generally defined by the squared Euclidean distance $d(x, x^m) = (x - x^m)^T (x - x^m)$. However, the euclidean distance does not consider how the data spread out, and may let the largest length scale among data points dominate the dissimilarity function. Therefore, the Mahalanobis distance $d(x, x^m) = (x - x^m)^T \Lambda^{-1} (x - x^m)$, where Λ is the covariance matrix, could be used to rescale all length of scales to be essentially equal.

The algorithm classifies a feature vector x_n given training data x^m where

$$m^* = \arg \min_m \{d(x_n, x^m)\}, \quad 1 \leq m \leq k. \tag{2.13}$$

However, the algorithm becomes more computationally expensive as the dimension of the feature vector increases. Therefore, principle components analysis (PCA) is introduced [?] to reduce the dimension by replace $\{x\}$ with a low-dimensional projection $\{y\}$. Hence, the dissimilarity function is denoted by $d(y_n, y^m)$. However, this method may not be helpful to separate classes from each other while getting the lower dimensions. Hence, another approach called linear discriminant analysis is also introduced in [145] to reduce the dimension of feature vectors while resulting in separation among classes.

2.4.2.3 Linear Discriminant Analysis

In supervised learning method where distinctive class information is available, the dimension of a feature vector can be reduced even while continuing to obtain a solid classification analysis. A supervised linear projection is defined as $y = W^T x$ where W is the projection matrix, $\mathcal{L}$ is the dimension of y, and $\dim\{W\} = \mathcal{D} \times \mathcal{L}, \mathcal{L} < \mathcal{D}$. Recall that $\mathcal{D}$ denotes the dimension of feature vector x. Since each user state class s is defined with a Gaussian model $p(x_s) = \mathcal{N}(x_s; m_s, S_s)$, the Gaussian model along with linear projection turns into $p(y_s) = \mathcal{N}(y_s; \mu_s, \sigma_s^2)$ where $\mu_s = W^T m_s$ and $\sigma_s^2 = W^T S_s W$.

The most efficient projection matrix creates a minimal overlap among the projected distributions, which can be achieved when the projected means are maximally separated and the projected variance are not large enough. Hence, the objective equation is known via maximizing the Fisher criterion [17]:

$$\frac{(\mu_s - \mu_{\acute{s}})^2}{\pi_s \sigma_s^2 + \pi_{\acute{s}} \sigma_{\acute{s}}^2} \rightarrow \mathcal{F}(W) = \frac{W^T (m_s - m_{\acute{s}})(m_s - m_{\acute{s}})^T W}{W^T \left(\pi_s \sigma_s^2 + \pi_{\acute{s}} \sigma_{\acute{s}}^2\right)^T W} = \frac{W^T A W}{W^T B W}, \quad (2.14)$$

where π_s is the fraction of data set in class s, $s \neq \acute{s}$, $A = (m_s - m_{\acute{s}})(m_s - m_{\acute{s}})^T$, and $B = \pi_s \sigma_s^2 + \pi_{\acute{s}} \sigma_{\acute{s}}^2$.

In the case of more than one dimension and more than two classes, Fisher's projection method (2.14) is generalized by canonical variates method, which takes $p(x) = \mathcal{N}(x; \mu_s, \Lambda_s)$ and replaces it with $p(y) = \mathcal{N}(W^T x; W^T \mu_s, W^T \Lambda_s W)$. Then, the following matrices are defined:

- Between class scatter: $A = \sum_{\forall s} n_s (\mu_s - \mu)(\mu_s - \mu)^T$ where μ is the mean of all data set and n_s is the number of data points in class s.
- Within class scatter: $B = \sum_{\forall s} n_s B_s$ where $B_s = \frac{1}{n_s} \sum_{u=1}^{n_s} (x_u^s - \mu_s)(x_u^s - \mu_s)^T = \Lambda_s$.

By assuming B is invertible, the Cholesky factor $\tilde{B}$ is defined by $\tilde{B}^T \tilde{B} = B$. In addition, defining $\tilde{W} = \tilde{B}W$ yields to have $W = \tilde{B}^{-1}\tilde{W}$. Then, the latest Fisher criterion becomes

$$\mathcal{F}\left(\tilde{W}\right) = \frac{\left(\tilde{B}^{-1}\tilde{W}\right)^T A \tilde{B}^{-1}\tilde{W}}{\left(\tilde{B}^{-1}\tilde{W}\right)^T \tilde{B}^T \tilde{B} \tilde{B}^{-1}\tilde{W}} = \frac{\tilde{W}^T \tilde{B}^{-T} A \tilde{B}^{-1}\tilde{W}}{\tilde{W}^T \tilde{W}}, \quad (2.15)$$

which subjects to $\tilde{W}^T \tilde{W} = I$.

Since it is symmetric, the term $\tilde{B}^{-T} A \tilde{B}^{-1}$ in (2.15) turns into a special case of the real-valued Eigen decomposition form: QEQ^T, called Schur decomposition, where E is a diagonal matrix, which contains eigenvalues. Hence, $\tilde{W}$ is set to hold relevant eigenvectors. Finally, the projection matrix becomes

$$W = \tilde{B}^{-1}\tilde{W}. \quad (2.16)$$

To differentiate user states, the newest (i.e., lower-dimensional) form of data classes and feature vectors are modeled by (2.11) and (2.12).

2.4.3 Online Processing: Dynamic Training

For an online classification algorithm, one of the most important things is to reduce computational burden and stay away from a large amount of data manipulations.

The computational complexity requires $\mathcal{O}\left(\eta \mathcal{L} \mathcal{D}^2\right)$, $\mathcal{O}\left(\mathcal{L}^2 \mathcal{D}\right)$, and $\mathcal{O}\left((\mathcal{L}+c)^2 \mathcal{D}\right)$ times for GMM, k-NN, and LDA with Schur decomposition, respectively, where η is the number of iterations during EM algorithm in GMM and c is the total number of user state classes. In this sense, the parameters related to GMM, k-NN, and exceptionally LDA algorithms need to be dynamically updated in an efficient way rather than just computing relevant system parameters all over again in the case where either new training data samples are inserted into an existing class or a new data class is added/deleted. Especially, matrix multiplications, which take $\mathcal{O}(c \mathcal{L} \mathcal{D})$ time, need to be manipulated with ease during the update process.

Here is the suggested update for supervised classification algorithms:

■ Adding new data to an existing class i: ($\hat{n}_s$: the number of added training samples)
  − Common properties for all classification methods
    • $\hat{\mu}_s = \mu_s + \Delta_{\mu_s}$
    • $\Delta_{\mu_s} = \left(\left(\sum_{u=n_s+1}^{n_s+\hat{n}_s} x_u^s\right) - \hat{n}_s \mu_s\right) \Big/ \left(n_s + \hat{n}_s\right)$
  − Only additional for LDA
    • $\hat{\mu} = \dfrac{\left((n_s+\hat{n}_s)\mu + \sum_{\forall s}\sum_{u=n_s+1}^{n_s+\hat{n}_s} x_u^s\right)}{\left(\sum_{\forall s} n_s + \hat{n}_s\right)}$
    • $\hat{A} = \sum_{\forall s}\left(n_s + \hat{n}_s\right)\left(\hat{\mu}_s - \hat{\mu}\right)\left(\hat{\mu}_s - \hat{\mu}\right)^T$
    • $\hat{B}_s = \dfrac{1}{n_s+\hat{n}_s}\sum_{u=1}^{n_s+\hat{n}_s}\left(x_u^s - \hat{\mu}_s\right)\left(x_u^s - \hat{\mu}_s\right)^T$
    • $\hat{B} = \sum_{\forall s}\left(n_s B_s + n_s \Delta_{\mu_s}\Delta_{\mu_s}^T + \sum_{u=n_s+1}^{n_s+\hat{n}_s}\left(x_u^s - \hat{\mu}_s\right)\left(x_u^s - \hat{\mu}_s\right)^T\right)$
■ Adding/deleting a class $\{s^*\}$
  − Common properties for all classification methods
    • Create/delete $\mu_{\{s^*\}}$ and $\Lambda_{\{s^*\}}$
  − Only additional for LDA
    • $\hat{B} = B \pm n_{\{s^*\}} B_{\{s^*\}}$
    • $\hat{A} = A + n\Delta_\mu \Delta_\mu^T \pm n_{\{s^*\}}\left(\mu_{\{s^*\}} - \hat{\mu}\right)\left(\mu_{\{s^*\}} - \hat{\mu}\right)^T$
    • $\Delta_\mu = \hat{\mu} - \mu = \pm n_{\{s^*\}}\left(\mu_{\{s^*\}} - \mu\right)/\left(n \pm n_{\{s^*\}}\right)$

Note that after update process completes, only for LDA algorithm, the linear projection matrix needs to be recomputed.

2.4.4 Statistical Tool–Based Classification

HMMs are only introduced as a statistical tool–based classification in this section. HMM-based human postural behavior and activity detection is the mostly used statistical tool in HAR-objected applications. In HMMs, a system parameter called observation emission matrix is represented with the help of (2.11) by

$$b_{s,O_t} = p\left(O_t/q_t = s\right) = \sum_{k=1}^{K} p_{sk}\mathcal{N}\left(O_t; \mu_{sk}, \Lambda_{sk}\right), \qquad (2.17)$$

where s, O_t, and q_t are a user state (i.e., a data class), an instant observation (i.e., feature vector), and a user state instance in a sequence, respectively. The traditional model basically considers observations (i.e., input feature vector) Gaussian based and draws an instant feature vector from cross-relationships between observations and user states to decide the most likely inference of an instant user state. The user state inference, according to (2.12), is done by checking for Gaussian membership of observations, and it is then selected as the suitable user state outcome regulated by majority voting in the classification.

On the other hand, HMMs utilize heavy computations, Baum–Welch method (forward–backward algorithms) [224], while evolving its chain that produces user state inferences in decision epoch times. Therefore, to improve HMMs for online processing, a similar system matrix as used in (2.17) can be constructed in light of our proposed method. This matrix is given by

$$b_{s,O_t} = \begin{bmatrix} 1 & 0 \\ 0 & 0 \end{bmatrix} \otimes \left(\begin{bmatrix} 1 & 0 \\ 0 & 1 \end{bmatrix} R_{in}^{Euc.} \begin{bmatrix} 0 & 1 \\ 1 & 0 \end{bmatrix} + R_{out}^{Euc.} \right)$$
$$+ \begin{bmatrix} 0 & 0 \\ 0 & 1 \end{bmatrix} \otimes \left(\begin{bmatrix} 1 & 0 \\ 0 & 1 \end{bmatrix} R_{in}^{MAD} + \begin{bmatrix} 0 & 1 \\ 1 & 0 \end{bmatrix} R_{out}^{MAD} \right), \qquad (2.18)$$

where $\otimes$ is the Kronecker product; $R_{in/out}^{Euc.}$ is the percentage of points that stays in and out of radius within the fixed search algorithm for Euclidean distance analysis to differentiate user states *sitting*, {*in*}, and *standing*, {*out*}; and $R_{in/out}^{MAD}$ is the same algorithm approach, but at this time, it is based on MAD analysis to differentiate user states *walking*, {*in*}, and *running*, {*out*}.

In addition, another important system parameter used in HMMs, user state transition matrix, is also defined by using our proposed method as

$$a_{s,\acute{s}} = \begin{bmatrix} 1/3 & 1/3 & 1/3 & 0 \\ 1/3 & 1/3 & 1/3 & 0 \\ 1/4 & 1/4 & 1/4 & 1/4 \\ 0 & 0 & 1/2 & 1/2 \end{bmatrix}$$

where s and $\acute{s}$ denote user states, which are ordered as in *sitting, standing, walking,* and *running*. In most studies, this system matrix is formed by user intervention after examining a full data record of user activities in off-line process, and specifying a general trend of user with respect to specific user states. However, in our proposed method, this matrix is held fixed with equal probabilities as default. It is because that it is not possible to give a specific formation to present user state transitions. This could alter from one user to another. Therefore, we focus on the creation of observation emission matrix more. According to the defined user state transition matrix in our method, there is no possibility to transit from *sitting* to *running*, from *standing* to *running*, or vice versa. The rest of the elements in the matrix has equal probability with respect to other state transitions.

2.5 Performance Evaluation

To demonstrate the effectiveness of the proposed classification method, experiments are carried out by using Blackberry RIM Storm II 9550 smartphone as a target device. Blackberry Java 7.1 SDK is used for programming purpose of implementations, and Eclipse is used as a software development tool. Storm II consists of three-axial accelerometer sensor named ADXL346 from Analog Devices. The experiments are performed by eight different individuals with around ∼16 h accelerometer data recordings analysis in total *per each method*, refer to Table 2.2. For instance, Figure 2.4 shows a 10 min recording of the collected sensory readings from the sensor and draws the track of user state recognitions provided by our proposed method with respect to changing context in the readings.

The target device is considered to be put in trousers pocket. A change in the orientation of the device, such as rotation, is an important design drawback for the most of classification algorithms, especially for those that solely rely on exploiting a specific axis information. Since the sensor is not placed fixed, it would produce some distortion over acceleration axes. Upward or downward position of the device causes *x*-axis flipped to *y*-axis or vice versa. Therefore, the device is placed fixed in many studies. Any change in orientation could cause false truthfulness to happen in activity

Table 2.2 Diversity in Participants Who Involve Experiments

Age	Gender	Number per Gender	Data Length per Subject (h)
18–30	Male	2	2
	Female		
30–40	Male	1	2
	Female		
>40	Male	1	2
	Female		

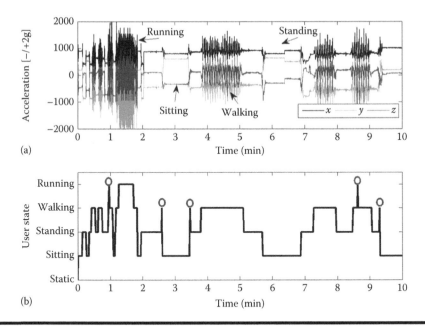

Figure 2.4 **The context inference from the accelerometer sensor: (a) a 10 min recording of three-axial acceleration signals while user posture changes, and (b) the corresponding user state representations before smoothing is applied.**

recognitions. The applied classification method in this chapter is not affected much by the rotation of the device since it does not depend on fixed threshold values in context recognition process. As a worst-case scenario, whenever the device changes its rotation, the update process will handle the adaptation problem as long as the rotation does not occur all the time. For example, if a rotation occurs, user state *sitting* might start being selected as *standing*, and this would give a false truthfulness in the differentiation of user states until user state *walking/standing* is not perceived. Note that in our proposed algorithm, user state *walking/standing* gives out user state *standing* since their data signal levels flow similarly.

With the utilization of the proposed classification method, the accelerometer sensor is sampled at $f_s = \{100, 50, 25\}$ Hz. The samplings are windowed with specifications of $L = 3f_s$ and 50% overlap value. Exceptionally, when $f_s = 100$ Hz is taken, L could be $2f_s$ since lower sampling frequencies cannot resolve inference problems when window size is not adequate. The proposed method infers user states from obtained contextual information through the accelerometer sensor with a perfect accuracy as shown in Figure 2.4. In addition, the user's quick movements during state transitions may lead to false statements in the recognition process; especially, any user transition between sitting/standing/walking might be detected as walking or any user transition from/to walking might be detected as running. In such cases, a basic *smoothing* technique is applied by taking a majority voting scheme by a sliding window with a specific length of user state history to prevent from having false truthfulness in user state recognitions. Hence, the circles in Figure 2.4b is corrected since the preceding and proceeding user states are different from what is perceived.

User state recognition analysis is examined through Figure 2.2 along with Equations 2.12, 2.13, 2.16, and 2.18 for each classification method. According to the results, Table 2.3 shows the confusion matrix for user state recognitions under

Table 2.3 Confusion Matrix 1: User State Recognition under Different Classification Methods at 100 Hz Sampling

Method at 100 Hz		a	b	c	d
DT	a	98.2	1.8	0	0
	b	1.4	94.5	4.1	0
	c	0	2.7	93.8	3.5
	d	0	0	8.3	91.7
GMM	a	93.8	4.4	0.6	0
	b	9.6	86.2	4.2	0
	c	0.6	3.7	89.5	6.1
	d	0	0	10.1	89.9
k-NN	a	94.5	4.4	1.1	0
	b	2.1	89.7	8.2	0
	c	0	6.6	82.1	11.3
	d	0	0	9.8	90.2
LDA	a	93.2	6.2	0.6	0
	b	8.5	83.5	8	0
	c	0.5	6.2	81.7	11.6
	d	0	3.3	12.4	84.3
HMM	a	95.3	4.7	0	0
	b	4.1	92.4	3.5	0
	c	0	1.8	91.5	6.7
	d	0	0	9.7	90.3

Note: a, sitting; b, standing; c, walking; d, running.

different classification methods at 100 Hz from accelerometer sensor samplings. The proposed classification method, labeled as DT, achieves a great differentiation in user state recognitions because the applied methodology well analyzes the acceleration signals and exploits sufficient features in order to make such differentiations in user states. In addition, other existing methods succeed very reasonable truthfulness in user state recognitions. It is because that online processing allows them to have updated training classes for the clustering problem instead of having fixed data references. More significantly, it also achieves adaptability toward some heterogeneities observed over acceleration signals, such as distortion due to the rapid movement or change in orientation. Only LDA algorithm seems to have worse outcomes in the user state recognition problem, which might result from the size of the feature vector. Since the feature vector in this study is set to a length of 15, it may not resolve the clustering problem after size reduction due to the projection. Note that most studies mentioned in Section 2.1 have a very large size of feature vectors, for example, size of over 40 features. In summary, existing classification methods fall behind in comparison with the proposed method even if they benefit from all signal processing elements utilized in a feature vector while differentiating user state classes.

Moreover, Table 2.4 shows how proposed classification method responds under slower sampling frequencies. The method still achieves a solid differentiation between *sitting* and *standing*, whereas there are some confusions between *walking* and *running*. Having a lower number of samplings and variant signal characteristics of actions such as *walking/running*, it would be difficult to have a pure data frame for each user state representation. Hence, clustering problem becomes more challenging to be resolved.

Table 2.4　Confusion Matrix 2: DT under Different Sampling Frequencies

DT		a	b	c	d
@50 Hz	a	95.2	4.8	0	0
	b	3.2	93.1	3.7	0
	c	0	3.8	86.5	9.7
	d	0	0	15.9	84.1
@25 Hz	a	93.1	6.9	0	0
	b	5.4	88.3	6.3	0
	c	0	9.4	78.3	12.3
	d	0	0	20.7	79.3

Note: a, sitting; b, standing; c, walking; d, running.

Table 2.5 Battery Lifetime With Respect To Constant Application Use under Different Classification Algorithms Without Update

Method	Battery Lifetime (H)
DT	8.5
GMM	3
k-NN	5.5
LDA	4
HMM	6

On the other hand, to be able to see the effect of each classification algorithm on the battery depletion, an application is implemented on the target device. The application runs from the point where 1400 mAh smartphone battery is fully loaded until it totally depletes. Only one classification algorithm without update process is employed at each application run. While applications are running, the device is left in a standby mode and only connected to a 3G network. Also, the accelerometer sensor is set to aggressive sampling where $f_s = 100$ Hz and DC $= 100\%$. The results of applications are given in Table 2.5. According to results, proposed method achieves the longest battery lifetime. It is because proposed contextual inference model exploits the characteristics of accelerometer signals and applies a sufficient number of signal processing features as needed. It does not apply all features at the same time like other classification methods use. Thereby, LDA and GMM together have shorter battery lifetime since they both first create feature vectors after sensory data acquisition and test these vectors with high-dimensional user state class matrices to check the membership of vectors in correspondence with any user state classes.

In addition to battery lifetime comparison, Table 2.6 is provided to well examine and compare classification algorithms in terms of computational complexity during context inference with/without update process taken place on their system parameters. As can be seen, our proposed method proves its lightweightiness property by having a lower time span to process sensory data until inferring desired context as outcome, and it also outperforms other methods even if update is applied. To mention the other classification methods, LDA takes less process time than GMM while inferring context thanks to its complexity reducing method. However, it uses GMM-based training data sets and applies projection on them to reduce complexity in computations. Therefore, update time of LDA's system parameters is longer than GMM's. k-NN and HMM together show very close results in computation time. However, it is normally expected from HMM to have a longer process time span since the training of system parameters is needed in update process. Remember that

Table 2.6 Comparison of Classification Methods With Respect To Average Process Time

Method	Process Time (ms)		Update Included
	Mean	*Std.*	
DT	5	0.9	–
	6	1.0	✓a
GMM	12	0.6	–
	15	2.1	✓a
	22	3.0	✓b
k-NN	7	0.7	–
	8.5	1.3	✓a
	12	1.5	✓b
LDA	8.5	0.5	–
	20	2.7	✓a
	27	3.2	✓b
HMM	6.4	0.6	–
	8.3	1.2	✓a

Note: a, proposed update; b, regular update.

our proposed system creates the observation emission matrix in HMM, and that makes pull process time down.

In summary, the proposed method achieves solid user state differentiations under variant sampling frequencies by showing an above 90% overall accuracy at each f_s. It also compares the outperforming result by showing an 10% overall enhancement for each user state at 100 Hz with the widely used GMM-, k-NN-, LDA-, and HMM-based classification methods. In addition, the proposed method infers user states from the obtained context through the accelerometer sensor with almost a perfect accuracy at 100 Hz, as an example shown in Figure 2.4b. For slower sampling frequencies, the method still makes high accurate differentiations in user states. On the other hand, the proposed method outperforms other classification methods by achieving less computational complexity and more battery lifetime.

As a conclusion, this chapter provides an online classification method to detect mobile device–based user-centric postural actions (called *user states: sitting, standing, walking, and running*) through the smartphone accelerometer sensor. A novel DT-based unsupervised learning method is developed for this purpose.

The proposed classification method effectively exploits the context provided by acceleration signals with an adequate number of signal processing techniques, and fixed-radius neighbors search algorithm. Hence, there is no need for creating high-dimensional feature vectors to be fed into pattern recognition algorithms to cluster the desired user state classes, which allows our method to gain the lightweightedness property. Furthermore, the proposed method does not need any a priori information about user state classes. It also provides training data classes to assist other widely used existing classification methods (GMM, k-NN, LDA, and HMM). Finally, the chapter improves these computationally heavyweight methods for online processing by providing a flexible update method on their system parameters.

To demonstrate the effectiveness of the proposed classification method and to prove its ability to make solid differentiations among user states even under different sampling frequencies, the experiments are carried out successfully through a smartphone accelerometer sensor. In summary, the proposed method achieves solid user state differentiations under variant sampling frequencies by showing an above 90% overall accuracy at each f_s, and it also outperforms GMM-, k-NN-, LDA-, and HMM-based classifications not only by showing an 10% overall enhancement for each user state at 100 Hz, but also by providing an extended battery lifetime.

Thereby, this chapter could resolve the trade-off existing between context accuracy and computational power in resource-constraint mobile sensing platforms. For the future work, the definition of user states can be extended by detecting more postural actions. Especially, additional lightweight online unsupervised-based detection algorithms have to be discovered for any mobile device–based sensor to be able to respond to the defined trade-off in mobile computing.

Chapter 3

Context-Aware Framework: A Basic Design

Human beings involve in a vast variety of activities within a very diverse context. A specific context can be extracted by a smartphone application, which acquires relevant data through built-in sensors. A desired activity within the context is then inferred by successful algorithmic implementations. Unfortunately, all of these operations put a heavy workload on the smartphone processor and sensors. Constantly running built-in sensors consume relatively much more power than a smartphone does for fundamental functions such as calling or text messaging. Therefore, mobile device batteries do not last a long time while operating sensors simultaneously.

However, some application fields like medical (see [28,205]) or personal sensing (see [25,114,228]) could use mobile devices as measurement devices. Suppose that a patient with heart disease needs an application to keep track of his or her heartbeats by a wearable sensor. The relevant application would monitor and evaluate data samples; more importantly, it could notify health centers in case an emergency situation occurs [130]. Another example could be marked by studies that recognize stress level since a balanced stress level has been studied to be an important factor to improve the quality of life [44]. Consequently, context-aware applications are becoming essential in our day-to-day life, which in return implies a greater power consumption required by smartphones. In this sense, a framework is required to create a control mechanism for sensor utilizations and to help context-aware applications work their functionalities properly.

This chapter proposes an inhomogeneous (time-variant) hidden Markov model (HMM)–based framework in order to represent user states by defining them as an outcome of either the recognition or estimation model. The framework also applies different sensory sampling operations in order to examine the device battery lifetime. With this method, sleeping time for a sensor can be extended by entering its idle operating mode frequently. While the sensor is in idle mode, the user might either keep or change his or her current activity. Thereby, a statistical model is required to track *time-variant* user activity profiles in order to predict the best likely user state that fits into instant user behavior. As a result, user states are either recognized as an inference of actual sensor readings or as an estimation of the missing inference. The ultimate goal of this chapter is to find a proper way to balance the trade-off while representing user states accurately as well as making sure that power efficiency is maximized.

The following highlight some key elements introduced by this chapter:

- This research intends to create and clarify an effective HMM-based framework to guide the development of real-time operating future context-aware applications.
- The framework accepts that user behavior changes in time; thereby, it assumes that HMM parameters are inhomogeneous (i.e., time variant). As a result, there is no a priori assumption revealed on system parameters such as how HMM evolves in terms of the information belonging to the probability of HMM state transitions.
- Adaptability problem is introduced for inhomogeneous user behaviors, and a relevant solution is given by the uncertainty of entropy rate. It is shown that the convergence of entropy rate could be used to notify a specific user behavior.
- An effective online unsupervised user state recognition algorithm for postural actions *sitting* and *standing* for context extraction through accelerometer data is provided in order to infer relevant activities within the provided context and also to conduct the observation analysis of HMM.
- By changing sampling frequencies in sensory operations, the trade-off analysis is examined. The connection between the context inference under different sampling frequencies and its effect on the convergence of entropy rate is discovered. Accordingly, the slower sampling methods could cause a failure in the convergence of entropy rate. Thereby, the discovery could be used to make a prediction on the actual accuracy of an HAR-based application performance in a real-time environment since there is not an exact solution to compare the actual user behaviors with the recognized behaviors. With this discovery, a feedback mechanism can be built to monitor the convergence of entropy rate while manipulating sensory sampling operations. If the convergence stabilizes, then the period of sensory samplings is extended or vice versa.
- Missing observations occurred during the slower sensory samplings are found by naive Bayesian approach within HMMs.

■ A proper simulation model is built around the accelerometer sensor so that the trade-off between accuracy in user state representations and efficiency in power consumption could be examined in detail.
■ A smartphone application using the accelerometer sensor is implemented to show the effectiveness of the proposed framework.

The outline of the chapter is as follows: Section 3.1 includes a summary of prior works in this field, including a discussion and recommendations on the ongoing research. In Section 3.2, the proposed framework is constructed in light of the purposes defined earlier. Sections 3.3 and 3.4 are reserved for results obtained by simulations and a smartphone application in order to validate the proposed framework.

3.1 Discussions

Many studies can be found in which a framework is proposed to capture and evaluate sensory contextual information. Most of the studies rely on the recognition of user activities and definition of common user behaviors. For instance, gesture recognition of users is well studied using video cameras. The applied methods in relevant studies are based on statistical models, which this chapter also intends to use. However, none of these studies engage themselves to model a common framework in order to construct a base structure for future context-aware applications. They would rather have canalized solutions to solve their own unique applications instead of a generalized approach. Therefore, these studies mostly focus on a specific sensor to discover possible target applications in order to exploit contextual data. A generic framework that fulfills requirements set by all types of context-aware applications was not identified. In contrast, all of the studies put the importance on evident trade-off, which is triggered by reducing power consumption while being intended to continuously receive accurate sensor contextual data.

From the literature search, it is important to refer to Wang et al. [220,221] who proposes a sensor management system, which is called energy-efficient mobile sensing system (EEMSS). This system models user states as a discrete time Markov chain and improves a device battery life by powering a minimum set of sensors and also by applying duty cycling into sensor operation. However, sensors have fixed duty cycles when they are active, and they are not adjustable to different user behaviors. Also, given system is predetermined and not time variant. Another study that analyzes hierarchical sensor management systems is introduced with the name of *SeeMon* in [116]. This system achieves energy efficiency and satisfies less computational complexity by performing continuous detection of context recognition when changes occur during context monitoring. Moreover, [238] demonstrates advantages of a dynamic sensor selection scheme for accuracy–power trade-off in user state recognition. From a power efficiency standpoint, Rachuri et al. [177] use different sampling period schemes for querying sensory data in continuous sensing mobile systems to evaluate accuracy–power trade-offs.

In addition, the use of entropy rate as an optimization criterion within the concept of HMMs to address a solution in order to reduce power consumption is introduced in [124] and implemented in [125]. These studies accept the off-line decision process to attain an optimal sampling policy through recorded HMM observations with known transition probabilities among states. The policy aims at selecting most informative subsequences of observations by measuring the uncertainty of expected entropy rate with respect to a power consumption constraint. By this policy, the time intervals where the most informative subsequences are selected define the length of idle times in sensory operations. Unfortunately, the policy gives a deterministic sampling strategy, and the given strategy is valid for time-invariant systems by providing the example of defining measurement epochs to build a temperature time series during the day. However, the optimal sampling strategies would work only if the weather season does not change since it accepts the transition probabilities among temperature measurements are fixed; thereby, this solution does not satisfy the trade-off requirement needed by HAR-based applications, which rely on actively changing distinctive user behaviors.

3.2 Proposed Framework

An HMM [175] can be applied to a system that aims to recognize user states, as shown in Figure 3.1. In this system, sensor readings (i.e., extracted user contexts through mobile device–based sensors) are seen as inputs. These readings undergo a series of signal processing operations and eventually end up with a classification algorithm in order to provide desirable inferences about user behaviors/profiles for context-aware applications. A required classification algorithm differs in terms of explanation of extracted user context through a specific sensor. Outcomes of the algorithm are represented in a matrix whose elements show probability weights for possible user state selections. Finally, selection criteria are set to differentiate between user states.

Classification algorithms produce observations (i.e., *visible states*), ϑ, of HMM. Among observations, only one observation is expected to provide the most likely differentiation in the selection of instant user state representation. This observation is marked as instant observation, which also indicates the most recent element of observation sequence of HMM. On the other hand, user states are defined as *hidden states*, S, of HMM since they are not directly observable but only reachable over visible states. Therefore, each observation has cross-probabilities to point any user state. These cross-probabilities build an emission matrix, b_{jk}, which basically defines decision probabilities of picking user states from available observations.

In addition, a user state might not be stationary since a general user behavior changes in time. Thus, it is expected from a user state either to transit into another

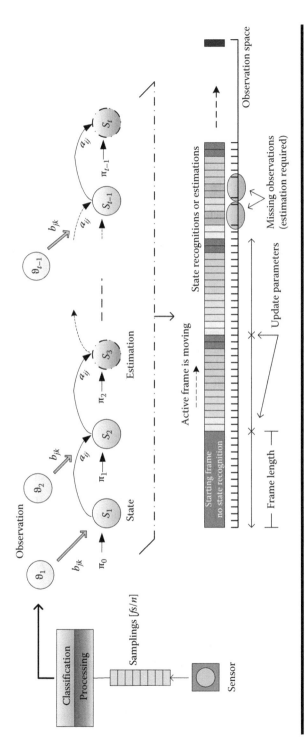

Figure 3.1 Operation of the proposed framework.

user state or to remain the same. These occurrences build a time-variant user state transition matrix, a_{ij}, which defines transition probabilities among the user states.

Note that one sensor model is considered for the sake of generalization. In reality, to recognize a user state, it might require multiple sensory observations.

3.2.1 Preliminaries

First-order HMM is proposed for creating a statistical tool to show dependencies of states at discrete time t that are influenced directly by a state at discrete time $t - 1$* [35,196]. Discrete time is used to specify sensor readings that occur periodically in a system.

HMM is characterized by the following elements:

■ *Hidden process*: A set of hidden states is defined as a discrete time process with a finite space of N,

$$S_{[1:t]} = \{S_1 = i, S_2, \ldots, S_t\}, \quad \forall i \in \{1, \ldots, N\}.$$

Recall that the system can revisit a user state at different system times and also not every user state needs to be visited.

■ *Initial hidden state probability*: An irreducible and aperiodic Markov chain that begins with its ergodic distribution

$$\pi_i = Pr(S_0 = i), \quad \begin{cases} \forall i \in \{1, \ldots, N\}, \\ \pi_i \geq 0, \\ \sum_{i=1}^{N} \pi_i = 1. \end{cases}$$

■ *State transition probability*: a is described as $\{N \times N\}$ state transition matrix where each element a_{ij} of a is equal to a transition probability from state i to state j,

$$a_{ij} = Pr(S_t = j \mid S_{t-1} = i), \quad \begin{cases} \forall i,j \in \{1, \ldots, N\}, \\ a_{ij} \geq 0, \\ \sum_{i=1}^{N} a_{ij} = 1. \end{cases}$$

There is no requirement that transition probabilities must be symmetric ($a_{ij} \neq a_{ji}$) or a specific state might remain the same in succession of time ($a_{ii} = 0$).

---

* In an mth-order Markov process, state at t has dependencies with states at $\{t - n, t - n + 1, \ldots, t - 1\}$.

- *Visible process*: A set of observations is defined as a discrete time process with a finite space of K,

$$\vartheta_{[1:t]} = \{\vartheta_1 = k, \vartheta_2, \ldots, \vartheta_t\}, \quad \forall k \in \{1, \ldots, K\}.$$

- *Observation emission probability*: b is described as $\{N \times K\}$ observation emission matrix where each element b_{jk} of b is equal to a cross-probability between hidden state and emitted observation:

$$b_{jk} = Pr(\vartheta_t = k \mid S_t = j), \quad \begin{cases} \forall j \in \{1, \ldots, N\}, \\ \forall k \in \{1, \ldots, K\}, \\ b_{jk} \geq 0, \\ \sum_{k=1}^{K} b_{jk} = 1. \end{cases}$$

HMM parameters are usually denoted as a triplet $\lambda = \{a_{ij}, b_{jk}, \pi_i\}$.

3.2.2 User State Representation

User state representation engine infers an instant user behavior in light of prior knowledge of a human behavior pattern and availability of sensory observation at decision time. If sensory observation exists, the applied process is called recognition method; otherwise, estimation method. In other words, estimation method is applied whenever power efficiency is taken into consideration by a system, seen in Figure 3.2.

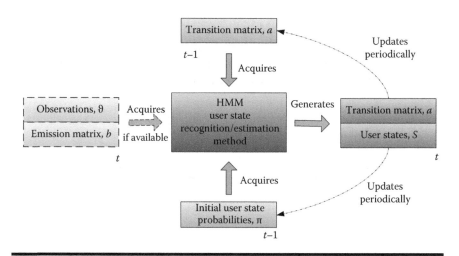

Figure 3.2   User state recognition/estimation method.

The probability of a specific observation sequence is given by

$$Pr(\vartheta \mid \lambda) = \sum_{i=1}^{N} Pr(\vartheta \mid S, \lambda) Pr(S \mid \lambda)$$

$$= \sum_{i=1}^{N} \pi_0 \prod_{t=1}^{T} Pr(\vartheta_t \mid S_t) Pr(S_t \mid S_{t-1})$$

$$= \sum_{i=1}^{N} \pi_0 \prod_{t=1}^{T} a_{ij} b_j(\vartheta_t = k). \tag{3.1}$$

By implementing Bayes' theorem together with (3.1), a sequence of hidden states can be formulated by

$$Pr(S \mid \vartheta, \lambda) = \frac{Pr(\vartheta \mid S, \lambda) Pr(S, \lambda)}{Pr(\vartheta, \lambda)}. \tag{3.2}$$

Then, inference of a hidden state at time t in (3.2) is given by

$$Pr(S_t = i \mid \vartheta_{[1:\tau]}),$$

where $\tau = t - 1$, t or T is termed as "predicted", $\mathcal{P}$, "filtered", $\mathcal{F}$, and "smoothed", $\mathcal{S}$, probabilities of S_t, depending on the observation sequence of $\vartheta_{[1:t-1]}$, $\vartheta_{[1:t]}$, or $\vartheta_{[1:T]}$, respectively.

The filtered probabilities of S_t have already been named user state recognition method in this chapter. Thus, the relevant probability of an instant user state recognition can be found by either evaluation method or decoding.

Evaluation method, aka forward and backward algorithm [175], see Figure 3.3, is proposed to find the most likely one-step ahead or one-step back user state in a hidden chain. Evaluation method relies on updating probability weights iteratively that decides which user state is selected to represent instant user activity.

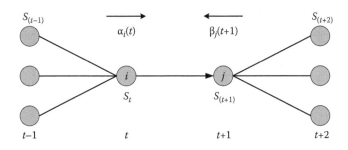

Figure 3.3 Forward–backward algorithm.

The corresponding probability weights are α for forward iterations and β for backward iterations. α_t is the probability of current occurrence of a user state, S_t, generated from one-step previous occurrence, S_{t-1}. On the other hand, with reverse analogy, β_t is defined as the probability of transition occurrence of S_{t-1} from S_t.

From the inferences of (3.2) since it has inductive calculations by using ϑ_t, S_t, and S_{t-1} each term, α and β are expressed as follows:

■ $\alpha_t = \sum_j \alpha_{t-1} a_{ij} b_j (\vartheta_t = k)$ with condition of $\alpha_0 = 1$ for initial state, π_0 at $t = 0$.
■ $\beta_t = \sum_j \beta_{t+1} a_{ij} b_j (\vartheta_{t+1} = k)$ with condition of $\beta_T = 1$ for final state, π_T at $t = T$.

The term of $a_{ij} b_j (\vartheta_t = k)$ represents a user state transition triggered by a given observation.

Since the recognition process of user states evolves in real time by context-aware applications, forward algorithm is employed to assign a proper user state in order to specify current user activity whenever a new observation is made.

$$\hat{S}_T = \arg \max_{1 \leq i \leq N} [\alpha_T] \tag{3.3}$$

selects the most likely user state representation at a given time with the existing probability of $Pr(\hat{S}_T) = \max_{1 \leq i \leq N} [\alpha_T]$.

On the other hand, to make sure that recognitions are made true, backward algorithm can also be employed. By this method, the accuracy of previous user state recognition is validated. However, this method can be seen redundant due to the fact that it consumes additional computational power.

Another user state recognition method is decoding, aka Viterbi algorithm [216], see Figure 3.4, which recursively finds the most probable hidden state chain by the given history of sequences for both observations and user states with system parameters, λ.

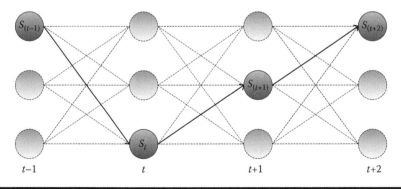

Figure 3.4   Viterbi algorithm.

Let $(\delta_t = i)$ be defined as the probability of the most probable path termination for a user state $(S_t = i)$:

$$(\delta_t = i) = \max_{S_1,\dots,S_{t-1}} Pr(S_1 \dots S_{t-1}(S_t = i); \vartheta_1 \dots \vartheta_t \mid \lambda), \qquad (3.4a)$$

$(\delta_t = j)$ can be calculated recursively by

$$(\delta_t = j) = \max_{1 \leq i \leq N} [(\delta_{t-1} = i) a_{ij}] b_j(\vartheta_t) \qquad (3.4b)$$

with the initialization of $(\delta_1 = i) = \pi_i b_i(\vartheta_1) 1 \leq i \leq N$ and termination of $\hat{S}_T = \arg\max_{1 \leq i \leq N}[(\delta_T = i)]$ where the existing probability of $Pr(\hat{S}_T) = [\hat{\pi}_T] = \max_{1 \leq i \leq N}[(\delta_T = i)]$.

In addition to using filtered probabilities to recognize user states, predicted probabilities are used to estimate user state if necessary. When power saving methods are taken into consideration, there will be some time intervals during sensor operation in which no sensor readings are obtained. As a result, system cannot receive a relevant observation. In that case, the inference of instant user state will be based on estimation method not on recognition method.

User state estimation method uses predicted probabilities. Therefore, a posteriori probabilities need to be derived from given existing system parameters, see Table 3.1 and Figure 3.5.

Predicted probabilities are found by

$$\mathcal{P}_t(j) = Pr(S_t = j \mid \vartheta_{[1:t-1]}, \acute{\vartheta}_t)$$
$$= Pr(S_t = j, \vartheta_t = k \mid \vartheta_{[1:t-1]})$$
$$= \sum_j a_{ij} \mathcal{F}_{t-1}(i) \sum_k b_j(\vartheta_t = k)$$
$$= \sum_j a_{ij} \mathcal{F}_{t-1}(i), \qquad (3.5a)$$

where $\mathcal{F}_t(i) = \alpha_t(i)$ is taken.

Table 3.1 Filtering User States While No Observation Received

Filter at $t-1$	$Pr(S_{t-1} = j \mid \vartheta_{t-1})$ $\downarrow$
Prediction at t	$Pr(S_t = j \mid \vartheta_{t-1})$ $\downarrow \vartheta_t$
Filter at t	$Pr(S_t = j \mid \vartheta^t)$

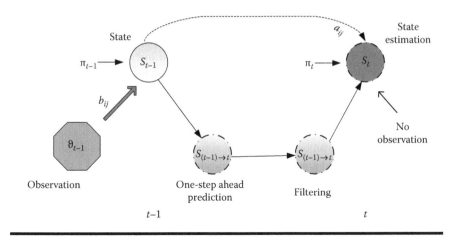

Figure 3.5 Prediction/filtering/smoothing.

Alternatively, $\mathcal{P}_t(j)$ can be found by assigning the most likely visionary observation instead by accepting there is a missing observation:

$$\mathcal{P}_t(j) = \sum_j a_{ij}\mathcal{F}_{t-1}(i)b_j(\vartheta_t = k_{predicted}). \tag{3.5b}$$

$\mathcal{P}_t(j)$ can be extended as $\mathcal{P}_t(j, k)$ to show a dependency on future predicted observations:

$$\mathcal{P}_t(j, k) = \sum_j a_{ij}\mathcal{F}_{t-1}(i)b_j(\vartheta_t = k). \tag{3.5c}$$

Then, the most likely observation is selected according to assigning each possible observation as a final node to observation sequence as indicated in (5.10) while calculating the probability of sequence existence

$$(\vartheta_t = k_{predicted}) = \arg\max_k \sum_j \mathcal{P}_t(j, k) \tag{3.6}$$

with the probability of $Pr(\vartheta_t) = \max_k \sum_j \mathcal{P}_t(j, k)$.

3.2.3 System Adaptability

The most important feature of context-aware applications is being capable of adapting themselves to user behaviors. User context differs in time, and the corresponding user state also does. Since user behavior shows various patterns from one user to another, a sequence of user states for each user will be arranged in a different formation with respect to variant user state transitions occurring throughout time.

For instance, one user might remain in the same user state for a long time; whereas, others might be more active by changing their user states frequently. Therefore, it cannot be expected from relevant user state transition matrix to remain stationary. User state transition matrix evolves in time and must adapt itself to user choices.

3.2.3.1 Time-Variant User State Transition Matrix

User state transitions can be represented as simple random walk on a graph. A finite, simple, and undirected graph is a finite collection of vertices, V, and a collection of edges, E, where each edge connects two different vertices and any two vertices are connected by at most one edge [35,196], such as the graph shown in Figure 3.6.

Let us notate $v_1 \sim v_2$ as vertices v_1 and v_2 are adjacent or an edge connects the two vertices.

User states in HMM are vertices of the graph. The chain chooses a new user state randomly from among neighbor user states adjacent to current user state.

Transition matrix for this chain is given by

$$a_{ij} = \frac{1}{d(v_i)}, \quad v_i \sim v_j,$$

where $d(v_i)$ is the number of vertices adjacent to $d(v_i)$. For example, if $d(v_i)$ is 0, a_{ii} becomes 1.

This transition matrix is a default system parameter that is predefined in application for all users. Starting from that point, transition matrix will be evolving in time in response to user behaviors/profiles.

3.2.3.2 Time-Variant Observation Emission Matrix

The system always receives an updated version of the emission matrix at each discrete time when a new context is conceived thanks to the resulted classification algorithms. Therefore, the emission matrix always includes an active condition of cross-probabilities among user states and observations.

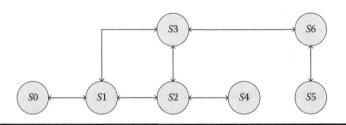

Figure 3.6   An example of user state transitions.

3.2.3.3 Update on System Parameters

The system has to update the user state transition matrix periodically according to obtained observations and recognized/estimated user states. There is no finite solution to find an optimal set of updated *a* and *b*. Boltzmann method or numerous weight adjustment methods can be found in the literature for this purpose. In this study, a generalized expectation maximization algorithm is considered for updating process, which is forward–backward algorithm or Baum–Welch method [19,175]. This method relies on updating weights iteratively to estimate new system parameters.

The process of how weights are calculated is explained and described in Section 5.2.1. With the combination of α and β, system parameters can be estimated. For this purpose, γ_t is defined to present the probability of transition from S_{t-1} to S_t in the presence of observation sequence, ϑ_t:

$$\gamma_t = \frac{\alpha_{t-1} a_{ij} b_{jk} \beta_t}{Pr(\vartheta_t = k \mid S_t, \lambda)}. \tag{3.7}$$

The updated version of elements belonging to user state transition matrix is found using (3.7), which is defined by dividing the expected number of transitions from S_{t-1} to S_t at any time to the total expected number of transitions from any user state to S_t:

$$\hat{a}_{ij} = \frac{\sum_{t=1}^{T} \gamma_t}{\sum_{t=1}^{T} \sum_k \gamma_t}. \tag{3.8}$$

In addition, emission matrix can also be estimated as

$$\hat{b}_{jk} = \frac{\sum \gamma_t}{\sum_{t=1}^{T} \gamma_t}. \tag{3.9}$$

However, the estimation of $\hat{b}_{jk}$ is not needed to estimate since system obtains this probability matrix as an outcome of required classification algorithms to process context.

Equation 3.8 is repeatedly calculated until the difference between newly estimated a_{ij} and current a_{ij} is less than a predetermined converge criteria. However, this algorithm runs only once when needed in this study because it consumes considerable computational power. Plus, an update for system parameters is invoked regularly to be able to satisfy adaptation to user behaviors faster; therefore, a_{ij} would converge in anyway sooner or later.

3.2.3.4 Entropy Rate

Entropy is a measure of uncertainty in a stochastic process. It quantifies the expected value of information contained in a specific realization of any random variable.

The value of entropy rate shows predictability of a random distribution. As long as entropy rate gets closer to 0, outcomes of distribution become more predictable. In this study, entropy rate is used to track the user state transition matrix. Since the transition matrix is set fixed as a default for all users, the system has to adapt to unique user behaviors in time by tracking changes in transition matrix. When entropy rate converges into a stable value, it points out that the system could manage to set required adjustment on adaptation [52,62].

Entropy rate for an HMM is given by

$$H(S_t) = \lim_{t \to \infty} H(S_t \mid S_{[1:t-1]}) = \lim_{t \to \infty} H(S_t \mid S_{t-1})$$

$$= \sum_i H(S_t \mid S_{t-1} = i) Pr(S_{t-1} = i)$$

$$= \sum_i \left(-\sum_j a_{ij} \log a_{ij} \right) \pi_i = -\sum_{ij} \pi_i a_{ij} \log a_{ij}. \qquad (3.10a)$$

With time-variant property, entropy rate becomes

$$H(S_T) = \frac{1}{T} \sum_{t=1}^{T} H(S_t) \qquad (3.10b)$$

in time sequence of T.

3.2.3.5 Scaling Problem

Computational complexity while calculating system parameters causes a crucial underflow problem. When time goes by during the evolution of HMM chains, both $\alpha_t(i) \overset{t}{\Rightarrow} 0$ and $\beta_t(i) \overset{t}{\Rightarrow} 0$ start to head to zero at an exponential rate since a_{ij} and b_{jk} include elements being lower than 1. Therefore, both variables need to be scaled:

$$\hat{\alpha}_{(i,t)} = \frac{\alpha_{(i,t)}}{\prod_{\tau=1}^{t} \sum_i \alpha_{(i,\tau)}}, \qquad (3.11a)$$

$$\hat{\beta}_{(i,t)} = \frac{\beta_{(i,t)}}{\prod_{\tau=1}^{t} \sum_i \alpha_{(i,\tau)}}, \qquad (3.11b)$$

where $\kappa_t = 1/\sum_i \alpha_t(i)$ is defined as a scaling coefficient or a scaling factor in the study of [175].

3.3 Simulations

Simulations are carried out in MATLAB® in order to examine the defined trade-off between power consumption and accuracy in user state representations in light of the proposed framework for context-aware applications. Some case scenarios are created so as to indicate the framework is still valid under different system parameters. For the sake of simplicity, a two-user state consisting HMM chain is considered. However, more complex models can be applied as well by using same system approach.

3.3.1 Preparations

The required HMM is constructed with an initial user state probability, π_0:

$$\pi_0 = \begin{bmatrix} 0.95 & 0.05 \end{bmatrix}, \tag{3.12a}$$

and an initial user state transition matrix, $a_{ij}^{default}$:

$$a_{ij}^{default} = \begin{bmatrix} 0.5 & 0.5 \\ 0.5 & 0.5 \end{bmatrix}. \tag{3.12b}$$

$a_{ij}^{default}$ is set fixed for all user profiles initially. It is expected from user state transition matrix to adjust itself according to different user profiles so that adaptability problem that arises in context-aware applications could be solved.

In order to claim that system provides adaptability, different user profiles are generated by assigning various probabilities to user state transition matrix, a_{ij}:

$$a_{ij}^{[1:6]} = \begin{bmatrix} 0.1 & 0.9 \\ 0.9 & 0.1 \end{bmatrix}, \begin{bmatrix} 0.25 & 0.75 \\ 0.75 & 0.25 \end{bmatrix}, \begin{bmatrix} 0.5 & 0.5 \\ 0.5 & 0.5 \end{bmatrix}, \begin{bmatrix} 0.9 & 0.1 \\ 0.1 & 0.9 \end{bmatrix},$$
$$\begin{bmatrix} 0.75 & 0.25 \\ 0.25 & 0.75 \end{bmatrix}, \begin{bmatrix} 0.5 & 0.5 \\ 0.1 & 0.9 \end{bmatrix}. \tag{3.12c}$$

It can be seen that first five matrices have symmetrical user profile; however, the last one does not.

In addition, observation emission matrix is built by

$$b_{jk}^{[1:2]} = \begin{bmatrix} 0.75 & 0.20 & 0.05 \\ 0.05 & 0.20 & 0.75 \end{bmatrix}, \begin{bmatrix} 0.05 & 0.20 & 0.75 \\ 0.75 & 0.20 & 0.05 \end{bmatrix}. \tag{3.12d}$$

Given matrices show that three different classification results help a decision process to select a proper user state for an instant user activity representation. In other words, same selection criteria are valid every time for which user state is most likely to be chosen in the presence of its cross-relations among observations. For example, given b_{jk} indicates that first and third observations have relatively significant weights for the decision process. During simulation, these matrices remain the same in order to make healthy statements on system response to different user profiles.

3.3.2 Applied Process

Figure 3.1 indicates how the proposed system runs. There is a moving frame acting like a queue structure to store new and recent observations. Initially, the frame is being filled with observations until it notifies full. After that, system updates a_{ij} and prepares itself for future operations such as actively running user state recognition or estimation methods. Since it would cause an insufficient number of observations to select proper user state representations, no operation is executed while initial frame is being filled. Hence, it is not allowed to run energy saving algorithms while the initial frame is in progress.

The frame keeps rolling in time by inserting a new instant observation and rejecting the oldest observation simultaneously. Having a frame like queue structure enables to store a short-term memory of recent observation history and to preserve the redundant waste of computational power. The increase in the number of observations puts more workload on computations required for applied algorithms during user state representations and the update of system parameters. Therefore, the length of the frame is an important system parameter to be set proper. During simulations, this value is set to 60 observations per frame.

System parameters, (3.8) and (3.11), are updated periodically whenever the frame advances as long as its length. This process continues until the system is terminated.

3.3.3 Power Consumption Model

The system makes an observation after a predefined number of sensor samplings are acquired. Then, user state is recognized with the help of extracted context from samplings. Actual sampling time in sensor operation can be extended in order to prolong a mobile device battery lifetime. Sampling intervals are modeled as $I_i = n/f_s$ where n and f_s are an integer value and sampling frequency, respectively. I_i defines a waiting time between two consecutive sensor samplings. During simulations, $n = \{1, 2, 4, 8\}$ and $f_s = 100$ Hz are taken.

Given the probability of user states and interval waiting time for a corresponding user state, the expected waiting time for an upcoming sensor sampling is calculated by

$$E[I_t] = \sum_i Pr(S_t = i)(I_t = i). \tag{3.13}$$

Since I_i is considered fixed for all user states throughout simulations, being at any user state does not change a relevant waiting duration to acquire a new sensor sampling.

Reasonably speaking that the expected energy consumption at each sensor sampling is inversely proportional to waiting time (3.13):

$$E[C_t] \propto \frac{1}{E[I_t]}. \tag{3.14}$$

For instance, if $n=1$ is taken for each user state, energy consumption turns out the highest since sensor sampling is being made at each available time slot. Otherwise, whenever $n > 1$, there come time slots at which no sampling is made.

The least power-consuming sensor on today's smartphones is the accelerometer [22]. Therefore, the accelerometer sensor is considered to use in simulations and implementation of a real-time application.

The accelerometer sensor needs to be modeled in order to examine power efficiency achieved at each different sampling strategy. Table 3.2 provides modeling parameters belonging to accelerometer used in an application. Drawn current values at specific sampling frequencies give an idea of how much power could be consumed in different sensor operation modes of accelerometer [1].

In this sense, let Ω_{sample} and Ω_{idle} be given as default sensor properties for power consumption per unit time during sensing and during running idle, respectively [236]. Note that only drain current value I_{DD} is an effective modeling parameter to determine power consumption through sampling channel under stable drain voltage V_{DD} where power is formulated as $P = VI$ in physics.

Energy consumption during sensing is then formalized as

$$\Theta_{sampling} = \sum_{m=1}^{\# \ of \ samplings} \delta(m)\Omega_{sample}, \tag{3.15}$$

where $\delta(m)$ is Kronecker delta function that indicates sampling is being made.

Also, energy consumption while the sensor is in idle mode is given by

$$\Theta_{idle} = \sum_{m=1}^{\# \ of \ estimations} \delta(m)\Omega_{idle}. \tag{3.16}$$

Table 3.2 Current Consumption versus Data Rate in Accelerometer, ADXL346

($V_{DDI/O}$ = 1.8 V, V_S = 2.6 V)	
Data Rate (Hz)	I_{DD} (µA)
100	140
50	90
25	55
12.5	40
Autosleep mode	23
Standby mode	0.2

According to Table 3.2, accelerometer drain current flowing at the lowest data rate 12.5 Hz draws roughly 200 times more than it does in standby mode. This information reveals that the total energy consumption to acquire samplings is much more greater than the one while the sensor is being idle, $\Theta_{sample} \gg \Theta_{idle}$. Assuming that the sensor becomes idle between two consecutive sampling operations, total energy consumption wasted during a waiting time is ignored.

In summary, in the presence of (3.15) and (3.16), the fact that expected waiting time is inversely proportional to the number of samplings gives a clue of

$$E[I] \propto \frac{1}{\Theta_{sampling}} \propto \Theta_{idle}.$$

Note that computational power required to extract contextual inference from sensor samplings is ignored.

3.3.4 Accuracy Model

The probability of error occurred during either the recognition or estimation of user state is calculated by

$$e_t = 1 - Pr(\hat{S}_t). \tag{3.17a}$$

This information yields to find the expected recognition error throughout the observation space O with a number of occurrences $\#O$

$$E[e^{rec.}] = \frac{1}{\#O} \sum_{t=1}^{O} e_t^{rec.}. \tag{3.17b}$$

The expected estimation error uses arithmetic mean method. However, it is assumed that t_f is where the first sampling is made. Then, the weight corresponding to an error occurred where the first estimation is made should have lower proportion than the weight corresponding to an error occurred where the last estimation is made because of the fact that while time goes by and an estimation is being made one after another, the accuracy of estimations is expected to degrade. Therefore, the relevant weight for any estimation point is a reciprocal of the time distance to the next available sampling time slot. In that case, harmonic mean becomes more appealing to finding the expected estimation error.

Whenever $n > 1$, the expected estimation error between two consecutive samplings is given by

$$E[e^{est.}] = \frac{1}{\#O} \sum_{t_f=1}^{O} \left(\frac{1}{I_i - 1} \sum_{t=t_f+1}^{t_{max}=t_f+I_i-1} \frac{t_{max} - t + 1}{e_t^{est.}} \right)^{-1}. \tag{3.17c}$$

Finally, accuracy can be found using (3.17) by

$$\varphi\% = \left(1 - (E[e^{rec.}] + E[e^{est.}])\right) * 100. \tag{3.18}$$

3.3.5 Parameter Setups

A waiting time for two consecutive samplings is set to $\{n_1, n_2\} = \{1, 2, 4, 8\}$, where $\{n_1, n_2\} \propto I$ with respect to which user state is represented, S_1 or S_2. That a pair of (n_1, n_2) is selected as $(1, 1)$ means that there is no power saving method applied. In contrast, the selection of $(8, 8)$ means that almost 87.5% of observations inside of the moving frame mentioned in Section 3.3.2 will be estimated according to (3.6).

The total observation number is set to 3600. Recall that the length of the moving frame has been already set to 60. According to which user profile is chosen (i.e., a specific a_{ij}), user states are found by Viterbi algorithm (3.4) with already synthetically generated Markovian observations. These user states are marked as original user states. While the proposed framework is operating, original user states are compared to the user states (3.3) obtained by recognition or estimation methods for the sake of accuracy (3.18).

A simulation starts for each user scenario with default system settings (3.12). In addition, all possible power saving methods are applied repeatedly on observation sequences as long as the proposed system runs and finishes a process of finding proper user state representations.

3.3.6 Results and Discussions

According to simulation results, Figure 3.7 shows how entropy rate could give a clue of identifying a specific user profile, and Figure 3.8 also shows how applied power saving methods affect the convergence of entropy rate and the accuracy of instant user state representations.

First, adaptability to any user profile is considered in the form of convergence of entropy rate. As stated in Section 3.2.3, entropy rate (3.10) is calculated with transition matrix, a_{ij}. Transition matrix, which is initially fixed for all user profiles, gets adjusted to an assigned user profile when time goes by. With the explanation of entropy rate, small difference in entropy rate reveals high prediction of how much closer transition matrix gets into relevant user profile. Therefore, if entropy rate converges into a specific value, which means time-variant user state transition matrix becomes stationary (i.e., time invariant). In this sense, Figure 3.7 shows how the system achieves adaptability to different user profiles under variant power saving methods. Discussions on this graph can be made as follows:

■ Symmetrically constructed user state transition matrices and their horizontal-flipped forms draw almost similar trajectories with respect to any change in the convergence of entropy rate, $(a^{(1)} \approx a^{(4)})$ and $(a^{(2)} \approx a^{(5)})$.

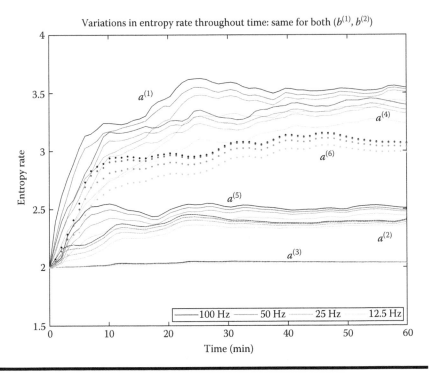

Figure 3.7 Simulation: entropy rate versus variant user profiles.

- Observation emission matrices and their horizontal-flipped forms respond in a similar way to the updating process of user state transition matrix, $(b^{(1)} \approx b^{(2)})$.
- Entropy rate can be a very distinctive factor to identify different user profiles.
- Frequently changing user states like $a^{(3)}$ have the lowest entropy rate since it is for sure that the frequentness of user state transitions will be more predictable.
- Aggressive sampling method (i.e., sampling at 100 Hz) helps user state transition matrix to adapt itself to relevant user profile very quickly and produces clear results to track where entropy rate converges. In contrast, decrease in sampling frequency causes slower adaptability and late convergence.

Second, the accuracy of user state representations at different sampling methods is examined for all user profiles. Figure 3.8. indicates accuracy rate versus earned power efficiency by sampling methods. The following assumptions can be evaluated from this graph:

- Aggressive sampling achieves the most accurate user state selections, whereas this method consumes the highest power.

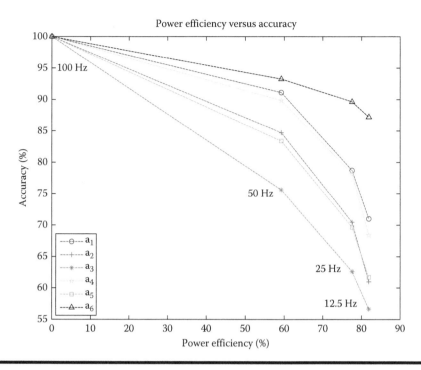

Figure 3.8   Simulation: power consumption versus accuracy.

- Other sampling methods elevate power efficiency while satisfying a reasonable accuracy:
  - Sampling at 50 Hz results in power efficiency of 60% in return for an accuracy range from 75% up to 96%, depending on user profiles.
  - At 25 Hz, power efficiency goes up to 78%; however, accuracy range goes down as in from 64% up to 91%.
  - Finally, the slowest sampling method at 12.5 Hz hits up the highest power efficiency by 82% while accuracy falls in a range from 55% up to 87%.
- The lowest accuracy is obtained by the third user profile $a^{(3)}$ since it has equal probability for both user states. In that case, the system becomes uncertain when it comes to a point of decision on proper user state selection.
- Interestingly, symmetrically constructed user state transition matrices and their horizontal-flipped forms have same accuracy model versus power efficiency, $(a^{(1)} \approx a^{(4)})$ and $(a^{(2)} \approx a^{(5)})$.
- Asymmetrically constructed user state transition matrix gives the best solution to the trade-off by achieving the accuracy of over 90% for all sampling methods.
- The highest adaptation the system gets to a specific user profile, the better accuracy the system achieves on user state recognitions.

3.4 Validation by a Smartphone Application

A real-time application is implemented in order to demonstrate the effectiveness of the proposed framework. Blackberry RIM Storm II 9550 smartphone is chosen as a target device. Blackberry Java 7.1 SDK is used for programming language, and Eclipse is used as a software development tool.

Storm II consists of three-axis accelerometer named ADXL346 from Analog Devices. This sensor operates at 2.6 V as supply voltage and 1.8 V as drain voltage. Its current flow varies under different operation modes and data rate selections (refer to Table 3.2). Turn-on and wake-up times are determined by data rate; they are approximately defined by $\tau + 1.1$ in milliseconds, where $\tau = 1/(\text{data rate})$.

3.4.1 Observation Analysis

Observation analysis is carried out through a smartphone accelerometer sensor. In Figure 3.9, three-axis acceleration information for postural movements, such as *sitting*, *standing*, *walking*, and *running*, is plotted. As applied in simulations, only two-user-state scenario is taken. These are *sitting* and *standing*. Inference related to

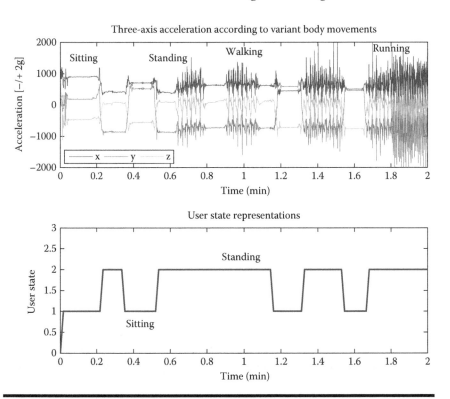

Figure 3.9 Three-axial accelerometer signals: the two-user-state case.

walking and *running* is considered as *standing* since *walking* and *running* activities cause more variations over acceleration signal belonging to *standing* activity.

To differentiate one activity from another, so many studies can be found in the literature (refer to Chapter 2). Studies proposing online solutions mostly use decision tree–based classifications with setting predefined fixed thresholds in order to cluster different states. On the other hand, some studies provide off-line solutions after recording relevant observation data. These studies propose a creation of high-dimensional feature vectors at first by applying many signal processing techniques in order to extract signal characteristics such as energy, entropy, mean, rms, and variance regardless of analyzing signal in detail in terms of what is really supposed to do so that a proper differentiation could be made. Then, feature vectors undergo classification and/or clustering algorithms to match themselves with one of the activities.

Nonetheless, applying complex processing techniques requires much computational power. Indeed, it may also cause rapid depletion in any mobile device battery. The differentiation of two-user-state scenario likewise applied in simulations may seem to be a less expensive method in the computation of feature vectors. However, the characteristics of observation data must be well analyzed under any condition in order to stay away from redundant computational workload. In this sense, this chapter proposes a combined usage of HMMs and pattern recognition techniques. The applied method is very applicable to work online processing in order to actualize the proposed framework.

3.4.1.1 Construction of Observation Emission Matrix

Observation emission matrix b_{jk} is built after an online classification method is applied. The applied method is presented in Figure 2.2. Two moving frame structures are used to store both recent history of sensor samplings and recent history of observations. The first frame has a length of 200 sensor samplings. Samplings are acquired by sensors and filled into the frame with a 50% overlap value. Thus, it is aimed that transition from one state to another will not be missed. On the other hand, the second frame has a length of 60 observations.

The recognition process of user state *sitting* and *standing* is explained in detail in Chapter 2; however, the output of this process sources the observation emission matrix of the proposed framework as follows:

$$b_{jk} = \begin{bmatrix} 1 & 0 \\ 0 & 1 \end{bmatrix} [prob.\ of\ sitting] + \begin{bmatrix} 0 & 1 \\ 1 & 0 \end{bmatrix} [prob.\ of\ standing]. \tag{3.19}$$

3.4.2 Applied Process

The system operates as explained in Sections 3.3.1 and 3.3.2. Default system parameters π_0 and $a_{jk}^{default}$ are set initially. The length for the moving frame to store observations is set to 60 observations, which equals 1 min in system time. Therefore, system parameters are updated periodically whenever the frame advances as long as its length. The initial time for system construction is set 2 min. This duration is basically reserved to let classification algorithms run properly and let the system adjust initial adaptability to the user. After initial 2 min long sampling insertions at 100 Hz, any power saving method can be applied. In that case, it takes {1, 2, 4, 8} s to insert a new observation if {100, 50, 25, 12.5} Hz sampling frequencies are adjusted, respectively.

The same user activity profile is performed throughout one and a half hour application running time for each power saving method.

3.4.3 *Performance Evaluation*

First, Figure 3.10 shows the convergence of entropy rate throughout application running time for each power saving method at different sampling frequencies. Aggressive sampling method that takes 100 Hz as sampling frequency draws the actual track of entropy rate. Circles over this track in Figure 3.10 indicate difference in user behaviors. Since user states such as *sitting* and *standing* are recognized, the frequentness of

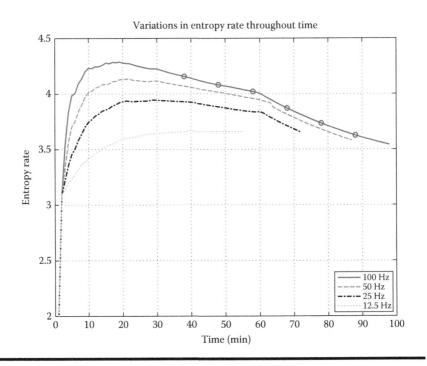

Figure 3.10 Experiment: entropy rate analysis.

transition from one state to another cannot be much due to the nature of human. Therefore, user state transition matrices over time are desired as

$$a_{ij}^{[1:6]} = \begin{bmatrix} 0.9 & 0.1 \\ 0.1 & 0.9 \end{bmatrix}, \begin{bmatrix} 0.85 & 0.15 \\ 0.1 & 0.9 \end{bmatrix}, \begin{bmatrix} 0.8 & 0.2 \\ 0.1 & 0.9 \end{bmatrix} \begin{bmatrix} 0.75 & 0.25 \\ 0.1 & 0.9 \end{bmatrix},$$
$$\begin{bmatrix} 0.6 & 0.4 \\ 0.1 & 0.9 \end{bmatrix}, \begin{bmatrix} 0.5 & 0.5 \\ 0.1 & 0.9 \end{bmatrix}.$$

As discussed in simulations, entropy rate converges late while samplings are collected at sampling frequencies except for 100 Hz. That is also the reason why accuracy rate decreases. The most significant assumption can be obtained from Figure 3.10 is entropy rate cannot sometimes converge into any point where the plot lines belonging to $f_s = \{12.5, 25, 50\}$ Hz stop. When the frequentness of state transitions increases, sampling frequency may not be fast enough to capture the activeness of user profile. Therefore, the system cannot find any proper user state transition matrix to define instant user activity profile. For instance, $a^{(6)}$ has equal probabilities for both residual frequentness in user state and its transition to other user state. Thereby, the specific user activity profile may be enough for being recognized at 100 Hz but not at other sampling frequencies. Note that at 12.5 Hz, 87.5% of observation space is estimated. Another significant point is the blue line on the graph gets closer to $a^{(6)}$ in Figure 3.10 since both transition matrices in application and simulation start to converge into the same pattern. Therefore, it is pointed out that the convergence of entropy rate belonging to an HMM-based HAR framework could distinguish a specific user activity profile. In addition to that, the linkage between the entropy rate and the accuracy of the recognitions could be made as follows: assume that a simple threshold is defined for entropy rate in Section 3.2.3 by $\varepsilon_{e_p} = [\mu_{e_p} - \sigma_{e_p}, \mu_{e_p} + \sigma_{e_p}]$ where μ_{e_p} and σ_{e_p} are mean and standard deviation of e_p, respectively. Hence, an accuracy notifier is set to inform whether or not current recognitions in user states are done accurately by

$$\phi(s, t) = \frac{1}{(t - s + 1)} \sum_{\tau=s}^{t} 1_{(e_p^\tau \in \varepsilon_{e_p})}.$$

Second, by using the accuracy notifier, the trade-off between accuracy in user state representations and power consumption is given in Figure 3.11. Aggressive sampling method has the best accuracy value of 100%, whereas power consumption has the worst efficiency. Sampling at 50 Hz frequency (red line) provides 82% accuracy against 42% power consumption as long as relevant entropy rate converges. Accuracy rate is over 50%, which means applied HMM works properly and estimates missing observations properly enough. When an user profile has less frequent transitions among user states, accuracy rate is seen over 90%. On the other hand, at a time slot where entropy rate loses information, the sampling method at 100 Hz frequency has consumed almost 87% of its power. Thus, efficiency in power consumption at

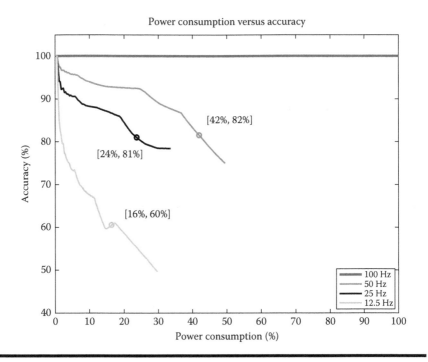

Figure 3.11 Experiment: power consumption versus accuracy.

50 Hz frequency becomes $(87-42)*100/87 = 51\%$. Power efficiency can be healed more if adaptability is satisfied earlier since a drastic fall is seen in the beginning of curves on the graph. In addition, when entropy rate converges in a fixed value, the curves become concave shaped because the number of false user state recognitions is expected to decrease. After losing entropy rate, the system retains previous user state transition values and continues running. Therefore, a rapid decrease can be seen after a circle is marked on any curve. Other sampling methods have (81%, 67%) and (60%, 70%) pairs of accuracy rate versus power efficiency for 25 and 12.5 Hz, respectively, where they are applicable. From application results, it can be concluded that if adaptability to user profile is sufficiently satisfied, different sensor sampling methods can be applied adaptively by periodically checking for the convergence of entropy rate. The lower variance value entropy rate gets, the slower sampling period the system can adjust, or vice versa.

Third, Figure 3.12 demonstrates battery lifetime for each power saving method. The target device has 1-year-old 1400 mAh battery named DX-1. Note that a used phone is examined to find a regular daily usage. The application starts running with fully charged battery at each sampling method. While the application is running, the device is in standby mode and connected to a 3G network. According to the results, the target device battery depletes after approximately {9, 15, 24, 28} h while

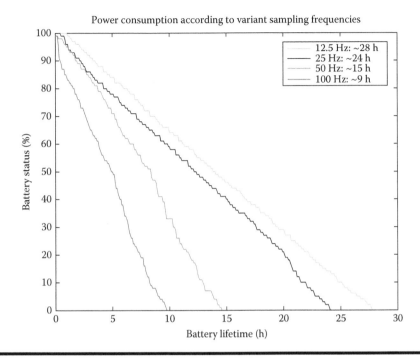

Figure 3.12   Experiment: battery depletion.

operating at {100, 50, 25, 12.5} Hz sampling frequencies, respectively. In a standby mode, the device itself lasts up to 55 h. Note that the Blackberry Java 7.1. SDK only reveals remaining battery status information.

In simulations, power consumption per unit sampling at each sampling frequency, which is proportional to (3.14), is modeled as

$$\Theta_{n*12.5\text{Hz}} = n * \Omega_{sample} + (8 - n) * \Omega_{idle}. \tag{3.20}$$

In order to compare power consumption between simulations and applications, the following inequality derived from (3.20) needs to be approximately satisfied:

$$\frac{\Theta_{100\text{Hz}}}{\frac{1}{9} - \frac{1}{55}} \approx \frac{\Theta_{50\text{Hz}}}{\frac{1}{15} - \frac{1}{55}} \approx \frac{\Theta_{25\text{Hz}}}{\frac{1}{24} - \frac{1}{55}} \approx \frac{\Theta_{12.5\text{Hz}}}{\frac{1}{28} - \frac{1}{55}}$$

In summary, this chapter presents a generic system framework within the area of mobile device–based context-aware applications. It focuses on the inhomogeneity and the user profile adaptability while examining the trade-off between accuracy in contextual inference from sensory data and required power consumption due to data acquisition and computational processing. The inhomogeneity is characterized by time-variant system parameters, and the user profile adaptability challenge is modeled using the convergence of entropy rate in conjunction with the inhomogeneity. Simulations are run, and a smartphone application is implemented in order to demonstrate how entropy rate converges in response to distinctive time-variant user profiles under different sensory sampling operations. In addition, user state representations are either recognized or estimated while various energy saving strategies are being applied. During the recognition process, a sufficient number of signal processing techniques are applied to find out the best context-exploiting methods on the sensory signal instead of applying computationally harsh pattern recognition methods. Moreover, the power saving consideration is taken at the low-level sensory operations rather than just applying less complexity in computations or changing transferring methods of data packets in the application. In summary, the present research aims at creating and clarifying an HMM-based framework to guide the development of future context-aware applications by proposing an effective method to achieve a fine balance in the defined trade-off analysis.

Chapter 4

Energy Efficiency in Physical Hardware

The use of mobile devices, such as smartphones, is constrained by battery life. With the ever-increasing computing power and hardware development in mobile devices and slow growth in the energy densities of the battery technologies used in these devices, topics such as extension of battery lifetimes and estimation of energy delivery by batteries have been one of the primary focuses in the mobile computing research field. Hence, modeling power consumption profiles belonging to new generation mobile devices with the knowledge of the battery behavior will be important for energy optimization and management in resource-constrained mobile computing systems. The battery behavior is not consistent with respect to energy required by the device since the energy drawn from the battery is not always equivalent to the energy consumed by the device itself. In addition, the impact of different usage patterns on devices needs to be investigated to link to the projected effect on the power consumption. Modeling the battery's nonlinearities and understanding the correlation between the usage patterns and the battery depletion lead to discovering suboptimal energy reduction strategies, which help continual improvement existing within the concept of the context-aware mobile computing.

This chapter studies the battery modeled under the scope of the battery nonlinearities with respect to variant discharge profiles. In addition, the energy consumption behavior of some smartphone sensors is analytically modeled, including a real-time application carried out for the accelerometer sensor to investigate the behavior in detail. Energy consumption profiles are created by assigning different pairs of duty cycles and sampling frequencies during the sensory operations.

Finally, a Markov reward process is integrated in order to model the energy consumption profiles and represents the cost by each profile as an accumulated reward. The accumulated reward is also linked to the battery modeling to make a connection between the usage pattern on sensors and the battery behavior.

New generation mobile devices with sensing capabilities, such as smartphones and tablets, will constitute a significant part of future mobile technologies. With built-in sensors being reconfigured and repurposed, these mobile devices can provide highly proactive services within the concept of human-centric or participatory sensing, which support computationally pervasive and emerging context-aware mobile applications. However, a major challenge standing up to these sensor-rich devices is resource limitation in terms of power, memory, and bandwidth as compared to the capabilities of PCs and servers. In this sense, the design of mobile device–based context-aware middleware emerges in needs not only to create abstract models for the representation of the interested phenomena for the application services but also to exploit heterogeneous and unobtrusive physical world as well as providing energy efficient optimal sensor sensing and actuating solutions.

Due to the ever-increasing computing power and hardware development in mobile devices compared with the slow growth observed in the stored capacity of energy densities in the mobile device–based battery technologies, the usage of mobile devices is constrained by battery lifetime. Especially, continuously capturing user context through sensors in a context-aware application imposes heavy workloads on computations and hardware, for example, the processor and relevant hardware peripherals, which, in return, makes the battery drain rapidly. Thereby, the topics such as the extension of battery lifetime, estimation of energy delivery or battery discharge, and optimal energy management have drawn much research interest in mobile computing. In this sense, the examination of nonlinear battery behaviors becomes crucial in terms of creating optimal sensor management systems. Correspondingly, the battery lifetime mostly depends on energy consumption rate; discharge profile, that is, usage pattern; and battery nonlinearities. At the high energy consumption rate, the effective residual battery capacity degrades and results in having a shorter battery lifetime. However, any precautionary change in the usage pattern could extend the battery lifetime. For instance, lowering the average energy consumption rate at any point of time could be one of the changes. More importantly, physical nonlinearities in batteries could recover the lost capacity while a very small amount of energy is consumed.

By this means, this chapter examines battery modeling to investigate battery behaviors and nonlinearities. Then, it continues by modeling the energy consumption of smartphone sensors, and it takes the accelerometer sensor as an example. Both simulation and smartphone application models are provided to see the effect of variant sensory operations on the battery discharge. By doing this, the linkage between a change in energy consumption profile wasted by context-aware applications and battery behavior to respond to this change is exposed. Having this knowledge, a reward process is integrated to create a sensor management system. The system aims at bridging sensor use by applications and battery behaviors on application loads. Finally, three different sampling methods are proposed on the evolution of the given reward process to achieve energy efficiency, yet context-aware applications maintain to provide accurate services. A smartphone application is implemented to validate given sensor management system.

4.1 Discussions

The battery behavior is not consistent with respect to energy required by the device since it is the fact that the energy drawn from the battery is not always equivalent to the energy consumed by the device itself. In this regard, many different approaches have been used to model the battery properties such as the electrochemical models, electrical-circuit models, and analytical models. However, these models provide the same battery lifetime for all load profiles, and they give better results for constant continuous loads but not for variant or intermittent loads. In this sense, stochastic models are presented to model batteries in an abstract manner by the discretization of the battery charge and creation of probabilistic transitions among discharge level caused by variations in workloads.

In addition, many studies have been put forward to extend battery lifetime in mobile sensing. Accordingly, most works done so far emphasize setting a minimum number of sensors by a mobile application with fixed duty cycles, using different deterministic sampling period schemes, and maximizing power efficiency by solely applying less complexity in computations or by changing transferring methods of data packets. However, the impact of different usage patterns on devices needs to be investigated to link to the projected effect on the power consumption. Especially, modeling the battery nonlinearities together with an understanding of the relation between energy-wise usage patterns and battery depletion may lead to discovering optimal energy reduction strategies in order to help continual improvement in context-aware mobile services.

Second, this study suggests opportunistic power saving methods at low-level sensory operations in mobile sensing so that battery lifetime could be extended. To be able to accomplish that, the energy consumption behavior of smartphone sensors are analytically modeled in this chapter. Significantly, a smartphone application is carried out for the accelerometer sensor to investigate this behavior in detail. According to the proposed model, energy consumption profiles are created by assigning different pairs of duty cycles and sampling frequencies in sensory operations. Third, a Markov reward process is integrated to evaluate the energy consumption profiles and represent the energy cost caused by each profile as an accumulated reward. The accumulated reward is also linked to the battery modeling to make a connection between energy-wise usage pattern on sensors and battery behavior. Finally, with an understanding of nonlinearity observed on the batteries in response to variant sensory operations, a fine efficiency in power consumption is achieved by proposing three different methods on the evolution of the reward process while employing a human activity recognition (HAR)–based context-aware smartphone application.

The outline of the chapter is as follows: Section 4.2 provides a battery modeling that is very feasible to project into the mobile device batteries. Section 4.3 models sensory operations in terms of energy consumption and creates different load profiles during the operations to find out their effects on the total energy cost by taking the smartphone accelerometer sensor as an example. Section 4.5 makes a connection between battery nonlinearity and sensor utilization to analyze battery discharge profiles triggered by energy cost ocurring during sensory operations. Finally, Section 4.6 uses this connection to examine changing sensory operations to achieve a fine achievement in energy efficiency by providing an HAR-based context-aware smartphone application.

4.2 Battery Modeling

The energy stored in batteries is expressed by the product of two quantities: voltage (*Volt*, V) and capacity (*Ampere-Hour*, Ah). The battery lifetime mostly depends on the energy consumption rate; the discharge profile, for example, the usage pattern; and battery nonlinearities. At the high energy consumption rate, the effective residual battery capacity degrades, resulting in having a shorter battery lifetime. However, any precautionary change in the usage pattern could extend the battery lifetime. More importantly, physical nonlinearities in batteries could recover the lost capacity while no or a very small amount of energy is consumed.

Battery modeling can help to predict the battery behaviors and then to extend the battery lifetimes. In this regard, many different approaches have been used to model the battery properties. The electrochemical models [61,78,129] have been developed to describe chemical processes that take place in batteries. These models are known as the most accurate models to predict the battery behaviors; however, these models are much complicated to be used in the applications belonging to contemporary mobile devices by including nonlinear differential equations as a function of time and position of some battery properties, such as the voltage and current, the potentials in the electrolyte and electrode phases, and reaction rate and current density in the electrolyte. In addition, electrical-circuit models [88] were proposed to simulate batteries. These models seem simpler than electrochemical models in terms of computational complexity; however, it requires much effort to configure the relevant electrical-circuit model corresponding to a specific battery and also requires a vast quantity of experimental data to better model the battery behaviors. Moreover, analytical models [191] are described to model batteries at a higher level of abstraction instead of electrochemical and electrical-circuit models. The major properties of the battery characteristics are given by equations. These models mostly consider batteries in an ideal case, which would have a constant voltage running and a constant capacity profile for every load throughout the discharge. In an ideal case, $L = C/I$ where the lifetime (L) is calculated with a constant capacity load (C) over the running current (I). In constant, the voltage could drop during discharge and the effective capacity observed lower under a heavy-usage pattern in reality. Therefore, an approximation is proposed by introducing Peukert's law in [179], which proposes $L = a/I^b$ where a and b are considered as approximately the battery capacity and integer value (e.g., ideally 1), respectively, in order of showing nonlinearity. However, this Peukert's law would provide the same battery lifetime for all load profiles. The model would give good results for constant continuous loads, but not for variant or interrupt loads. In this regard, an extended Peukert's law, $L = a/(\frac{1}{L} \int_0^L I_t dt)^b$, is also proposed in the same study to give a new analytical battery model in terms of handling nonconstant discharge profiles, that is, variant loads. Furthermore, stochastic models [70,159] are presented to model batteries in an abstract manner like analytical models by discretizing the battery charge and creating probabilistic transition among discharge levels caused by variations in workload. A very detailed study in battery modeling can be found in [112,178,181].

A battery consists of electrochemical cells that drive electrochemical reactions in order to convert chemically stored energy into electrical energy. A cell includes two electrodes, an anode and a cathode, and the electrolyte, which separates the two electrodes, as shown in Figure 4.1. The electrolyte may be liquid as in lead–acid batteries or solid as in lithium-ion batteries. During the discharge, an oxidation reaction occurs at the anode. By this reaction, a reductant (R_1) donates m electrons, which become available to be released into the connected circuit. On the other hand, at

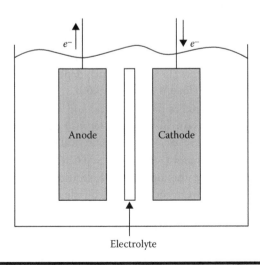

Figure 4.1 A battery cell.

the cathode, a reduction reaction occurs. By this reaction, m electrons are received by an oxidant (O_2):

$$R_1 \rightarrow O_1 + me^-$$

$$O_2 + ne^- \rightarrow R_2$$

Lithium-ion batteries are widely used in notebook computers and cellular phones due to their high energy density and lightweightedness. For example, relevant chemical reactions for a lithium-ion battery with the positive electrode ($Li_yMn_2O_4$) and the negative electrode (Li_xC_6) are given in [191] as

$$Li_{y-n}Mn_2O_4 + nLi^+ + ne^- \rightleftharpoons Li_yMn_2O_4$$

$$Li_nC_6 \rightleftharpoons Li_0C_6 + nLi^+ + ne^-$$

The theoretical capacity of the battery is a measure of the maximal charge. The ions at the anode diffuse into the cathode when current is drawn from the battery. If the current drawn is too high, the speed of diffusion is slower than the rate of the ions reacted at the cathode. This results in reduction occurring at the outer surface of the cathode and access to the inner ions impossible; hence, a drop in the output voltage sourced by the battery is observed. As the intensity of the current drawn increases, the loss of capacity due to the nonuniform deviation in the ion concentration becomes significant, and thereby, the cell voltage decreases, which is called rate capacity effect [178]. At the lower current drawn or when the discharge process occurs in some intermediate or periodic time scale, the ions could have enough time to diffuse into the inner cathode and let the charge recovery process take place. Therefore, the reacted ions at the cathode become uniformly distributed. This nonlinearity is called recovery effect [179,181], which depends on the discharge profile and the time length while no load is applied [49,60].

Let C and $\acute{C}$ are considered as the theoretical and nominal capacity values of a fully loaded battery, respectively. In addition, let $x(t)$ denote the level of available charge and $v(t)$ denote the level of available theoretical capacity of the battery with the conditions of $t \in [0, T]$ and $(v(0), x(0)) = (C, \acute{C})$. According to the Nernst equation in electrochemistry, the logarithm of electric charge determines the terminal voltage that exists between the pair of electrode terminals, the potential E is determined by $E = E_0 - K_e \ln C$ where C is the concentration of electroactive species at the electrode, E_0 is the equilibrium potential, $K_e = RT_a/nF$ with R the ideal gas constant, T_a absolute temperature, $n = 1$ the valency of the lithium-ion battery reaction, and F Faraday's constant. By Faraday's first law, the mass of active material altered at an electrode is directly proportional to the quantity of electrical charge that is transferred at the electrode in the battery reaction. Thus, it identifies the capacity of the cell as a product of C. As a result, the terminal voltage E_t of the cell at time t is given by

$$E_t = E_0 + K_e \ln \tilde{x}(t), \quad 0 \le t \le t_0 \tag{4.1}$$

where the normalized and dimensionless $\tilde{x} = x(t)/C \in [0, 1]$ is a measure of capacity, then the battery is full where $\tilde{x}(t) = 1$ and the battery is empty where $\tilde{x} = 0$. Also, t_0 notifies the battery life at which E_t in (4.1) reaches a cutoff voltage E_c and battery stops functioning. For lithium-ion battery, $E_0 = 3V$ and $E_c = 2V$ where $E_c \le E_0$.

The kinetic battery model (KiBaM) is the most powerful analytical battery model represented, first, in [143] and widely used in the recent studies [48,112,182]. The name kinetic is given to the model because of chemical processes taken place during the discharge. KiBaM considers the stored charge to be distributed over two wells, the available-charge well and the bound-charge well, as shown in Figure 4.2. The bound-charge well supplies electrons only to the available-charge well, whereas the available-charge well supplies electrons directly to the connected load. The rate of charge flow between these wells depends on the conductance parameter k and the difference in heights of two wells h_1 and h_2. The capacity ratio is denoted as parameter c and corresponds to the friction of total charge stored in the available-charge well. Recall that $x(t)$ denotes the available capacity of the battery and $v(t)$ denotes the total capacity where $x(0) = \acute{C}$ and $v(0) = C > \acute{C}$, so $y(t) = v(t) - x(t)$ becomes the bound charge. On the other hand, the KiBaM was primarily developed to model lead–acid batteries. Since these types of batteries have a flat discharge profile, there are some shortcomings of KiBaM to model lithium-ion batteries, which are widely used in today's mobile devices. However, KiBaM could be still examined for issues such as the battery lifetime, the capacity rate, and the recovery effect [112,182]. To be able to extend the battery model for lithium-ion cells, a solid state diffusion must

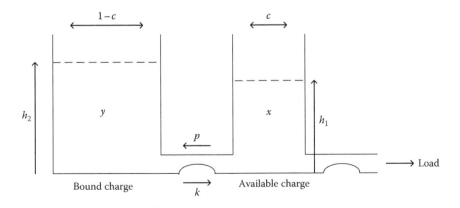

Figure 4.2 The two-well KiBaM.

be added into KiBaM. In solid state, electroactivated at the electrodes experience a drift motion diffusion in addition to random diffusion [55]. The drift motion can be added into flux as a negative charge, that is, degradation on the conductance parameter k.

During the battery operation, the current drawn due to discharge is denoted by $i(t) \geq 0$ with the average discharge rate of $\hat{\lambda} = \lim_{t \to \infty} \frac{1}{t} \int_0^t i(s)ds$ if the limit exists. Then, the unit change in the charge stored in both wells is given by the differential equations:

$$
\begin{aligned}
\frac{dx(t)}{dt} &= -i(t) + k(1-p)(h_2 - h_1) \\
\frac{dy(t)}{dt} &= -k(1-p)(h_2 - h_1)
\end{aligned}
\tag{4.2}
$$

with initial conditions of $x(0) = c \cdot C = \acute{C}$, $y(0) = (1-c) \cdot C = C - \acute{C}$, $h_1 = x(t)/c$, and $h_2 = y(t)/(1-c)$. Also, $p \in [0, 1]$ denotes a fraction of the flow of charge that has been released from and sent back to the bound-charge well. A very detailed study for further equation derivations can be found in [115].

When the battery supplies continuous discharge, the available-charge well would be reduced rapidly, the difference of the height in both wells would grow since there is no time to move charge from the bounded-charge well into the available-charge well, and the battery would not last long. However, when the load is removed, a remedy charge flows from the bounded-charge well into the available-charge well until h_1 and h_2 are balanced. This gives the idea of why a recovery process takes place when an intermittent charge is applied by variant loads.

By using (4.2), the total discharge process becomes independent from the charge flow gradient:

$$
v(t) = x(t) + y(t) = C - \int_0^t i(s)\,ds, \quad t \geq 0
\tag{4.3}
$$

By replacing $i(t)dt$ with some measure of $\Lambda(dt)$, then $v(t) = C - \Lambda(t)$. Equation 4.2 turns into

$$
\begin{aligned}
dx(t) &= -\Lambda(dt) + k(1-p)\left(\frac{y(t)}{(1-c)} - \frac{x(t)}{c}\right)dt \\
dy(t) &= -k(1-p)\left(\frac{y(t)}{(1-c)} - \frac{x(t)}{c}\right)dt
\end{aligned}
\tag{4.4}
$$

The equivalent differential equation solution for (4.4) then becomes

$$x(t) = cv(t) - (1-c)\int_0^t e^{-k(1-p)(t-s)/c(1-c)}\Lambda(ds)$$

$$y(t) = (1-c)v(t) + \int_0^t e^{-k(1-p)(t-s)/c(1-c)}\Lambda(ds)$$

(4.5)

If a cell is subject to variant loads, the current drawn would vary with different discharge rates by examining (4.3) accordingly; thereby, (4.5) has solutions as follows:

■ *Case 1*: The constant discharge, $\Lambda(t) = \lambda t$, where $v_\lambda(t) = C - \lambda t$ on the bivariate dynamic system of $(v_\lambda(t), x_\lambda(t))$:

$$x_\lambda(t) = cv_\lambda(t) - C_\lambda(1 - e^{-k(1-p)t/c(1-c)})$$

$$C_\lambda = \lambda c(1-c)^2/k(1-p)$$

(4.6)

■ *Case 2*: The periodic regularly spaced pulsed discharge, $\Lambda(t) = \lambda r \sum_{j=1}^{t/r}\delta_{jr}$, where λr denotes the released charge during the two consecutive pulses in $r > 0$ time intervals on the system of $(v^{(r)}(t), x^{(r)}(t))$:

$$x^{(r)}(t) = cv^{(r)}(t) - (1-c)\lambda r \sum_{j=1}^{t/r} e^{-k(1-p)(t-jr)/c(1-c)}$$

$$= cv^{(r)} - C_\lambda^{(r)}(1 - e^{-k(1-p)(C-v^{(r)})/\lambda c(1-c)})$$

(4.7)

With the evaluation of geometric sum, $C_\lambda^{(r)} = \lambda r(1-c)/(1-e^{-k(1-p)r/c(1-c)})$ gives the bursting points of the discharge profile due to the periodically drawn load.

Figure 4.3 shows an example for investigating the KiBaM behavior under different load profiles and at fixed system parameters. The load profiles are characterized by mixture pairs of sampling frequency, f_s, and the duty cycling on the load. Thereby, the load is defined by $\lambda = 2f_s$ where $f_s = \{50, 100\}$ Hz, and $r = n\Delta t$ where $n = \{1/2, 3/4, 1\}$. For instance, if $n = 1$, it means that the load has a constant discharge profile, that is, 100% duty cycling, whereas if $n \in \{1/2, 3/4\}$, it means that the duty cycle values of $\{50\%, 75\%\}$ are applied on the load. In addition, the same power consumption rate per unit time is considered during discharge. On the other hand, the battery parameters for KiBaM are chosen as in $C = 1400$ mAh, $c = 0.625$, $p = 0.1$, and $k = 4.5E^{-5}(1/s)$. These parameters can differ from one battery to another.

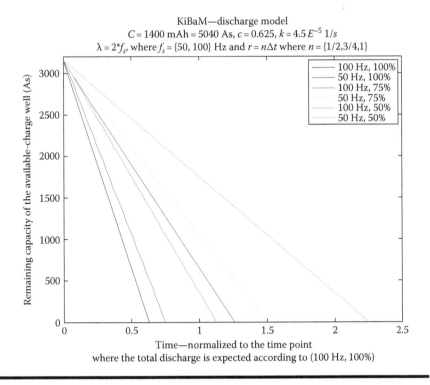

Figure 4.3 **The KiBaM discharge model: an example.**

However, by analyzing the given example, it is intended to see how differently a battery discharges with respect to variant load profiles.

Figure 4.3 is normalized to the time point where the total discharge is expected according to the full depletion in C where $f_s = 100$ Hz and 100% for duty cycle. According to the results, obtaining the depletion time less than 1 means that the battery seems as if it was depleted even if it still has charges in storage. In contrast, the battery lifetime is extended when the depletion time is greater than 1. As a conclusion, two hypotheses can be made from the example in Figure 4.3. First, the constant aggressive loading by (4.6) affects the discharge profile severely and yields to deplete the device battery faster even if the battery still has a sufficient stored charge. The second hypothesis by (4.7) is that battery recovery effect takes place when load gets lighter. The effect increases the available-charge well and prolongs the battery lifetime.

4.3 Modeling of Energy Consumption by Sensors

Sensors on mobile devices can be classified into two categories depending on operation methods. The first category consists of sensors, such as accelerometer and microphone, which when turned on to operate can run as long as needed.

They need an external command to finish their operations and to be turned off. When sampling operation is in progress, the relevant sampling period in the operation can be adaptively changed if power considerations are taken. On the other hand, the second category consists of sensors such as GPS, Wi-Fi, and Bluetooth. When these sensors are turned on, they follow their own dedicated protocols to operate and be in idle position after the required work is done. Therefore, the idea of setting different sampling periods might not be an option for this category. Exceptionally, although Bluetooth is selected in the second category while scanning nearby users, it might also be considered as a member of the first category as well while its spectrum is sensed and analyzed with different sampling periods.

The cost of the energy consumed during any sensor operation not only depends on instant energy consumption per operation but also depends on the duration of operation itself. In Figure 4.4, sensor operation structure for both categories is illustrated. The structure starts with an initialization block that is in charge of waking the sensor up and then waiting for an acknowledge response informing that the sensor is ready. For example, the study in [221] states that for GPS operation, it is required at least 10 s to successfully synchronize with satellites. For other sensors, especially the first-category sensors, a little time duration would be sufficient to power sensors up and then to set initial system requirements before sampling operations begin. The second block is called processing. This block is dedicated to provide the mentioned efficiency in energy consumption, which this chapter proposes. In this block, sensors start to capture user contextual information and continue to do the same operation repeatedly. The third block terminates sensor's active duty. After all these three blocks are operated, the sensor is shut down until a new duty is assigned.

The processing block is where the time length for duty cycle and sampling period are adjusted dynamically for a sensor. Energy consumption is reduced by carefully assigning duty cycles and sampling periods; however, these assignments cause a trade-off between reduced energy consumption and accurate sensing. If successive sampling intervals are too long, there would not be a sufficient number of samplings to present real conditions, and eventually it would cause user contextual information

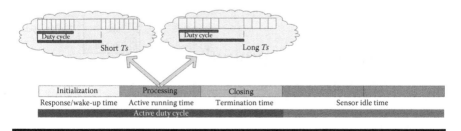

Figure 4.4 **Sensory operations.**

to be sensed incorrectly. On the other hand, in the case where intervals are too short, energy saving would not be satisfied. The same approach can also be applied to sensor sleeping time intervals. A longer sleeping time interval would reduce energy consumption; nonetheless, the detection latency will be increased so that false detections could occur.

4.3.1 Preliminaries

Assume that a first-category sensory operation is modeled by certain time parameters, such as t_w, t_s, t_c, and t_r are given for a wake-up/initialization time, which could be a termination time as well, a total time per sampling, a total time for operation cycle, and a total time throughout sensor running, respectively. In addition, Ω_s and Ω_i are given as constant default sensor properties for power consumption to make a sampling and to run idle, respectively [236].

DC stands for duty cycle, which indicates the active sensor operation (i.e., time interval in which actually sensor samplings are being made) within t_{cycle}. Thus, the number of sampling occurrences is found by $N_s = DC * t_c / T_s$ where $0 \leq DC \leq 1$ and T_s is sampling period (i.e., inversely proportional to sampling frequency, $1/f_s$), which defines a waiting time between two consecutive sensor samplings, see details in Figure 4.5.

Then, a total energy consumption throughout sensor running is approximately given by

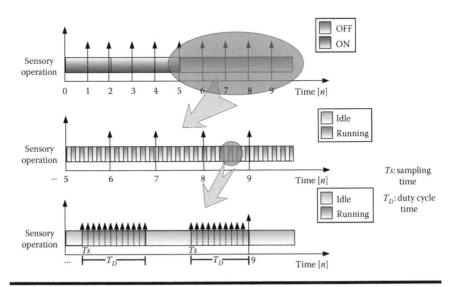

Figure 4.5 Duty cycling and sensor sampling.

$$\Theta_{total} \approx \left[(DC * t_c) \left(\sum_{k=1}^{N} \left(\sum_{(k-1)Ts}^{(k-1)Ts+t_s} \Omega_s + \sum_{(k-1)Ts+t_s}^{kTs} \Omega_i \right) \right) \right.$$

$$\left. + ((1-DC) * t_c)\Omega_i \right] \left(\frac{t_r - 2t_w}{t_c} r \right)$$

$$\approx \left[N_s t_s \Omega_s + (t_c - N_s t_s)\Omega_i \right] \left(\frac{t_r - 2t_w}{t_c} \right) \qquad (4.8)$$

while ignoring power consumption wasted during the initialization and termination of the sensor.

4.3.2 Modeling of Sensory Operations

Sensor operation can be modeled as 1-Burst process, also called ON–OFF sensory operation. This process is a special case of Markov-modulated Poisson processes. This special case is called IPP and has two states: ON and OFF, as shown in Figure 4.6. According to the process, the traffic is Poisson $\{F(x) = 1 - e^{-\lambda x}\}$, but the traffic is generated at deterministic intervals in ON state with a constant rate λ_{on} and a length of mean time, that is, transition time, $1/w_{on}$. In contrast, there is no traffic in OFF state, and the intensity of residency in this state is given by w_{off}.

The traffic in IPP can be seen as a discrete-event simulator for samplings in sensory operations. Thus, the intensity rates become $\lambda_{on} = f_s$, $w_{on} = (DC * tc)^{-1}$, and $w_{off} = ((1-DC) * tc)^{-1}$.

Note that alternatively the burst periods can be modeled by Weibull distribution $\{F(x) = (1 - e^{-\lambda x^{\alpha}})\}$ where $\alpha > 1$ yields to have more deterministic variations. Then, sampling intervals, that is, interarrival time in traffic, $T = 1/\lambda_{on}$, are generated. In addition, the silence periods can be derived from Pareto distribution, which is known as tail process, $\{F(x) = (1 - (k/x)^{\alpha})\}$ where $\alpha > 1$ yields to have

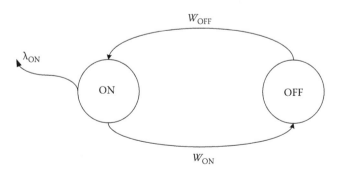

Figure 4.6   Interrupt Poisson process (IPP).

more deterministic variates. On the other hand, in the case of no silence periods, Erlang-K model, which is stochastically the sum of K times *i.i.d.* random variables with each having a Poisson distribution, can be considered by setting $\lambda_{on} = 2f_s K$ and the expected frequentness of consecutive ON/OFF times becomes $K/(2f_s K)$.

4.4 Validation by a Smartphone Application

The least power consuming sensor in today's smartphones is the accelerometer [22]. Therefore, the accelerometer sensor is used in the implementation of a real-time application.

The Blackberry RIM Storm II 9550 smartphone is chosen as the target device for a real-time context-aware application. The Blackberry Java 7.1 SDK is used for programming, and Eclipse is used as a software development tool. Storm II consists of three-axis accelerometer named ADXL346 from Analog Devices. This sensor operates at 2.6 V as supply voltage and 1.8 V as drain voltage. Its current flow varies under different operation modes and data rate selections (refer to Table 3.2). The drawn current values at specific sampling frequencies give an idea of how much power could be consumed in different accelerometer sensor operation modes. Turn-on and wake-up times are determined by data rate, and a relevant formula is given approximately by $\tau + 1.1$ in milliseconds, where $\tau = 1/(\text{data rate})$ [1].

By using IPP sensory modeling together with the data obtained through Table 3.2, and (4.8) with parameter setting of $t_c = 2s$, the power consumption ratio in the sensor drain per each operation cycle under variant DC and f_s values are shown in Table 4.1. According to the results, the smartphone accelerometer sensor

Table 4.1 Power Consumption Ratio in the Sensor Drain per Each Operation Cycle

$(DC\ (\%), f_s\ (Hz))$	Ratio
(100, 100)	4.45
(50, 100)	2.58
(100, 50)	2.85
(50, 50)	1.80
(100, 25)	1.75
(50, 25)	1.24
(100, 12.5)	1.26
(50, 12.5)	1

Note: $t_C = 2s$, and the comparison applied based on (50%, 12.5 Hz).

consumes 4.45 times more power per each operation cycle in aggressive sampling mode in comparison with the most nonaggressive sampling mode.

The accelerometer sensor needs to be modeled to examine power efficiency achieved under different sampling and duty cycling strategies. By using (4.2) and (4.8), the power consumption model within each t_c can be considered as follows:

$$\Theta_{t_c} = \sum_{0}^{DC*t_c} (L_s(x,y) - R_s(x,y)) + \sum_{DC*tc}^{tc} (L_i(x,y) - R_i(x,y)) + \sum_{0}^{tc} L_b(x,y)$$

$$(4.9)$$

- (x,y) is the bivariate dynamic battery system parameters, which define capacity values stored inside the bound-charge well and the available-charge well in KiBaM.
- L_s and L_i are denoted as the discharged load when sensor samplings are being made and the sensor is being idle, respectively:
  - If $DC = 1$, then the sensor makes samplings continuously. This means that the effect of L_i can be ignored due to the constant discharge profile. Thus, recall that the model follows (4.6).
  - If $DC \in [0, 1)$, then the sensor makes samplings in defined intervals. In this case, the effect of L_i cannot be ignored so that the model follows (4.7).
- R_s and R_i are *battery recovery effects* in KiBaM to define the remedy charge flowing from the bound-charge well to the available-charge well when sensor samplings are being made and the sensor is being idle, respectively.
- L_b stands for the background load occurring instantly within the smartphone operation. For instance, while the application is running, the device is in standby mode and is only connected to a 3G network. There is no other system functionality being executed while the sensor operates.

The application runs until initially fully loaded 1 year long used smartphone battery depletes. Only one constant pair of sampling frequency and duty cycle is applied as operation parameters to the accelerometer sensor at each application run. Sampling intervals are modeled as $I_i = n/f_s$ where n and f_s are an integer value and sampling frequency, respectively. I_i defines a waiting time between two consecutive sensor samplings; $n = \{1, 2, 4, 8\}$ and $f_s = 100$ Hz are taken. On the other hand, values of $\{0.5, 0.75, 1\}$ are taken for DC. t_c is also taken as 1 s.

Results are shown in Figure 4.7. Note that the Blackberry Java 7.1. SDK only helps to reveal the remaining battery status. According to results, applying a more aggressive sampling methodology causes faster battery depletion. In addition, the lower value of DC makes the battery recovery effect more significant and thus prolongs the battery lifetime.

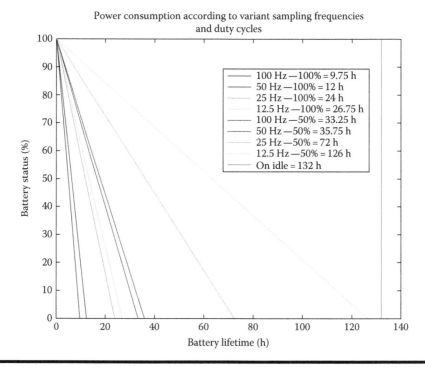

Figure 4.7 **The battery depletion due to variant sampling frequencies and duty cycles within the operation of the accelerometer sensor (samples are taken at every 20 min).**

According to (4.8), energy consumption per time of $(n_{max}/f_{s_{max}} = 8/100)$ under different sampling frequencies is modeled as

$$\Theta_{n*12.5\text{Hz}} = n * \Omega_{sample} + (n_{max} - n) * \Omega_{idle} \tag{4.10}$$

Then, with the help of (4.10), (4.9) turns into

$$\Theta_{t_c} = \frac{DCt_c}{n_{max}/f_{s_{max}}}(\Theta_{n*12.5\text{Hz}} - r_s) + \frac{(1 - DC)t_c}{1/f_{s_{max}}}(\Omega_{idle} - r_i) + l_b \tag{4.11}$$

where r_s, r_i, and l_n are considered having a stable energy consumption rate per unit time.

Since the parameters r_s and r_i in (4.11) cannot be verified through smartphone programming, in order to compare energy consumption between the analytical model and the application, the following inequality needs to be approximately satisfied:

$$\frac{\Theta^{real}_{100Hz,DC=1}}{\Theta^{sim}_{100Hz,DC=1}} \approx \frac{\Theta^{real}_{50Hz,DC=1}}{\Theta^{sim}_{50Hz,DC=1}} \approx \frac{\Theta^{real}_{25Hz,DC=1}}{\Theta^{sim}_{25Hz,DC=1}} \approx \frac{\Theta^{real}_{12.5Hz,DC=1}}{\Theta^{sim}_{12.5Hz,DC=1}}$$

If DC is not equal to 1, the effects of r_s and r_i becomes more significant. Hence, the inequality shown below

$$\frac{\frac{1}{9.75}-\frac{1}{132}}{\Theta^{sim}_{100Hz,DC=1}} \approx \frac{\frac{1}{12}-\frac{1}{132}}{\Theta^{sim}_{50Hz,DC=1}} \approx \frac{\frac{1}{24}-\frac{1}{132}}{\Theta^{sim}_{25Hz,DC=1}} \approx \frac{\frac{1}{26.75}-\frac{1}{132}}{\Theta^{sim}_{12.5Hz,DC=1}}$$

prove a valid connection with a small margin error between the analytical model and the application in terms of power efficiency achieved. Relevant error would stem from computational workload on the processor and nonlinear functionality of the battery. With the help of these facts, the accelerometer sensor is analytically modeled with sufficient success. This information reveals that many sensors whose operation method is similar to accelerometer, such as microphone, gyroscope, pulse meter, and so forth, can be modeled in a similar way.

4.5 Sensor Management

In this section, the battery discharge profiles are seen within the concept of Markov reward process. Suppose that an inhomogeneous semi–Markov chain is given as a statistical tool for handling sensor managements. The chain consists of a finite state space $S=\{1,\ldots,N\}$, the state transition density matrix Q, and the state transition matrix P where $Q,P \in \mathbb{R}^{N\times N}$. In addition, a reward structure can be attached to this ongoing chain and can be considered a random variable associated with the state occupancies and transitions. Thus, the reward can depend on the time of entrance in a state defined in this chain. $r(s,t)$ is given where the reward is accumulated from s to t, $t \geq s$.

This process considers *reward* being paid/received at each time that system passes for a given state. Rewards are defined in two different ways. The first, called permanence/rate reward, represents the reward given for the permanence in a state and is denoted by ψ. On the other hand, the second, called transition/impulse reward, represents the reward given for a state transition and is denoted by γ. When the reward increases at a given rate while hanging in a state, it is referred to as rate reward accumulation, whereas when the reward increases instantly at a state transition of the underlying process, it is referred to as impulse reward accumulation. The reward processes can be positive or negative and discounted or nondiscounted. Therefore, a variable called interest/discount rate, denoted by ϱ, is introduced into the reward processes within the definition of discount function, φ.

The general evolution equation for reward process for inhomogeneous semi–Markov chain is given by

$$V_i(s, t) = (1 - H_i(s, t)) \sum_{v=s+1}^{t} \psi_i(s, v - s)\varphi(s, v)$$

$$+ \sum_{l} \sum_{v=s}^{t} b_{il}(s, v)\varphi(s, v)(\gamma_{il}(v) + V_l(v, t)) \qquad (4.12)$$

The left-hand side (LHS) represents the expected present value of all received/paid discounted rewards from time s to t given that process enters into state i at time s, whereas the first element of right-hand side (RHS) represents the rewards in case there is no state transition from the state i to any from time s to t. The second element represents the rewards after a possible state transition occurs.

Equation 4.12 can be redefined for an immediate case where the total reward is an aggregation of rewards earned both at previous time and at current time as the following structure:

$$V_i^{(t)}(s) = V_i^{(t-1)}(s) + \varphi_i(s, t) \sum_{l} p_{il}^{(t-1)}(s)\psi_l(s, t) + \sum_{j} p_{lj}(t)\gamma_{lj}(s, t) \quad (4.13)$$

which, that is, collects the reward by either continuity in the same state or transition to another state.

The interest rate, ϱ, is a constant value; however, it can change by implying forward rates, ϱ_x. Each time that system is in state i, it is paid a reward ψ_i, which should be discounted for each epoch at time s. Thus, the paid/received rewards change in time:

$$\varphi(s, h) = \begin{cases} 1, & \text{if } s = h \\ \prod_{x=s+1}^{h} (1 + \varrho_x)^{-1}, & \text{if } s < h \end{cases} \qquad (4.14)$$

with the condition of $0 < \varphi(s, h) \leq 1$.

The permanence reward, $\psi_i(s, t)$, may vary in time or set fixed as $\psi_i.(t - s)$.

4.5.1 Battery Case

Assume that reward is seen as power consumption per unit time while a mobile device battery is discharging, and states are defined as the battery discharge profiles. Due to the present power consumption being independent from future power consumption in a mobile device discharge model, the discount factor would be 0. The immediate reward is also ignored because it could be seen as a difference of permanence rewards during a state transition.

The total accumulated reward while residing in state i from time s to t follows the difference equation of (4.13) as in

$$\Delta_t(v_i(s,t)) = \psi_i(t, v_i(s,t)) \qquad (4.15)$$

with the distribution of $F^V(t,v) = Pr\{V(t) \leq v\}$.

For modeling a battery, two different rewards could be considered. By recalling (4.2) along with (4.15), the first reward indicates the power consumption in each state i, whereas the second reward belongs to degradation in maximum battery capacity, that is, the recovery effect, which makes a remedy charge flow migrate from the bound-charge well into the available-charge well in KiBaM:

$$\begin{aligned} \Delta_t(v_{i,1}(s,t)) &= \psi_{i,1}(v_{i,1}(s,t), v_{i,2}(s,t)) \\ &= I_i - k(1-p)(h_2 - h_1) \\ \Delta_t(v_{i,2}(s,t)) &= \psi_{i,2}(v_{i,1}(s,t), v_{i,2}(s,t)) \\ &= k(1-p)(h_2 - h_1) \end{aligned} \qquad (4.16)$$

where $h_2 > h_1 > 0$ and $v_{i,1}(s,0) = v_{i,2}(s,0) = 0$.

The joint distribution of the accumulated rewards for a specific state i in (4.16) becomes

$$F_i^{(V_1,V_2)}(t, v_1, v_2) = Pr\{S(t) = i, V_1(t) \leq v_1, V_2(t) \leq v_2\} \qquad (4.17)$$

with boundaries of $\min\{v_1, v_2\} = \{0,0\}$ and $\max\{v_1, v_2\} = \{c.C+v_2, (1-c).C\}$ since the battery always has a predefined capacity C, which is distributed by a fraction factor c over two wells in KiBaM.

Therefore, the battery gets empty by evaluating (4.17) when $V_1(t) \geq \acute{C} + V_2(t)$,

$$Pr\{V_1(t) \geq \acute{C} + V_2(t)\} = \sum_{v_1=0}^{\acute{C}+v_x} \sum_{v_2=0}^{v_x} \sum_{i \in S} F_i^{(V_1,V_2)}(t, v_1, v_2) \qquad (4.18)$$

where $v_x \leq C - \acute{C}$. If $v_x \neq C - \acute{C}$ when the battery gets empty, it gives a clue that a constant high load was being applied to the battery and that made the recovery effect not to take place.

4.5.2 Sensor Utilization Case

Assume that a set of DC and a set of f_s are given by $\{1, 0.75, 0.5\}$ and $\{100, 50, 25, 12.5\}$ Hz, respectively. In addition, let the state space lie over two subspaces, which are sets of DC and f_s, $S = \{S_{DC} \times S_{f_s}\}$. Thus, the state space is defined by $S = \{S_{\{1,100\}}, S_{\{1,50\}}, \ldots, S_{\{0.75,100\}}, \ldots, S_{\{0.5,12.5\}}\}$.

The corresponding reward for each state can be obtained by using (4.8) and Table 4.1. The power consumption at each f_s is proportional to flowing drain current, I_{DD}, under a stable drain voltage supply due to $P = VI$. Thus, the reward for staying in a state can be defined as

$$\psi_{\{DC=j,f_s=k\},1} = \Theta_{\{DC=j,f_s=k\}}/\Theta_{\{(DC=1,f_s=100\}} \tag{4.19}$$

where $0 < \psi_{\{j,k\},1} \le 1$ since a pair of $(DC = 1, f_s = 100)$ is the most aggressive sensor utilization method in terms of power consumption.

The ascending order of $\psi_{\{j,k\}\to\{i\},1}$, $\forall j \in DC$, $\forall k \in f_s$ according to Table 4.1 defines state characterization: $S_i = \{S_{\{0.5,12.5\}} = 1, \ldots, S_{\{1,100\}} = N\}$ where $N = $ length$(DC) \times$ length(f_s).

The second reward can be found by derivation from (4.2) and (4.6) if a state transits into another state at s:

$$\psi_{j,2}(s, t) = \frac{c(1-c)}{k}(\psi_{i,1} - \psi_{j,1})(1 - e^{-k(t-s)/c(1-c)}) \tag{4.20}$$

where $t \ge s$ and $\psi_{i,1} > \psi_{j,1}$ since the recovery effect takes place whenever a lower load is applied. To this end, assume that a semi–Markov chain represents the evolution of changing sensory operation methods. The chain consists of a finite state space $S = \{1, \ldots, N\}$, the state transition density matrix $q \in Q$, and the state transition matrix $p \in P$. q represents jump or transition rates from user state i to user state j at time t. Whenever $i = j$, it means that the current user state remains unchanged; that is, a dummy transition occurs. Also, $p_{il}(s, t) = Pr(S(t) = l \mid S(s) = i)$ where $i, l \in S$, and $t \ge s$ represents a user state transition probability matrix, which accepts the relation of $\lim_{t \downarrow s} \partial p_{il}(s, t)/\partial t = q_{il}(s)$. The chain can revisit a user state at different system times, and also not every user state needs to be visited. Hence, there is no requirement that user state transition probabilities must be symmetric ($p_{il} \ne p_{li}$), or a specific state might remain the same in succession of time ($p_{ii} = 0$).

In addition, a reward structure can be attached to this ongoing chain, and it can be considered a random variable associated with the state occupancies and transitions. The reward can be seen as power consumption per unit time while a mobile device battery is discharging, thereby, it is denoted by the same ψ, and S is then redefined as the battery discharge profiles/states. As a result, the total reward, that is, total power consumption, depends on the total visiting time in state i. Then, it can be said that the reward ψ_i belonging to state i is proportional to the aggregation of (4.19) and (4.20).

Finally, the general evolution of a semi–Markov reward process to describe power consumption caused by sensory operations is attached to (4.18) and given by

$$V_l(s, t) = V_i(s, t - 1) + \sum_{l \in N} p_{il}(s, t - 1)\psi_l(s, t) \tag{4.21}$$

The LHS, V, represents the expected present value of all received rewards from time s to t given that process enters into state i at time s, whereas the first element of the RHS represents the aggregation of rewards earned both at previous time, and the second element of the RHS is the reward obtained from either continuity in the same state or transition to another state.

This chapter investigates how any change in sensory operations affects the power consumption profiles triggered by the sensor and depletion on the battery. Understanding the nonlinear battery behavior with respect to diverse operation methods in sensors, a tolerable power consumption balance could be achieved while employing context-aware services in resource-constrained mobile devices.

4.6 Performance Analysis

An HAR-based context-aware application is examined to investigate the power efficiency caused by the sensor utilization with respect to the recognition accuracy on interested context. The study in Chapter 2 is adopted for context recognition by using smartphone accelerometer, and accordingly, some user postures such as *sitting, standing, walking,* and *running* are chosen as interested context. Blackberry RIM Storm II 9550 smartphone with a fully charged 1400 mAh battery is used for experiments. For performance analysis, a similar user activity profile is performed by applying two proposed sensory sampling methods differently on an HAR-based context-aware application with a sufficient number of experiment repetitions (over 20 experiments for each sensor management method with variant users). Accordingly, a user profile begins with *sitting* and then *standing* each for 30 s (used for calibration), and then it transits into another posture randomly at the end of the following visiting times of {5, 10, 30, 60, 100, 300} s. The adopted recognition algorithm uses the smartphone accelerometer and recognizes the defined postural activities with a period of 1 s. In the first 1 min runtime, the accelerometer sampling parameters are set to $\{DC = 100\%, f_s = 100 \text{ Hz}\}$. Then, sensory sampling parameters are adaptively changed by the following proposed methods.

An action state space, $a = \{\text{decrease} = 1, \text{preserve} = 2, \text{increase} = 3\} \in \mathcal{A}$, is defined to regulate sensory operations, that is, to decrease, preserve, and increase power consumptions, respectively, while maintaining the application accuracy in context awareness. A 10% threshold value is defined for the accuracy margin to represent the tolerance where false recognitions are observed. Depending on the ratio of false recognitions, actions are applied. This ratio is calculated every 10 s. If the ratio of false recognitions occurring within the recent 10 s of application time is lower than the specified margin, then action #2 is taken to preserve the same setup for the applied sensory operations. In addition, if the ratio hangs in the same margin at least for a sufficient time t_{suff}, which is set to 20 s for the experiments, then action #1 is taken to reduce power consumption by estimating that observed postural activity is expected to stay on hold. In contrast, if the ratio of false recognitions is higher than the specified margin, then action #3 is taken to increase the power consumption in sensory operations by making more aggressive samplings. Thereby, a fine balance between the power consumption caused by the sensory operations and the application accuracy is attempted to achieve.

There are three different state transition methods applied for the Markov reward process defined by (5.28). Methods control power consumption by changing DC or/and f_s according to recognition accuracy observed in postural activities. Relevant adjustments are regulated by the action set of a.

4.6.1 Method I (MI)

This method tries to change DC in the first place rather than to change f_s and proposes how to wander over the defined space S according to actions a by

$$S_{\{j,k\}}(t) = \begin{cases} S_{\{j-1,k\}}(s), & a = 1, j \neq j_{\min}, \\ S_{\{j,k-1\}}(s), & a = 1, j = j_{\min}, k \neq k_{\min}, \\ S_{\{j+1,k\}}(s), & a = 3, j \neq j_{\max}, \\ S_{\{j,k+1\}}(s), & a = 3, j = j_{\max}, k \neq k_{\max}, \\ S_{\{j,k\}}(s), & \text{otherwise.} \end{cases} \quad (4.22)$$

4.6.2 Method II (MII)

This method, in contrast to Method I, makes the adjustments in f_s in the first place. Then, the relevant state transitions over S become

$$S_{\{j,k\}}(t) = \begin{cases} S_{\{j,k-1\}}(s), & a = 1, k \neq k_{\min}, \\ S_{\{j-1,k\}}(s), & a = 1, k = k_{\min}, j \neq j_{\min}, \\ S_{\{j,k+1\}}(s), & a = 3, k \neq k_{\max}, \\ S_{\{j+1,k\}}(s), & a = 3, k = k_{\max}, j \neq j_{\max}, \\ S_{\{j,k\}}(s), & \text{otherwise.} \end{cases} \quad (4.23)$$

4.6.3 Method III (MIII)

State transitions are executed according to the ascending order of power consumption rates shown in Table 4.1. Hence, both DC and f_s could be changed simultaneously by this method as in

$$S_{\{i\}}(t) = \begin{cases} S_{\{i-1\}}(s), & a = 1, i \neq i_{\min}, \\ S_{\{i+1\}}(s), & a = 3, i \neq i_{\max}, \\ S_{\{i\}}(s), & \text{otherwise.} \end{cases} \quad (4.24)$$

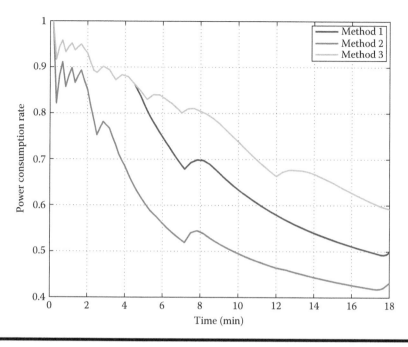

Figure 4.8 Power consumption ratio analysis in comparison to the aggressive sampling ($DC = 100\%$, $f_s = 100$ Hz) (results are averaged with respect to experiments).

Each method given by (5.29) through (5.31) is applied differently to the semi–Markov reward process for the similar user activity profile within the same experimental setups in order to analyze the trade-off between the power efficiency shown in Figure 4.8 and the application accuracy shown in Figure 4.9.

During the initial first 1 min period, the aggressive sampling method is applied on the sensory operations, which results in the highest application accuracy in the recognition process. After that, state transitions are regulated by proposed methods together with actions according to the ongoing user activity profile; thereby, the decrease is observed in the application accuracy. The ups and downs depicted in Figure 5.3 show the increase in power consumption to compensate the worsening of application accuracy and the decrease in power consumption to take an opportunistic sensory operation adjustment due to the stability observed in the application accuracy. On the other hand, even if Figure 4.9 depicts a drastic decrease in accuracy ratio initially due to obtaining a lower number of sensory samplings to infer user activities, the accuracy ratio then increases since better adaptation is achieved by user activity recognition algorithm as time passes. Among the proposed methods, a comparison can be made by MIII > MI > MII in terms of the power consumption ratio. Accordingly, the sampling in slower frequencies consumes higher power than the

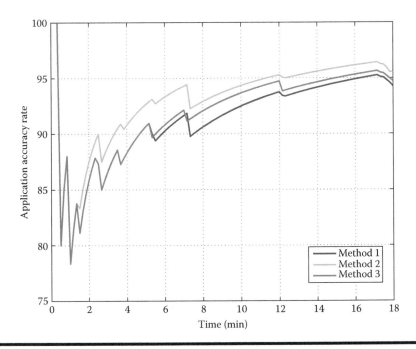

Figure 4.9 Accuracy ratio analysis in response to changing sensory operation method (results are averaged with respect to experiments).

sampling in lower duty cycles; however, it shows the opposite assumption in terms of the recognition accuracy. It is because that sampling in slower frequencies still obtain information about user activity where the sampling in lower duty cycles cannot do. On the other hand, MIII has the highest efficiency in the power consumption since it switches sensory operation modestly while achieving a fine accuracy in user state recognitions.

In general, the trade-off solutions achieve overall 50% enhancement in power consumption caused by the physical sensor work with respect to overall 10% decrease in accuracy ratio for user state recognitions.

As a conclusion, this chapter investigates mobile device–based battery behavior with respect to variant sensory operations in a smartphone application. In this manner, the chapter studies the battery nonlinearities by examining an effective battery model, called KiBaM, for various battery discharge profiles. The chapter also models sensory operations by providing the smartphone accelerometer as an example to analyze the linkage between battery discharge and power consumption caused by the sensor. With the understanding of nonlinearity observed on the batteries with respect to variant operation methods in sensors, a fine efficiency in power consumption is objected to achieve. Thereby, a Markov reward process is integrated to create energy consumption profiles in sensory operations and to represent the total energy cost by each profile as an accumulated reward. Finally, three different sensor employment methods are proposed on the evolution of reward process while employing an HAR-based context-aware smartphone application. It is shown that with the integration of the battery nonlinearities into the diverse operation methods in sensors, a fine power consumption balance is achieved while employing context-aware services in resource-constrained mobile devices.

Chapter 5

Context-Aware Framework: A Complex Design

The evolution of ubiquitous sensing on resource-constrained mobile devices has empowered the creation of context-aware middleware [144,227]. It emerges as a promising solution for the dynamic integration of highly complex and rich interactions in the virtual world and the physical world. With these capabilities, the new emerging network architecture would enhance data credibility, quality, privacy, and share-ability by encouraging participation at personal, social, and urban scales and would lead to discovering the knowledge about human lives and behaviors, and environment interactions/social connections by leveraging the deployment capacity of smart things (e.g., smartphones and tablets) in order to collect and analyze the digital traces left by users.

However, the heavy use of built-in smartphone sensors would bring new challenges, especially in resource-constrained hardware platforms. Continuously capturing user context through sensory data acquisitions and inferring desirable hidden information from the context would put a heavy workload on the smartphone processor and sensors. Thereby, these operations cause more power consumption than the device itself does during a regular run. Eventually, the battery of the smartphone would deplete rapidly.

The best energy saving algorithm to address power efficiency in context awareness would be the one that infuses into the low-level sensory operations by manipulating the frequentness of sensory sampling intervals. An adaptive sensor management mechanism that dynamically assigns duty cycles and sampling periods in a context-aware manner would reduce power consumption significantly. However, intervening sensory operations to achieve power efficiency jeopardizes the accuracy, that is, quality of service, provided by context-aware services. Therefore, it creates a trade-off between power consumption and accuracy provided by these services.

In this chapter, we propose a novel framework that allows running an human activity recognition (HAR)-based smartphone application while achieving a fine balance in the defined trade-off. The framework consists of a context inference module including an observation analysis block to acquire and infer the desired contexts through the smartphone accelerometer, a statistical machine to represent user activities, and a sensor management system to prolong the smartphone battery lifetime. Our objective is to improve the power efficiency of smartphones by dynamically adapting sensor sampling rates and duty cycles while supporting accurate recognition in user activities. More importantly, this research creates an effective hidden Markov model (HMM)-based framework that provides optimal power saving methods at the low-level sensory operations in order to guide the development of future context-aware applications. The following are a few distinctive key novelties exposed in this chapter:

- User profiles are considered time variant (inhomogeneity) in a provided statistical machine. Therefore, adaptability problem is defined for time-varying user profiles, and a relevant solution is given in the introduction of the entropy production rate. The entropy production rate is also used for the accuracy notifier in the context inference problem.

- The analytical modeling of the accelerometer sensor is provided and integrated into sensor management system. The system aims at utilizing a mixture pair of duty cycling and adaptive sampling regulated by three intuitive and two suboptimal sampling policies in order to prolong a mobile device's battery lifetime.

- Missing observations that occur due to power saving strategies are estimated under the regulation of inhomogeneous semi-Markovian process.

- A feedback control mechanism is integrated between context inference module and sensor management system in order to ensure that a fine balance is obtained for the trade-off.

- A smartphone application is implemented to show the effectiveness of proposed entropy production rate analysis in accuracy notification and the extension of battery lifetime under proposed sensor management system.

To summarize, this chapter considers the physical world as inhomogeneous. Therefore, the inhomogeneity is characterized by time-variant system parameters. Second, adaptability challenge in response to variant and rapid user activities is integrated as well using the convergence of entropy rate in conjunction with the inhomogeneity. Accordingly, entropy rate is used to make an assumption on the accurate working of system parameters regulated by an ongoing stochastic process.

Third, power saving considerations are taken at the low-level sensory operations. Fourth and most importantly, a machine learning structure regulates sensor management by estimating the trend of user preferences and opportunistically finding out stable moments in user activity. Thereby, sensor management could apply optimal sensing policies and change sensor sampling settings to respond to the defined trade-offs in context-aware application services. Finally, missing contextual inferences are estimated while energy saving strategies are being applied.

The rest of the chapter is organized as follows: Section 5.1 provides the aim and purpose of the proposed framework design. Section 5.2 explains the context inference module consisting of the analysis of sensory data and creation of the statistical machine to represent true user activities and behaviors. Section 5.3 includes the analytical model of sensor utilization and power saving solutions to balance the trade-off. Section 5.4 is reserved for performance analysis. In addition, the summary of important notations used throughout the chapter is listed in Table 5.1.

5.1 Proposed Framework

Context-aware sensing systems have been put forward to provide a required model for the recognition of daily-occurring human activities via observations acquired by various sensors built in mobile devices. These activities are inferred as outcomes of a wide range of sensor applications utilized in such areas of environmental surveillance, assisting technologies for medical diagnosis/treatments, and creation of smart spaces for individual behavior model. Key challenges faced in this concept is to infer relevant activity in such a system that takes raw sensor readings initially and processes them until obtaining a semantic outcome under some constrictions. These constrictions mostly stem from the difficulty of shaping an exact topological structure and from modeling uncertainties in the observed data due to saving energy wasted while physical sensor operations and processing of data are done. Finally, there is not a common framework system that covers all types of application settings, provides an adaptation toward changing context, and acquires a collection of asynchronous heterogeneous contexts to create different abstract entities. Even, none of the current frameworks succeed to have a full transparency, which eliminates direct involvement of an application in context modeling process, by imposing less computational workload on resource-limited mobile devices. In this direction, gathering diverse and asynchronous information and presenting it to the application would be the future work in context-aware framework research, which this chapter intends to enlighten. By this means, this chapter could help the exciting vision of *Internet-of-Things* [10] while creating a knowledge network that is of making autonomous logical decisions to actuate environmental objects and also to assist individuals, especially in a resource-constrained smart device. In addition, this research could give a solution to effective manage fusion of data gathered from multiple sensor applications.

Table 5.1   Summary of Important Symbols

Symbol	Definition (Section Where the Symbol Is First Used)
S_t	User state (5.2.1)
S_s^τ	Markov chain or sequence of user states (5.2.1)
ϑ_t	Observation (5.2.1)
ϑ_s^τ	Sequence of observations (5.2.1)
o	Observation emission matrix (5.2.1)
n, s, t, τ	Time indexes throughout the chapter (5.2.1)
i, j, m	Indexes for user states (5.2.1)
ξ	Inhomogeneous Markov process (5.2.1)
q_{ij}	User state transition rate (5.2.1)
Q	User state transition density matrix (5.2.1)
p_{ij}	User state transition probability (5.2.1)
P	User state transition matrix (5.2.1)
π_i	Initial user state probability (5.2.1)
F_{ij}	Probability of waiting time in a state (5.2.1)
H_i	Probability of leaving a user state (5.2.1)
d_i	A random time distribution (5.2.1)
$\mathcal{F}_j$	Filtered probabilities (5.2.1)
$\mathcal{P}_j$	Predicted probabilities (5.2.1)
$\hat{S}_t$	Estimation of user state (5.2.1)
N	Total number of user state transitions (5.2.1)
N_i	Total number of passages in a fixed user state (5.2.1)
e_p	Instantaneous entropy production rate (5.2.2)
ϕ	Accuracy notifier (5.2.2)
a	Actions (5.2.2)
t_{suff}	Sufficient time to trigger an action (5.2.2)
S^R or S^{R^2}	1D or 2D state space for reward process (5.3.1)

(Continued)

Table 5.1 *(Continued)* **Summary of Important Symbols**

Symbol	Definition (Section Where the Symbol Is First Used)
r, w	Indexes for states $\in S^R$ (5.3.1)
l, k	Indexes for $l \in DC$ and $k \in f_s$ (5.3.1)
$\Theta_{t_{span}}$	Total power consumption for a spanning time (5.3.1)
ψ_{SR}	Reward process attached to ongoing S^R (5.3.1)
V	Total received reward, that is, power consumption (5.3.1)
u	Optimal policies in CMDP and POMDP (5.3.4)
P^a	State transition matrix under actions (5.3.4)
I	Identity matrix (5.3.4)
λ	Belief vector (5.3.5)
R^a	Rewards according to actions (5.3.5)

To this end, this chapter proposes an inhomogeneous (time-variant) HMM-based framework in order to represent HAR-based user states by defining them as an outcome of either recognition or estimation model. A statistical tool–based classification, mostly using HMMs [120,243] or using AutoRegressive (AR) [93] models, is one of the foremost methods to infer context obtained via wearable or built-in smart device sensors in HAR-based applications. However, these studies mostly allow predefined and *user-manipulated* system parameter settings, such as arbitrary formation of context transition matrix in HMMs, or building filtering coefficients in ARs, which is not suitable for online processing due to increasing computational workload while enlarging the data size. Therefore, a statistical model is added into our approach to track *time-variant* user activity profiles in order to predict the best likely user state that fits into instant user behavior. The inhomogeneity is characterized by time-variant system parameters, and the user profile adaptability challenge is modeled using the convergence of entropy rate. Accordingly, an implemented smartphone application is provided to demonstrate how entropy rate converges in response to distinctive time-variant user profiles under different sensory sampling operations. The proposed framework is designed to be based on a statistical machine to obtain a better realization in context awareness in order to create adaptability to time-variant user preferences and behaviors, estimate missing context inferences in the presence of idle sensory operations, and also preserve the functionality against aperiodically received sensory observations.

Most importantly, which is the key of this study, a machine learning structure regulates sensor management opportunistically to figure optimal sensing policies, and change sensor sampling settings such as varying sensory sampling and duty cycling. By this, power efficiency could be achieved while satisfying the accuracy of context-aware application services.

The following two sections give further information about two interoperated core modules that our proposed framework has: context inference module and sensor management system.

5.2 Context Inference Module

The proposed context inference module consists of two main blocks as shown in Figure 5.1, which are sensory data acquisition and analysis, and a statistical machine. The first block receives *raw sensory readings* (i.e., extracted user contexts through mobile device–based sensors) as *inputs*. These readings undergo a series of signal processing operations and eventually end up with a classification algorithm in order to provide desirable inferences about user relevant information for context-aware applications. Note that the selection of classification algorithm in the inference process could differ due to the interested context obtained through a target sensor. The probabilistic outcomes of the classification algorithms source the inputs of the second block.

The second block choses a discrete time inhomogeneous hidden semi-Markov model (DT-IHS-MM) as the desired statistical machine. HMMs have been used to infer mobile device–based human-centric sensory context in HAR-based applications [175]. However, our approach intends to expand the properties of statistical machine so as to obtain a better realization in context awareness. First, the concept of Markov renewal process is adopted to describe the functionalities of user behavior modeling. Second, the inhomogeneity is introduced to characterize time-variant user behaviors so that the module could adapt itself to dynamically changing user behaviors. Third, the semi-Markovian feature is added to specify aperiodically received discrete time observations through sensory readings. Fourth, the estimation theory is included in case of missing sensory inputs. Finally, the entropy rate analysis is integrated to track the accuracy of context inferences because there is not an absolute solution to actually calculate the accuracy of a real-time running HAR-based context-aware application. Thereby, *the convergence of entropy rate* is considered as the *output* of the module, which will be used by the sensor management system introduced in Section 5.3.

The following sections include the explanations of main blocks in context inference module. The desirable statistical machine is put forward first since some system parameters declared in this block will be used during the introduction of the subsequent sensory data acquisition and analysis block.

5.2.1 Inhomogeneous Statistical Machine

Classification algorithms produce observations (i.e., *visible states*), ϑ_t, of DT-IHS-MM. Among given observations, the one that has the highest probability will make a

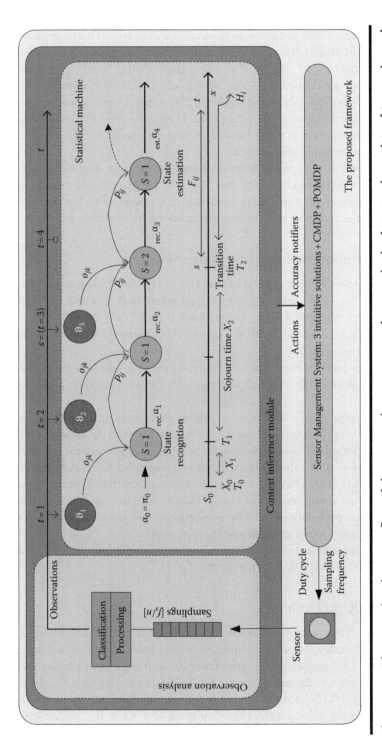

Figure 5.1 **The operational process flow of the proposed context-aware framework: the framework consists of two main modules, which are context inference module and sensor management system. Basically, context inference module acquires sensory data, extracts context, infers user states, and delivers recognition accuracy statistics to sensor management system. Then, sensory operations are adjusted by sensor management system to achieve a fine balance in power consumption and recognition accuracy.**

most likely differentiation in the selection of instant user behavior. This observation is marked as instant observation, ϑ_T, which also indicates the most recent element of observation sequence, ϑ_1^T, of DT-IHS-MM. On the other hand, user states, *sitting* and *standing*, are defined as *hidden states*, S, of DT-IHS-MM since they are not directly observable but only reachable over visible states. Therefore, each observation has cross probabilities to point a user state. These cross probabilities build an observation emission matrix, o, which basically defines decision probabilities to pick any user state from available observations.

In addition, the transition probabilities among user states might not be stationary since a general user behavior changes in time. Thus, it is expected from a user state either to transit into another user state or to remain in the same with a different probability. These occurrences build a time-variant user state transition matrix, p.

5.2.1.1 Basic Definitions and Inhomogeneity

Let an inhomogeneous Markov process exist as $\xi = \{\xi(t), \ t \geq 0\}$ with a user state space of $S = \{1, 2, \ldots, M\}$, and let $Q(t) = q_{ij}(t)$ where $\{i, j\} \in S$ and $t \geq 0$ be a transition density matrix of ξ. If Q satisfies both $0 \leq q_{ij}(t) \leq \infty$ and $q_i(t) = -q_{ii}(t) = \sum_{i \neq j} q_{ij}(t)$, then Q is called a conservative inhomogeneous transition density matrix function on S.

$q_{ij}(t)$ represents jump or transition rates from user state i to user state j at time t. Whenever $i = j$, it means that current user state remains unchanged or a dummy transition occurs.

Moreover, suppose that a user state transition probability matrix $P(s, t) = \{p_{ij}(s, t) = Pr(S(t) = j \mid S(s) = i)\}$ where $t \geq s \geq 0$ together with Q satisfies both forward and backward Kolmogorov's equations [163], which assume to have $\lim_{t \downarrow s} \partial p_{ij}(s, t)/\partial t = q_{ij}(s)$, then S becomes an *inhomogeneous Markov chain* with the transition density of Q. The chain can revisit a user state at different system times, and also not every user state needs to be visited. Hence, there is no requirement that user state transition probabilities must be symmetric ($p_{ij} \neq p_{ji}$) or a specific state might remain the same in the succession of time ($p_{ii} = 0$).

Furthermore, let an initial user state $\pi(t) = \{\pi_i(t) = Pr(S(t) = i)\}$ satisfy the Fokker–Planck equation [163]: $d\pi(t)/dt = \pi(t)Q(t)$.

5.2.1.2 Underlying Process

Let $\xi = \{\xi_n, \ n \in \mathbb{N}\}$ be redefined as an inhomogeneous irreducible discrete Markov process with a user state space of S. The process evolves from S_0 as initial user state and stays in there for a nonnegative length of time X_1 until it goes into another user state S_1. Then, it stays in the new user state for X_2 before entering into S_2, and so on. As indicated in [18,152], this process is a two-dimensional or bivariate stochastic process in discrete time called positive $(S-X)$ process: $(S-X) = ((S_n, X_n), n \geq 0)$ with the initial of $X_0 = 0$ where X_n is called the successive sojourn times.

X_n is the time spent in state S_{n-1} that defines interarrival times. There is also another time variable T_n introduced for the definition of system properties at which state transitions occur. This random time sequence is called renewal sequence, and it is given by $X_n = T_n - T_{n-1}$, $n \geq 1$ with the initial statuses of $\{X_0, T_0\} = \{0, 0\}$.

The Markov renewal process is now redefined over $(S - T) = ((S_n, T_n)$, $n \geq 0)$ by

$$Q_{ij}(s, t) = Pr(S_{n+1} = j, T_{n+1} \leq t \mid S_n = i, T_n = s), \qquad (5.1)$$

where T_n represents nth renewal time at which a user state transition occurs.

The probability of waiting time, also called conditional distributions of sojourn times, for each user state i in the presence of (5.1) and information about the successively followed user state is given by

$$F_{ij}(s, t) = Pr(T_n \leq t \mid S_{n-1} = i, S_n = j, T_{n-1} = s)$$
$$= \begin{cases} Q_{ij}(s, t)/p_{ij}(s), & p_{ij} \geq 0, \\ 1, & p_{ij} = 0. \end{cases} \qquad (5.2)$$

In addition, with the help of (5.1) and (5.2), the probability of the process leaving the user state i, also called sojourn times distributions in a given user state, from time s to t is introduced by

$$H_i(s, t) = Pr(T_n \leq t \mid S_{n-1} = i, T_{n-1} = s)$$
$$= \sum_j p_{ij}(s)F_{ij}(s, t) = \sum_{j \neq i}^{U} Q_{ij}(s, t). \qquad (5.3)$$

If $F(s, t) = F(t - s)$, $s \leq t$, then the kernel Q only depends on $t - s$, which it yields to have $Q(t - s) = pF(t - s)$ being called an inhomogeneous semi-Markov process. The semi-Markov process [54,171] indicates that the sojourn time belonging to each state might have a random distribution, $d_i(t)^*$, which can depend on the next user state to be visited. Thereby, this gives the probability of a user state transition occurring at time t:

$$b_{ij}(s, t) = \begin{cases} Q_{ij}(s, t) = 0, & t \leq s \\ Q_{ij}(s, t) - Q_{ij}(s, t - 1), & t > s. \end{cases} \qquad (5.4)$$

---

* The proposed solutions in Section 5.3 regulate sampling epoch times in sensory operations and change the defined time distribution accordingly.

Also, for each waiting time, a user state is occupied. Therefore, transition probabilities are defined with (5.3) and (5.4) by

$$p_{ij}(s, t) = Pr(S_t = j \mid S_s = i)$$

$$= \delta_{ij}(1 - H_i(s, t)) + \sum_{m \in M} \sum_{\tau=1}^{t} b_{im}(s, \tau) p_{mj}(\tau, t), \qquad (5.5)$$

where δ_{ij} represents the Kronecker symbol. The first element of right-hand side, where $d_i(t) = 1$ if $i = j$, notifies the probability of residing in user state i at time t without any change in context since time s; and the second represents the probability of a user state transition from state i in some way to user state j, and staying in this new user state at time t.

5.2.1.3 User State Representation

User state representation engine infers an instant user behavior in light of prior knowledge of a human behavior pattern and the availability of sensory observation at a decision time. If sensory observation exists, the applied process is called recognition method; otherwise, estimation method. In other words, estimation method is applied due to missing observations when power efficiency is taken into consideration at low-level sensory operations.

Let ϑ_t denote an observation at time t, which is associated with user state S_t, and let $o_i(\vartheta_t)$ be the probability of observing ϑ_t from given $S_t = i$. Thus, $o_i(\vartheta_s^t) = \prod_{t'=s}^{t} o_i(\vartheta_{t'})$ represents a sequence of emitted observations from time s to t, $s \leq t$. In addition, note that since the process flows in a discrete time and follows the first-order Markovian feature, a current user state S_t depends solely on the most recent user state S_{t-1}.

The inference of a hidden user state j at time t given the last known hidden user state i at time s, $s \leq t$ is presented by

$$Pr(S_t = j \mid S_s = i, \vartheta_s^\tau), \qquad (5.6)$$

where $\tau = t - s$. This equation is termed as *predicted* $\mathcal{P}$, *filtered* $\mathcal{F}$, and *smoothed* $\mathcal{S}$, probabilities of S_t, depending on the observation sequence of ϑ_s^{t-1}, ϑ_s^t, and ϑ_s^T, respectively, where $T > t$.

The recognition method uses filtered probabilities of S_t where it is derived from (5.6) as in $\mathcal{F}_j(s, t) = Pr(S_t = j \mid S_s = i, \vartheta_s^t)$ in the presence of a sufficient number of available observations. The probability of an instant user state recognition is found by the forward algorithm [175], which is proposed to find the most likely one-step-ahead user state in a hidden chain. The forward algorithm relies on updating a probability weight α inductively, which decides the probability of current occurrence of a user state, S_t, generated from the one-step-previous occurrence, S_{t-1}.

However, this method works well for traditional HMMs not for semi-Markovian featured models due to the random sojourn time distribution between two consecutive user states in the hidden chain. In this manner, an extended forward algorithm has been proposed in [133,234] by

$$\alpha_j(s,t) = \sum_{t'=s}^{t} \sum_{i} \left(\alpha_i(s, t-t')p_{ij}(s, t-t')d_j(t') \prod_{t''=1}^{t'} o_j(\vartheta_{t-t'+t''} = z) \right) \quad (5.7)$$

with the condition of $\alpha_i(s,t) = \pi_i$ if $t \le 0$.

Since the recognition process of user states evolves in real time, the forward algorithm assigns a proper user state to specify current user activity in the case where a new observation is made. On the other hand, to make sure that user state recognitions are made true, the backward algorithm, whose corresponding weight is denoted by β, is employed [175]. By this algorithm, the accuracy of previous user state recognitions is validated, that is, *smoothing*. However, applying this algorithm seems redundant as it consumes additional computational power on the mobile device batteries. The context-aware applications run in real time; thereby, there is no value of discovering what happened in the past again. Hence, the filtered probability becomes

$$\mathcal{F}_j(s,t) = \alpha_j(s,t)\beta_j(s,t') = \alpha_j(s,t), \quad t = t' = T. \quad (5.8)$$

Note that computational complexity while calculating system parameters causes a crucial underflow problem. When time goes by during the evolution of ξ, $\alpha_i(0,t) \overset{t}{\Rightarrow} 0$ starts to head to zero at an exponential rate since p_{ij} includes elements being lower than 1. Therefore, $\mathcal{F}_j(s,t)$ needs to be scaled [175] by a factor of $\prod_{t'=s}^{t} \sum_j \mathcal{F}_j(s,t')$.

In addition to using the filtered probabilities to recognize user states, the predicted probabilities are used to estimate user state in case of no observation received. When power saving methods are taken into consideration as studied in Section 5.2.2, there will be some time intervals during sensory operations in which no sensor readings are obtained. As a result, the framework cannot receive a relevant observation. In that case, the inference of instant user state is based on the estimation method not on the recognition method.

The predicted probabilities are found by

$$\mathcal{P}_j(s,t) = Pr(S_t = j \mid S_s = i, \vartheta_1^{t-1}, \vartheta_t)$$
$$= Pr(S_t = j, \vartheta_t = z \mid S_s = i, \vartheta_1^{t-1})$$
$$= \sum_j \mathcal{F}_i(s, t-1)p_{ij}(s, t-1). \quad (5.9)$$

Alternatively, (5.9) can be found by assigning the most likely visionary observation instead by accepting there is a missing observation:

$$P_{j,z}(s, t) = \sum_j \mathcal{F}_i(s, t-1) p_{ij}(s, t-1) o_j(\vartheta_t = z). \qquad (5.10)$$

Then, the most likely observation is selected according to assigning each possible observation as a final node to observation sequence while calculating (5.10) by

$$\hat{\vartheta}_t = \arg\max_z \sum_j P_{j,z}(s, t). \qquad (5.11)$$

Finally, instant user state estimation is found using (5.10) together with (5.11) by

$$\hat{S}_t = \arg\max_{1 \le j \le M}[P_{j,z}(s, t)]. \qquad (5.12)$$

Then, instant user state recognition is specified using (5.8) in the case where observations are available by

$$S_t = \arg\max_{1 \le j \le M}[\mathcal{F}_j(s, t)]. \qquad (5.13)$$

5.2.1.4 Time-Variant User State Transition Matrix

The most important feature of context-aware applications is being capable of adapting themselves to distinctive user behaviors. User relevant context differs in time, and the corresponding user state also does. For instance, one user might remain the same user state for a long time, whereas others might be more active by changing their user states frequently. Therefore, it cannot be expected from user state transition matrix to remain stationary under such conditions.

■ Default settings: User state transitions can be represented as simple random walk on a graph [35]. On this graph, a vertice, υ, represents a user state, and an edge represents an user state transition. Thus, ξ always starts evolving by a default transition matrix, which is

$$p_{ij}^{default} = \frac{1}{d(\upsilon_i)}, \quad \upsilon_i \sim \upsilon_j, \qquad (5.14)$$

where $d(\upsilon_i)$ is the number of vertices υ_j adjacent to υ_i. For example, if $d(\upsilon_i)$ is 0, $p_{ii}^{default} = 1$.

■ Update: A random variable $N(t) > n - 1 \leftrightarrow T_n \leq t$ is represented as the total number of jumps or transitions of the $(S - T)$ process during $(s = 0, t]$. Therefore, $N(t)$ is also called the discrete-time counting process of the number of jumps. Jumps or transitions may include any transition toward user state itself (i.e., virtual transitions).

By having the counting process, counting parameters can be calculated where $0 < \tau \leq t$ as follows:

■ The number of visits to user state i during $(0, t]$: $N_i(t) = \sum_{n=0}^{N(t)-1} 1_{\{S_n=i\}}$
■ The number of transitions from user state i to user state j during $(0, t]$: $N_{ij}(t) = \sum_{n=1}^{N(t)} 1_{\{S_{n-1}=i, S_n=j\}}$
■ The number of transitions from user state i to user state j during $(0, t]$ with the sojourn time, τ, in state i: $N_{ij}(\tau, t) = \sum_{n=1}^{N(t)} 1_{\{S_{n-1}=i, S_n=j, X_n=\tau\}}$

The empirical estimations of the user state transition matrix, p_{ij}, the conditional distributions of sojourn times, f_{ij}, and the discrete-time semi-Markov kernel, q_{ij}, are given in [47] by

$$\hat{p}_{ij}(t) = N_{ij}(t)/N_i(t),$$

$$\hat{f}_{ij}(\tau, t) = N_{ij}(\tau, t)/N_{ij}(t), \tag{5.15}$$

$$\hat{q}_{ij}(\tau, t) = N_{ij}(\tau, t)/N_i(t).$$

Given empirical estimations in (5.15) get close to nonparametric maximum likelihood estimations with having good asymptotic properties if they maximize the likelihood function of

$$\mathcal{L}(t) = \prod_{n=1}^{N(t)} p_{ij} f_{ij}(X_n) \left(1 - \sum_{j} \sum_{\tau=n}^{B(t)} q_{ij}(\tau) \right), \tag{5.16}$$

where $B(t) = t - X_{N(t)}$ is called age process showing the sojourn time in the last visited state $S_{N(t)}$.

With the evaluation of (5.16), the corresponding transition density kernel turns into

$$Q_{ij}(s, \tau_0, \tau) \overset{update}{=} \frac{Q_{ij}(s, \tau) - Q_{ij}(s, \tau_0)}{Q_{ij}(s, \tau_0)}, \tag{5.17}$$

where τ_0 is the elapsed time since the first entrance into user state i.

Finally, beginning from the default status in (5.14), the evolving inhomogeneous state transition probability (5.5) is updated by (5.17) together with (5.3) and (5.4) as in

$$p_{ij}(s, \tau_0, \tau) \overset{update}{=} \delta_{ij}(1 - H_i^*(s, \tau_0, \tau)) + \sum_{m \in M} \sum_{v=\tau_0}^{\tau} b_{im}^*(s, \tau_0, v) p_{mj}(s + v, \tau - v).$$

$$(5.18)$$

5.2.1.5 Adaptive Observation Emission Matrix

The least power-consuming sensor on today's smartphones is the accelerometer [22]. Therefore, the accelerometer sensor is considered to be used in the implementation of HAR-based applications. Blackberry RIM Storm II 9550 smartphone is chosen as a target device. Storm II consists of three-axis accelerometer named ADXL346 from Analog Devices [1]. While any application is running, the target smartphone is only connected to a 3G network and background operations are kept minimal.

For performance analysis first, two user states consisting, which are *sitting* and *standing*, and then four user states consisting, which are *sitting, standing, walking,* and *running*, statistical machines are considered for the framework. However, more complex models can be applied as well by using similar system approach. In Chapter 2, an unsupervised classification method to detect user-centric postural actions, such as sitting, standing, walking, and running, by smartphones is studied. By adopting these works into our current study, recognition between user states is made. Then, the observation emission matrix is constructed by adopted algorithm as follows:

■ For two user states,

$$o_{jz} = \begin{bmatrix} prob.\ of\ sitting \\ prob.\ of\ standing \end{bmatrix}.$$

$$(5.19)$$

■ For four user states,

$$o_{jz} = \begin{bmatrix} prob.\ of\ sitting \\ prob.\ of\ standing \\ prob.\ of\ walking \\ prob.\ of\ running \end{bmatrix}.$$

$$(5.20)$$

5.2.2 Accuracy Notifier and Definition of Actions

Supposing $\pi_i(0) > 0$ where $\forall i \in S$, the Markov process ξ_n evolves in bidirectional way over the distributions of $P_{[n,n+\acute{n}]}$ and $P_{[n,n+\acute{n}]}^-$ where $\forall n \in \mathbb{Z}^+$ and $\forall \acute{n} \in \mathbb{N}$, and the user state transition matrix also obeys a condition of $p_{ij} > 0 \leftrightarrow p_{ji} > 0$, then ξ_n satisfies

$$\lim_{t \downarrow s} \frac{\pi_i(s) p_{ij}(s, t)}{\pi_j(s) p_{ji}(s, t)} = 1, \tag{5.21}$$

which indicates that the inhomogeneous Markov process has instantaneous reversibility at time s, and hence, it yields to have $\pi(s)Q(s) = 0$.

Having the reversibility feature defined by (5.21), the instantaneous entropy production e_p^n of ξ at time n is given by

$$e_p^n = \mathcal{H}(P_{[n,n+1]}, \bar{P}_{[n,n+1]}) = \frac{1}{2} \sum_{i,j \in S} [\pi_i^n p_{ij}^n - \pi_j^n p_{ji}^n] \log \frac{\pi_i^n p_{ij}^n}{\pi_j^n p_{ji}^n}, \tag{5.22}$$

where $\mathcal{H}(P_{[n,n+1]}, \bar{P}_{[n,n+1]})$ is the relative entropy of the distribution of (ξ_n, ξ_{n+1}), $P_{[n,n+1]}$, with respect to the distribution of (ξ_{n+1}, ξ_n), $\bar{P}_{[n,n+1]}$.

By using (5.22), Figure 3.10 shows the convergence of entropy rate under some sensory operation parameters, such as a fixed duty cycle $DC = 1$ along with variant sampling frequencies $f_s = \{100, 50, 25, 12.5\}$ Hz. Aggressive sampling method, which takes 100 Hz as f_s, draws an actual track of the entropy rate. Circles over blue line indicate a difference in user behavior. Since user states, such as sitting and standing, are recognized in this application example, the frequentness of transition from one user state to another cannot be observed much due to the nature of human being, which requires high-energy effort by users throughout application running time. Therefore, user state transition matrices over time are desired as $p_{ij} =$
$\begin{bmatrix} 0.9 & 0.1 \\ 0.1 & 0.9 \end{bmatrix}, \begin{bmatrix} 0.85 & 0.15 \\ 0.1 & 0.9 \end{bmatrix}, \begin{bmatrix} 0.8 & 0.2 \\ 0.1 & 0.9 \end{bmatrix}, \begin{bmatrix} 0.75 & 0.25 \\ 0.1 & 0.9 \end{bmatrix}, \begin{bmatrix} 0.6 & 0.4 \\ 0.1 & 0.9 \end{bmatrix}, \begin{bmatrix} 0.5 & 0.5 \\ 0.1 & 0.9 \end{bmatrix}.$

According to the results obtained by an HAR-based smartphone application, the entropy rate converges late while samplings are collected at less than 100 Hz. This indicates the reason why accuracy ratio decreases as well. In addition, the entropy rate cannot sometimes converge into any point and it stops where the plot lines belonging to $f_s = \{12.5, 25, 50\}$ Hz. When the frequentness of user state transitions increases, sampling frequency may not be fast enough to capture the activeness of a user profile. Therefore, the system cannot find any proper user state transition matrix to define instant user activity profile.

After all these assessments on the characteristic of entropy rate analysis with respect to a changing user activity profile, let $e_p(s, t)$ denote a sequence of entropy rates from (5.22) in the time range of s up to t. Also, assume that a simple threshold is defined by $\varepsilon_{e_p} = [\mu_{e_p} - \sigma_{e_p}, \mu_{e_p} + \sigma_{e_p}]$ where μ_{e_p} and σ_{e_p} are mean and standard deviation of $e_p(s, t)$, respectively. Thereby, the first output delivered to the sensor management system by the statistical machine as shown in Figure 5.1 is named as accuracy notifier, which is defined by

$$\phi(s, t) = \frac{1}{(t - s + 1)} \sum_{n=s}^{t} 1_{(e_p^n \in \varepsilon_{ep})}. \tag{5.23}$$

Moreover, τ_{ii} denotes a return time, that is, elapsed total sojourn time, to user state i entering at s.

$$\tau_{ii} = \begin{cases} \min\{n = t - s, n \geq 1, S_t = i \mid S_s = i\}, \\ \infty, \quad S_t \neq i, \ t \geq 1, \end{cases} \tag{5.24}$$

represents the total amount of time until the process returns to the same user state i. Note that it may never return to the same state.

By considering that a time variable t_{suff} is assigned during application run to indicate a sufficient time interval in which user state i would not change, the second output is defined then using (5.23) and (5.24) by

$$a(t) = \begin{cases} 1, & \phi(s, t) \geq \phi, \tau_{ii} > t_{suff}, \\ 2, & \phi(s, t) \geq \phi, \tau_{ii} \leq t_{suff}, \\ 3, & \phi(s, t) < \phi, \end{cases} \tag{5.25}$$

where $\phi \in [0.5, 1]$ and $a(t)$ denotes the actions for sensory management introduced in Section 5.3.2.

5.3 Sensor Management Module

In this section, the effect of variant sensory load profiles on the depletion of mobile device battery is studied. Then, these battery discharge profiles are examined within the concept of Markov reward process. In addition, there are five novel solutions provided in this section for balancing the trade-off existing between accuracy in the user state recognitions and power consumption required by the recognition process.

5.3.1 Sensor Utilization

The smartphone accelerometer sensor is utilized in order to examine the power efficiency achieved under different sampling and duty cycling strategies. Assume that a set of DC and a set of f_s are given by $\{1, 0.75, 0.5\}$ and $\{100, 50, 25, 12.5\}$ Hz, respectively. Also, let a state space lie over two subspaces, which are sets of DC and f_s, as in $S^{R^2} = \{DC \times f_s\}$. Thus, the state space is defined as in

$$S_r^R = S_{\{l,k\}}^{R^2} = \{S_{\{1,100\} \to 1}^{R^2}, S_{\{1,50\} \to 2}^{R^2}, \ldots, S_{\{0.5,12.5\} \to W}^{R^2}\}, \tag{5.26}$$

where $S^{R^2} \rightarrow S^R : \{DC = l, f_s = k\} \rightarrow r$, $\forall l \in DC$, $\forall k \in f_s$, and $W =$ length $(DC) \times$ length(f_s).

The state space S^R, or S^{R^2}, is considered to represent different sensory operation methods supported by the accelerometer sensor in a sensor management system.

To be able to see the effect of S^R on the battery depletion, an application is implemented on the target device. The application runs from the point where the smartphone battery is fully loaded until it totally depletes. Only one constant pair of sampling frequency and duty cycle, that is, a state in S^R, is applied as sensory operation parameters to the accelerometer at each application run. A total time for sensory operation cycle, denoted by t_c, is taken as 1 s. For instance, where $f_s = 100$ Hz, $DC = 100\%$, and $t_c = 1$ s are taken, the total number of samplings per second becomes 100.

The application results are shown in Figure 4.8. Note that the Blackberry Java 7.1. SDK only reveals remaining battery status. According to results, more aggressive the sampling methodology is applied, the faster the battery depletes. In addition, the lower value of DC makes the battery recovery effect more significant, and thus, it prolongs the battery lifetime. However, the battery nonlinearities [182] are not intended to study in this chapter.

After the application results shown in Figure 4.7 together with [1] and our previous work [236], the sampling frequency– and duty cycle–dependent power consumption model in the accelerometer sensor operations can be defined as in

$$\Theta_{\omega * 12.5\,Hz} = \omega * \Omega_{sample} + (\omega_{max} - \omega) * \Omega_{idle},$$

$$\Theta_{t_c} = \frac{(DC)t_c}{\omega_{max}/f_{s_{max}}} \Theta_{\omega * 12.5\,Hz} + \frac{(1 - DC)t_c}{1/f_{s_{max}}} \Omega_{idle}, \qquad (5.27)$$

where $\omega = \{1, 2, 4, 8\}$, and Ω_{sample} and Ω_{idle} are defined as power consumption occurring during the operations where sensor makes samplings or runs idle, respectively, and t_c is a time span through a power cycle.

By using (5.27) and the application results obtained for Figure 4.8, Table 4.1 shows the power consumption ratio of each sensory operation methods by the accelerometer, where the aggressive sampling method, $DC = 100\%$ and $f_s = 100$ Hz, is taken as a normalizing factor.

To this end, assume that a semi-Markov chain represents the evolution of changing sensory operation methods, S^R, for a desired sensor management system. The chain consists of a finite state space $S^R = \{1, \ldots, W\}$, the state transition density matrix $q^R \in Q^R$, and the state transition matrix $p^R \in P^R$ where $Q^R, P^R \in \mathbb{R}^{W \times W}$. In addition, a reward structure can be attached to this ongoing chain, and it can be considered a random variable associated with the state occupancies and transitions. Moreover, assume that the reward, denoted by ψ, is seen as power consumption per unit time while a mobile device battery is discharging, and S^R is redefined as the battery discharge profiles/states. Thereby, the total reward, that is, total power consumption, depends on the total visiting time in a state r where $r \in S^R$. Then, it can be said that the reward ψ_r belonging to state r is proportional to the corresponding power consumption defined by (5.27).

Finally, the general evolution of a semi-Markov reward process to describe power consumption caused by sensory operations in the sensor management system is given by

$$V_w(s, t) = V_r(s, t - 1) + \sum_{w \in W} p_{rw}^R(s, t - 1)\psi_w(s, t). \qquad (5.28)$$

The left-hand side, V, represents the expected present value of all received rewards from time s to t given that process enters into state i at time s, whereas the first element of the right-hand side represents the aggregation of rewards earned both at previous time, and the second element is the reward obtained from either continuity in the same state or transition to another state.

5.3.2 Trade-Off Analysis

There are five different solutions proposed to respond to the defined trade-off between sensing accuracy and power consumption. The proposed solutions aim at reducing power consumption by intervening sensory operations. Therefore, the context inference framework always receives the manipulated sensory samplings and then tries to recognize user states accurately according to (5.12) and (5.13). After the recognition process is done, it releases $a(t)$ as in (5.25), which defines the actions to be taken on sensory operations. These actions force the proposed solutions to adjust a pair of duty cycle and sampling frequency dynamically while sensory sampling operations are actively operated. As a result, a feedback system is integrated into a cyber-physical sensor management system that balances the increase in power efficiency with the decrease in user state recognition accuracy.

Actions are defined as commands $\{1, 2, 3\}$ for sensor management, which are to *decrease*, *preserve*, and *increase* power consumption, respectively. If the entropy rate is not stable, it means user profile changes frequently, and corresponding entropy rate does not converge a specific value. Action #3 needs to be taken in this case to increase the power consumption in sensory operations by making more aggressive samplings. In contrast, if the entropy rate converges and hangs in a specific margin, then action #2 preserves the same setup for applied sensory operations. More significantly, if the same user profile has been observed at least for a sufficient time t_{suff}, then action #1 is taken to reduce power consumption by estimating that user profile is expected to stay on hold.

5.3.3 Intuitive Solutions

Intuitive solutions either reduce power consumption by decreasing DC or/and f_s or improve accuracy in user state recognition by increasing them. Relevant adjustments are regulated by the action set of $a(t)$. There are three different intuitive solutions proposed as follows.

5.3.3.1 Method I (MI)

This method tries to change DC in the first place rather than to change f_s. Let the pairs of DC and f_s lie over a space S^{R^2}, which is defined in a matrix of $\{DC, f_s\} \rightarrow \{l, k\}$, where $l \in DC$ and $k \in f_s$. Method I proposes how to wander over the defined space according to actions by

$$
S^{R^2}(l, k) = \begin{cases} S^{R^2}(l-1, k), & a = 1, l \neq l_{\min}, \\ S^{R^2}(l, k-1), & a = 1, l = l_{\min}, k \neq k_{\min}, \\ S^{R^2}(l+1, k), & a = 3, l \neq l_{\max}, \\ S^{R^2}(l, k+1), & a = 3, l = l_{\max}, k \neq k_{\max}, \\ S^{R^2}(l, k), & \text{otherwise.} \end{cases} \tag{5.29}
$$

5.3.3.2 Method II (MII)

This method, in contrast to Method I, makes the adjustments in f_s in the first place. Then, the relevant state transitions over S^{R^2} become

$$
S^{R^2}(l, k) = \begin{cases} S^{R^2}(l, k-1), & a = 1, k \neq k_{\min}, \\ S^{R^2}(l-1, k), & a = 1, k = k_{\min}, l \neq l_{\min}, \\ S^{R^2}(l, k+1), & a = 3, k \neq k_{\max}, \\ S^{R^2}(l+1, k), & a = 3, k = k_{\max}, l \neq l_{\max}, \\ S^{R^2}(l, k), & \text{otherwise.} \end{cases} \tag{5.30}
$$

5.3.3.3 Method III (MIII)

In this method, state transitions are executed according to the ascending order of power consumption ratios shown in Table 4.1. The definition of (5.26) is then recharacterized as in $S^R = \text{ascend}(S^R)$. Hence, both DC and f_s could be changed simultaneously:

$$
S^R(r) = \begin{cases} S^R(r-1), & a = 1, i \neq r_{\min}, \\ S^R(r+1), & a = 3, i \neq r_{\max}, \\ S^R(r), & \text{otherwise.} \end{cases} \tag{5.31}
$$

In summary, intuitive solutions (5.29), (5.30), and (5.31) regulate p^R and hence affect the evolution of (5.28).

5.3.4 Constrained Markov Decision Process–Based Solution

Constrained Markov decision process (CMDP) is applied into sensor management system by setting a Markov-optimal policy u. This policy controls sensory sampling operations by deciding which pair of DC and f_s to be assigned in the sampling process, and it randomizes the decisions over given actions.

The CMDP parameter set is provided as follows:

- *Decision epochs, O:* These are the outputs obtained from the context inference module. *State space, S^R,* and *action space, A,* are given by (5.26) and (5.25), respectively.
- *State transition probability, P_{rw}^a:* This probability matrix defines transition probabilities among states $\{r \rightarrow w\}$ while action a is taken:

$$
P_{rw}^a = \begin{cases}
\frac{1}{r-1}, & a = 1,\ w < r, \\
1, & a = 2,\ w = r, \\
\frac{1}{W-r}, & a = 3,\ w > r, \\
0, & \text{otherwise.}
\end{cases}
\tag{5.32}
$$

Remark that all transitions that form a specific state are set an equal probability according to the rule of actions. Different transition probabilities could bring an unfair selection of state.

- *Accuracy cost, c(r,a):* The accuracy cost is the retrieved error rate in user state recognitions while the context inference framework is running, which is defined by ϕ in (5.23):

$$
c(r, a) = 1 - \phi_r^a.
\tag{5.33}
$$

On the other hand, the default settings for the accuracy cost are ruled by the rate of missing sampling points under different system states where $\{(S = r)\} \rightarrow \{(DC = l) \times (f_s = k)\}$ and $\forall a \in A$:

$$
c(r, a)_{default} = c(\{l, k\}, a) = 1 - l + l\frac{k}{k_{\max}}.
\tag{5.34}
$$

Remark that the default settings are the maximum error rates, indeed.

- *Power consumption, d(r,a):* Power consumption ratio is the reward process ψ_r:

$$
d(r, a) = \psi_r, \quad \forall a \in A.
\tag{5.35}
$$

The policy aims to maximize the accuracy in user state recognitions subjected to the power constraints. Therefore, a CMDP distinguishes from a regular MDP in the added power consumption function d, which is related to the constraints V_y where $y \in [1, Y]$.

$\rho(r, a)$ is denoted in CMDP as the occupation measure by specifying the probability of a relevant state–action pair in the decision process that satisfies given constraints, whose probability distribution is given by

$$f(\gamma, u, r, a) = \sum_{t=1}^{\infty} Pr_{\gamma}^{u}(S_t^R = r, A_r = a),$$ (5.36)

where γ and u are defined as any initial distribution and any stationary policy, respectively.

Having (5.32), (5.33), (5.34), and (5.35), the constrained optimization problem is given by the following requirements:

$$\min_{\rho} \sum_{r} \sum_{a} \rho(r, a)c(r, a)$$

$$\text{subjects to} \sum_{r} \sum_{a} \rho(r, a)(\delta_w(r) - P_{rw}^a) = 0,$$

$$\sum_{r} \sum_{a} \rho(r, a) = 1,$$

$$\rho(r, a) \geq 0,$$ (5.37)

where $\forall r, w \in S^R, \forall a \in A, \delta_w(r) = \{1, r = w; 0, \text{otherwise}\}$.

Let u be the optimal policy that satisfies for all i, a:

$$u_r(a) = \frac{\rho(r, a)}{\sum_a \rho(r, a)}, \quad \forall r \in S, \forall a \in A,$$ (5.38)

whenever the denominator is nonzero. Since the occupation measure is derived from

$$\rho(w) = \gamma(w) + \sum_{r} \sum_{a(r)} \rho(w, a)P_{rw}^a$$

$$= \gamma(w) + \sum_{r} \rho(r) \sum_{a(r)} \frac{\rho(w, a)}{\rho(w)} P_{rw}^a$$

$$= \gamma(w) + \sum_{r} \rho(r) \sum_{a(r)} u_w(a)P_{rw}^a$$

$$= \gamma(w) + \sum_{r} \rho(r)P_{rw}(u),$$ (5.39)

it is concluded that ρ equals to $\gamma(I - P(u))^{-1}$ as defined in (5.37), and also to (5.36), where I is the identity matrix.

In addition, the following constraints are added into (5.37):

$$\sum_i \sum_a \rho(r,a) d^y(r,a) \le V_y, \quad y = 1, \ldots, Y, \tag{5.40}$$

where $V_y(t) = (1 \pm v)V_y(t-1)$ is given for the constraint according to which action is taken, such as $\{a = 1 : -v\}$ and $\{a = 3 : +v\}$ where $0 < v < 1$ and $\{a = 2 : v = 0\}$.

Finally, the constrained optimization problem is defined from (5.37) and (5.40) as $\{\min c$ subjects to $d^y \le V_y\}$, whose solution is described in [8,170], and solved based on linear programming as follows: Find the minimum $C^* \in C(\gamma, u)$ for u defined in (5.38), $\rho \in f(\gamma, u)$ defined in (5.39), $C(\gamma, u) = C(\rho(u))$ and each $D^y(\gamma, u) = D^y(\rho(u))$, where the expected cost is expressed as in

$$C(\gamma, u) = \mathbb{E}^u_\gamma \left\{ \sum_{t=1}^{\infty} c(S_t^R = r, A_t = a) \right\}$$

$$= \sum_{t=1}^{\infty} \mathbb{E}^u_\gamma c(S_t^R = r, A_t = a)$$

$$= \sum_{t=1}^{\infty} \sum_r \sum_{a_i} Pr(S_t^R = r, A_t = a) c(r, a)$$

$$= \sum_r \sum_{a_r} \sum_{t=1}^{\infty} Pr(S_t^R = r, A_t = a) c(r, a)$$

$$= \sum_r \sum_{a_r} f(\gamma, u, r, a) c(r, a). \tag{5.41}$$

In the similar way, for the constraints,

$$D^y(\gamma, u) = \sum_r \sum_{a_r} f(\gamma, u, r, a) d^y(r, a). \tag{5.42}$$

Under the policy u from (5.38) and derivation from (5.41) and (5.42), the expected average accuracy and power consumption cost are then defined by

$$\mathbb{E}^u[C] = \frac{1}{n} \sum_{n'=1}^{n} \mathbb{E}^u c_{n'}(i, a), \tag{5.43a}$$

$$\mathbb{E}^u[V] = \frac{1}{n} \sum_{\forall y} \sum_{n'=1}^{n} \mathbb{E}^u d^y_{n'}(i, a), \tag{5.43b}$$

where n' and n are instant and total decision epoch times, respectively.

5.3.5 Partially Observable Markov Decision Process–Based Solution

Partially observable Markov decision process (POMDP) also decribes an optimal solution in order to respond to the defined trade-off. The parameter set by POMDP has some similarities like the one provided by CMDP. The same states S^R, actions a, and state transitions P^a_{rw} are used in this model as well. A POMDP relies on an agent that takes some action $a \in A$ and hence makes the system move from state r to a new state w. Due to the uncertainty in an action, the state transition is modeled by P^a_{rw}. In addition, the agent makes an observation $x \in O$ to gather information for the decision on the new system state selection; thereby, state–observation relationship is probabilistically modeled by Z^a_{wx}. In each observation epoch, the agent takes action a in state r and then receives a reward $R(r, a)$.

The POMDP parameter set is given as follows:

■ *Decision epochs, O; State space, S^R; Action space, A;* and *State transition probability, P^a_{rw}:* These given the same as in Section 5.3.4.
■ *Observation emission probability, Z^a_{wx}:* The observation is the accuracy ratio provided by the context inference module (see Section 5.2.2):

$$Z^a_{wx}(t) = \frac{1}{|Z|} \begin{cases} \phi(t), & r = w, \\ (1 - \phi(t)), & r \neq w, \end{cases} \tag{5.44}$$

where $S^R_{(t-1)} = r, S^R_t = w, \forall a \in A, |Z| = \phi(t) + (W-1)(1-\phi(t))$, and $x = 1$ since there is only one observation, which is the accuracy ratio.
■ *Reward function, $R^a_r(t)$:* The reward process (i.e., power consumption) ψ_r is defined in Section 5.3.1:

$$R^a_r(t) = \psi_r, \quad \forall a \in A. \tag{5.45}$$

■ *Belief vector, $\lambda^a_r(t)$:* Since the internal state of the underlying POMDP is not directly observable, the knowledge of the internal state could be provided by a belief vector $\lambda^a_r(t) \in \Lambda$ in the presence of the history of all past decisions and observations. The belief vector gives the conditional probability of being in state r under action a prior to any state transition.

The belief vector is updated whenever a new knowledge comes in after incorporating the action and observation obtained at time t within the history set of $\mathcal{H}(t) = \{a(\tau), O(\tau)\}, \tau \in [1, t]$. The updated belief vector is obtained using (5.44) by the Bayes rule:

$$\lambda^a_w(t+1) = \mathcal{T}(\lambda(t) \mid a, O) = \frac{Z^a_{wx} \sum_i P^a_{rw} \lambda^a_r(t)}{\sum_x Z^a_{wx} \sum_r P^a_{rx} \lambda^a_r(t)}. \tag{5.46}$$

The goal defined by OPMDP is to develop an opportunistic sensor sampling strategy, which seeks a favorable trade-off balance between accuracy in sensing and energy efficiency. Hence, a sensing policy $u^* : \Lambda \rightarrow A$ is defined to map a belief vector λ_r to an action a. The policy u^* is presented by a sequence of functions $\{u^* = [\eta_1, \eta_2, \ldots, \infty]\}$ where η_t maps a belief vector $\lambda_r(t) \in \Lambda$ to an action $a \in A$ at time t over infinite horizon of POMDP.

From the time at the current belief vector is $\lambda(t)$, a value function $V_t(\lambda(t))$ is denoted to represent the minimum expected remaining reward, which can be earned under the assigned policies. This reward is obtained through immediate and future rewards. The optimal policy strikes a balance between earning immediate reward and obtaining a lean toward future decisions on the system.

The optimal strategy aims at minimizing the expected total reward, and it is defined together with (5.45) and (5.46) as in

$$u = \arg \min_u \mathbb{E}_u \left[\sum_{t=1}^{T} R_r^a(t) \mid \lambda(1) \right]. \tag{5.47}$$

Hence, the value function for total reward aggregation is given with the help of (5.47) as in

$$V_t(\lambda(t)) = \min_a \mathbb{E}[R^a(\lambda(t)) + \varphi V_{t+1}(T(\lambda(t) \mid a, S_r^a(t)))], \tag{5.48}$$

where $R^a(\lambda) = \sum_r \lambda_r R_r^a$ and $\varphi \in [0, 1]$ is a discount factor.

Due to the impact of the current action on the future rewards, the uncountable belief state lies over an infinite horizontal space. Therefore, specifying nonstationarity of the optimal policy or finding an optimal strategy for POMDP is often computationally prohibitive.

5.3.5.1 Myopic Strategy and Sufficient Statistics

Since finding an optimal strategy is computationally restricted, it is crucial to exploit the available POMDP and develop suboptimal strategies in order to reduce the complexity. Therefore, it is needed to show the a posterior of distribution of the belief vector under sufficient statistics. The belief vector (5.46) is then updated based on the chosen action under the following sufficient statistics:

$$\lambda_r(t+1) = \begin{cases} (\lambda(t)_r^T P_{rw}^a)^T, & d' = \{1, 3\}, \ r \neq w, \\ \lambda_i(t), & d' = 2, \ r = w, \\ 0, & \text{otherwise}, \end{cases} \tag{5.49}$$

where ^{T} is the matrix transpose.

In addition, a myopic policy is introduced to ignore the impact of current action on the future rewards by solely focusing on minimizing the immediate reward. This is due to the fact that power consumption caused by instant sensory operation settings does not rely on future diversity in the sensory operation methods. Thereby, the myopic policy makes $\varphi = 0$ in (5.48), and hence, it turns (5.47) into

$$S_*^R = \arg\min_r \mathbb{E}[R_r^a(\lambda_r^a(t))],$$

$$\text{subjects to} \quad \max(Z_{w,O=x}^a(t)) > \varepsilon, \tag{5.50}$$

where S_*^R is the chosen optimal state and ε denotes the minimum probability of given accuracy allowed by the process.

5.4 Performance Evaluation

A case study in an HAR application model is examined to investigate the defined trade-off by proposed sensor management system. The targeted smartphone is placed fixed on the user's hip area. A similar user activity profile is examined for each trade-off analysis by five different participants. They are three males and two females, whose ages range from 18 to 30. Accordingly, the HAR-based user activity profile begins with a random activity pattern of user states *sitting* and *standing* for a minute (used for calibration), and then any of the user states *sitting, standing, walking*, and *running* transits into the another one in the end of the following sojourn times of {5, 5, 10, 10, 30, 30, 60, 60, 100, 100, 300, 300} s. This procedure is also performed three times (approximately 50 min in total per method by each individual) to see the effect of having a transition from longer waiting time to shorter waiting time, or vice versa. The initial 1 min long application time is used for adaptation process, which is reserved to set required adjustments in the system parameters with respect to ongoing activity pattern. Note that system parameters already have default settings defined by (5.14). From that point, sensory operation parameters, which are duty cycle and sampling frequency, are updated with a 10 s period. In addition, t_{suff} is set to 20 s. Recall that as long as a continuing settlement time in any state gets longer than t_{suff}, sensor management system decreases power consumption, which jeopardizes the recognition accuracy of the activity pattern in return. The default sensory operation parameters are set to the aggressive sampling method, which is equal to the pair of {100%, 100 Hz} for {DC, f_s}.

The context inference module is set to recognize a user state with a period of 1 s under the aggressive sampling method. The underlying Markovian chain in this module has a finite horizon length of 60, which means 1 min long recent history of user states. Every 1 min, system parameters are updated according to (5.18). Except for the aggressive sampling method in sensory operations, the context inference module may not have a sensory observation at any time. For instance, in the case where the pair of {50%, 50 Hz} is selected for sensory operation parameters, the decision period to recognize a user state is extended to 4 s, which results in having three empty decision points to estimate missing user state recognitions.

The trade-off analysis is carried out for each sensor management method by each participant. The trade-off solutions by each method are averaged and then shown in Figure 5.2 for the analysis of power consumption ratio according to (5.28), (5.43b), and (5.48), and also in Figure 5.3 for the analysis of averaged recognition accuracy according to (5.23), (5.43a), and (5.50). In addition, the trade-off solutions by each method in both figures are noted by the suffixes "a" and "b" to demonstrate without/with some constraints added. The suffix "a" indicates the actual sensor management methods without any additional constraints. However, the suffix "b" sets extra rules on these methods. First, a 10% tolerance value is added into Methods I, II, and III to constrain the recognition accuracy ratio, which helps the prevention of drastic recognition errors. If this constraint is exceeded, sensory operation parameters are forced to set the default settings, that is, the aggressive sampling.

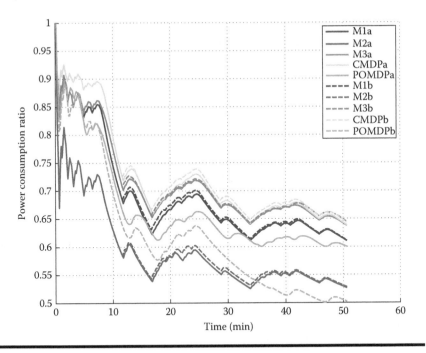

Figure 5.2 Averaged power consumption ratio in response to user profile: the evolution of power consumption efficiency in comparison to the most aggressive sensory sampling methods is shown for each proposed sensory operation method in response to the analyzed user profile. Overall 40% enhancement in power consumption caused by the smartphone accelerometer is achieved.

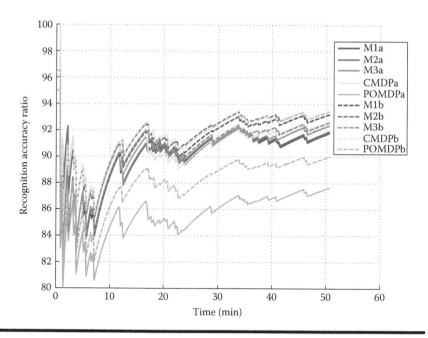

Figure 5.3 Averaged recognition accuracy ratio in response to user profile: having shown a drastic decrease initially due to the default system parameters, the recognition accuracy ratio heals gradually while the context inference module gets better adaptation toward the analyzed user profiles and ends up with an overall 10%–15% decrease in accuracy ratio for user state recognitions thanks to the proposed framework.

Second, for CMDP, there is another constraint set on the power consumption ratio to control the tendency of the decision process to take an immoderate decrease in power consumption. According to this regulation, current sensory operation setting must stay in ±25% of the present power consumption level at most for the next setting. Finally, additional constraint for POMDP, the update process of belief vector is reconfigured by adding the feature of $\lambda_i(t+1) = 1$ where $a = 2$.

In light of the preceding explanations, the following discussions can be made through both Figures 5.2 and 5.3:

■ Recognition accuracy ratio decreases significantly during the initial progress of context inference module since the framework begins running with default settings. Therefore, the adaptation process toward a user by the framework is not adequate yet. It is also because that any user exhibits a variant activity profile initially by changing user states regularly.

■ Both figures show ups and downs, that is, zigzag lines, to prove the defined trade-off. This is because sensor management system always seeks an opportunity to save in power consumption. However, this also jeopardizes the accuracy problem. In contrast, accuracy is healed by boosting power cost. Therefore, increase in power consumption compensates the worsening of the recognition accuracy ratio, whereas decrease in power consumption receives benefits from the adaptation feature if possible where the framework shows high accuracy.

■ When the time passes by, since the framework gets a better adaptation to the user activity profile, the recognition accuracy ratio increases even though power consumption ratio decreases. It is also because that all user activities are known by the framework at this point, and it will lead to the continuity of better enhancement on trade-off solutions.

■ While switching from longer waiting times to slower waiting times, second or third run of defined user activity pattern, accuracy decreases even if power consumption increases. It is because that the system has been fully aware that the same user activity has been continuing for a longer waiting period, and that is also giving a higher recognition accuracy compared with what it is currently in the presence of higher-pace variant user activities.

■ The recognition accuracy ratio may show a slight decrease if a state transition occurs after a long state visiting time, or the number of estimations in user state recognition increases after a slower sampling policy is attained. It is because that the entropy rate cannot converge into any stable point. In such cases, the framework attempts to fix the accuracy ratio.

■ Among intuitive solutions, a comparison can be made by MIII > MI > MII in terms of the power consumption ratios and by MI > MIII > MII in terms of the recognition accuracy ratio. Results show that the sampling in slower frequencies consumes higher power than the sampling in lower duty cycles; however, it shows the opposite assumption for the recognition accuracy. It is because that sampling in slower frequencies still obtains information about user activity while the sampling in lower duty cycles cannot do. On the other hand, MIII has the highest power consumption since it switches sensor operation modes modestly while achieving a fine accuracy in user state recognitions.

■ $MX_b > MX_a$ where $X = I, II, III$, and $CMDP_b > CMDP_a$ are met in terms of the power consumption ratio because the aggressive sampling is forced to apply in the case where severe errors occur in user state recognitions.

■ $POMDP_b$ makes a clear conclusion about the belief vector rather than $POMDP_a$ does when a sufficient visiting time elapses on a specific user state. Hence, the power consumption decreases since the conclusion notifies the continuity of the same user state.

■ MIII responds in a similar way CMDP does while trying to reach their optimal policies.

In general, our novel trade-off solutions achieve overall 40% enhancement in power consumption caused by the physical sensor work with respect to overall 10–15% decrease in accuracy ratio for user state recognitions thanks to proposed generic context inference framework. The novelty of our framework also comes from adaptability feature toward changing user behaviors along with online accuracy tracker while providing optimal adaptive sampling strategies within the research area of mobile device–based activity recognition. In contrast, some other recent studies within the same concept show enhancement in power efficiency by 20%–25% in [230], 5%–10% in [38], and 10%–30% in [204] while satisfying considerable recognition accuracy under nonadaptive, deterministic, and variant sampling frequency or duty cycle applying sensor sampling methods.

As a summary of this chapter, a novel comprehensive framework is presented within the futuristic concept of context awareness in mobile sensing. A statistical machine–based context inference model together with an intelligent sensor management system is created to recognize human-centric activities. This approach aims at achieving a fine balance between power consumption and recognition accuracy. The study takes the smartphone accelerometer sensor into the scope to show the effectiveness of proposed total system structure as well as leaving the door open for future improvements in the functionality of other smartphone sensors.

While creating the statistical machine, some features are taken into consideration, such as time-varying user activity profile, system adaptability to the changing profile, nonuniform time distribution of sensory sampling process due to the power saving precautions, and the estimation process where missing sensory observations exist. On the other hand, while creating the sensor management system, the analytical modeling of power consumption caused by the accelerometer is examined. Thereby, along with the collaboration of the statistical machine, a better balance is achieved for the defined trade-off throughout the chapter. For the trade-off analysis, some intuitive and optimal sensory operation solutions are provided in order to increase efficiency in power consumption, whereas the statistical machine tries to maintain the accuracy ratio provided by the framework.

Chapter 6

Probabilistic Context Modeling

Probabilistic models have emerged in an efficient way of representing random variables, dependencies, and temporal variations to create a suitable tool for behavior modeling. Several dynamic probabilistic models in terms of their effectiveness in learning sequential and temporal characteristics of a data sequence have been proposed. The foremost important probabilistic model is hidden Markov models (HMMs). An HMM is composed of hidden states (e.g., human activity patterns) and observations (e.g., featured sensor readings). It aims to model a sequence or a time series by learning characteristics of probability models belonging to state transitions and observations. This ubiquitous tool for modeling time series data has been widely used in areas of written and spoken language recognition, computational molecular biology, pattern recognition, machine learning, and computer vision. While HMMs are simple and efficient models for learning sequential data, their performances tend to degrade when activities become more complex with increasing data set and exhibit long-term temporal dependencies.

The intent of multiple sensor use in many complex context-aware applications results in a large number of parameter space and arises a need for modeling and recognizing more complex human-related activities and behaviors. Therefore, some extension versions of HMMs such as parallel HMMs (PaHMMs), factorial HMMs (FHMMs), coupled HMMs (CHMMs), and observation decomposed/multiple observation HMMs (OD/MO-HMMs), see Figure 6.1, have been increasingly employed to model different event sequences. Main difference between these models is topological structure of modeling observation-state and state-state probabilistic dependencies throughout the time. To mention briefly on these models, PaHMMs

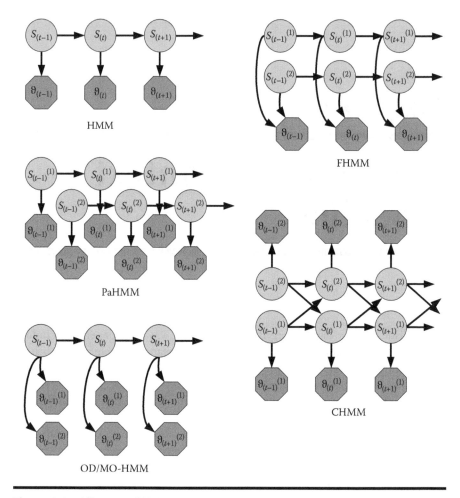

Figure 6.1 All types of HMMs (X-HMMs).

consist of multiple HMMs (channels) running independently without considering any interchannel state/observation dependencies. FHMMs decompose the state of HMMs into several metastates evolving independently but emitting joint observations. CHMMs capture causal–temporal influences among HMMs and evolve its chain over states in the form of compositional representations. OD/MO-HMMs emit either a set of subobservations or multiple independent observations over the same hidden chain.

There are two different dynamic structure models representing temporal dependencies: parallel and hierarchical. Such models like CHMMs and OD/MO-HMMs need multisource observations involved and required to make context inference in a fusion, whereas human behaviors can ensemble in a hierarchy based on multiscaled sensory observations. Hierarchical HMMs (HHMMs) have been developed in this manner in order to address these problems by introducing a hierarchical probabilistic model in which each level of hierarchy represents an activity at a particular level of abstraction. Activities can be formed as consequences of either temporal relations or spatial relations. First, one activity may either occur as a combination of actions having some rank-wise relations in a hierarchic structure whose layers reflect partial relations among activities, or it may occur as a view of abstraction existing over taxonomic hierarchical layers reflecting somewhat relations. Second, activities can have spatial character since they are seen as dynamic processes, which have their own internal flows and which might be influenced by others.

All these different Markovian models can also be seen as a particular case of dynamic Bayesian networks (DBNs), which are successfully able to handle time-varying signals and events of large spatial and temporal variability. As DBNs are generative models that are generally preferred for a large data set due to their better reliability on a dynamic model supported by state and observation likelihood functions, DBNs could provide a unified probabilistic framework to represent various graphical structures.

A special case of DBNs is proposed in this chapter for context awareness. Production layer of the propsed DBN consists of C number of different types of HMMs called X-HMMs. These channels may either run independently or have causal dependencies to capture atomic activities that are only obtained by sensory observations. Going up to upper layers, temporal correlations among layers are constructed. For instance, second layer, which is called relation layer, can have multiple independent temporal correlation chains. Therefore, c' number of channels are defined on this layer where $1 \leq c' \leq C - 1$. Finally, top layer has only one temporal relation, which can be seen as the highest interest of network.

To this end, this chapter aims to describe proposed generic model in detail. On one hand, it aims to give an inside-out summary of probabilistic models within generic model; on the other hand, it tries to give some new assumptions on these models.

6.1 Construction of Hidden Markov Models

HMMs are probably the most efficient framework used in context-aware sensing for modeling and classifying dynamic behaviors since they offer some features such as dynamic time warping, statistical learning, efficient algorithms for parameter estimation, a clear Bayesian semantics, and great adaptability and versatility in handling sequential signals. Therefore, they have been widely used under areas of speech and image processing in order to learn from data and handle the processing of time-varying signals. Moreover, Bayesian semantics makes it easy to compute with uncertainties. A detailed tutorial for conventional HMMs can be found in [175], an overview of HMMs in [67], a discussion on learning and inference in HMMs within understanding of Bayesian networks in [83], and concrete mathematical background behind HMMs in [35].

6.1.1 General Model

First-order HMM is a stochastic process that shows dependency of state at discrete time t that is influenced directly by a state at discrete time $t-1^*$. Underlying stochastic process, which is a sequence of states, is not observable, so it is called hidden chain. This process also influences another stochastic process that produces (emits) a sequence of observations.

HMM is characterized by following elements:

■ *Hidden process*: A set of hidden states are defined as a discrete time process with a finite space of $1, \ldots, N$:

$$S_{1:T} = \{S_1 = i, S_2, \ldots, S_T\}, \quad \forall i \in \{1, \ldots, N\} \tag{6.1a}$$

In hidden process, a state can be revisited at any discrete time and also not every state needs to be visited.

■ *Initial hidden state probability*: An irreducible and aperiodic Markov chain begins with its ergodic distribution:

$$\pi_i = Pr(S_0 = i), \quad \begin{cases} \pi_i \geq 0, \quad \forall i \in \{1, \ldots, N\} \\ \sum_{i=1}^{N} \pi_i = 1 \end{cases} \tag{6.1b}$$

■ *State transition probability*: a is described as $N \times N$ state transition matrix where each element a_{ij} of a is equal to a transition probability from state i to state j:

$$a_{ij} = Pr(S_t = j \mid S_{t-1} = i), \quad \begin{cases} a_{ij} \geq 0, \quad \forall i, j \in \{1, \ldots, N\} \\ \sum_{i=1}^{N} a_{ij} = 1 \end{cases} \tag{6.1c}$$

There is no requirement that transition probabilities must be symmetric ($a_{ij} \neq a_{ji}$) and a specific state might remain same in succession of time ($a_{ii} = 0$).

---

* In an nth-order Markov process, state at t has dependencies with states at $\{t - n, t - n + 1, \ldots, t - 1\}$.

- *Visible process*: A set of observations are defined as a discrete time process with a finite space of $1, \ldots, K$:

$$\vartheta_{1:T} = \{\vartheta_1 = k, \vartheta_2, \ldots, \vartheta_T\}, \quad \forall k \in \{1, \ldots, K\} \tag{6.1d}$$

- *Observation emission probability*: b is described as $N \times K$ observation emission matrix where each element b_{jk} of b is equal to a cross probability between hidden state and emitted observation:

$$b_{jk} = Pr(\vartheta_t = k \mid S_t = j), \quad \begin{cases} b_{jk} \geq 0, & \forall j \in \{1, \ldots, N\}, \forall k \in \{1, \ldots, K\} \\ \sum_{k=1}^{K} b_{jk} = 1 \end{cases}$$

$$\tag{6.1e}$$

HMM parameters are usually denoted as a triplet $\lambda = \{a_{ij}, b_{jk}, \pi_i\}$.

6.1.2 Parallel HMMs

PaHMMs consist of C independent HMMs with separate observation sequences. In other words, PaHMMs are essentially defined in the form of multiple independent HMMs running parallel. This kind of models combine multiple HMMs without the consideration of any relation among channel states.

Research for PaHMMs is mostly done in the area of American sign language (ASL) recognition. Major challenge being faced in the research of ASL recognition is how to develop methods that scale well with increasing vocabulary size. It is reported in [217] that there are two critical aspects of scalability problem. The first aspect is breaking down the signs into their constituent phonemes; the second one is modeling of these phonemes. According to study, ASL can be modeled by PaHMMs as independent processes because of these defined linguistic properties.

PaHMM is characterized by following edited elements in (6.1) in the presence of C independent HMMs where $1 \leq c \leq C$ and $1 \leq i, j \leq N^{(c)}$:

- *Initial hidden state probability*: $\sum_{i=1}^{N^{(c)}} \pi_i^{(c)} = 1$
- *State transition probability*: $\sum_{i=1}^{N^{(c)}} a_{ij}^{(c)} = 1$
- *Observation emission probability*: $\sum_{k=1}^{K} b_{jk}^{(c)} = 1$ where $1 \leq k \leq K^{(c)}$

6.1.3 Factorial HMMs

FHMMs combine multiple independent stochastic processes in a way where their outputs are superimposed. This model basically defines parallel running hidden chains (state channels) with joint observation sequence. The source of observation is separated with nonmutual information, for example, classification algorithms, to overlay on different state channels. FHMMs enable a state variable to be factored into multiple state variables. Therefore, FHMMs create C separate HMMs by forming C-dimensional state space that includes $N^{(c)}$ metastates at each dimension. Metastates are hidden states that are noncausally related to visible states. A well-detailed study regarding FHMMs can be found in [84].

FHMM is characterized as same as PaHMM except for a joint output:

- *Observation emission probability*: $\sum_{k=1}^{K} b_j^{(c)}(k) = 1$ where $1 \leq c \leq C$, $1 \leq i, j \leq N^{(c)}$, and $1 \leq k \leq K$

In addition to FHMMs, products of HMMs (PoHMMs) are a very different way of combining multiple state variables that have noncausal effect on observed variables, well studied in [32,146]. PoHMMs have an opposite property compared with FHMMs in terms of conditioning on a set of observations; however, hidden state chains are still independent of each other. Therefore, inference on each HMM is independent given observations due to undirected arcs from hidden states to observations.

6.1.4 Coupled/Joint HMMs

CHMMs include multiple interacting time series processes to enhance the capabilities of standard HMM by using more complex architectures since separate HMMs are not able to capture interactions among different models. One method of doing this, as indicated in [31], is taking Cartesian products of states and transition parameters among HMMs in order to create a mathematical framework for coupling operation. Coupling creates temporal and asymmetric conditional probabilities among Markov chains. Another approach is given in [242] that offers a new forward procedure and training algorithm to produce a joint conditional probability among chains with weights represented as coupling coefficients.

In CHMMs, the state of one HMM at time t depends on states of all models at time $t - 1$ including itself since multiple HMMs are coupled/joint together with regard to state transitions. Therefore, the influence of one chain on the other run through a causal link. For C number of HMMs coupled/joint together, the probability of state transitions becomes $Pr(S_t^{(c)} \mid S_{t-1}^{(1)}, S_{t-1}^{(2)}, \ldots, S_{t-1}^{(C)})$ instead of $Pr(S_t^{(c)} \mid S_{t-1}^{(c)})$ as seen in standard HMMs, which means transition matrix is the intersection of each individual channel.

The number of parameters is reduced by CHHMs, and its model is characterized as same as PaHMMs except for coupled/joint states:

- *State transition probability*: $a^{(c)} = \prod_{c'=1}^{C} a_{ij}^{(c',c)}$ where $1 \leq c', c \leq C$, $1 \leq i, j \leq N^{(c)}$, and (c', c) indicates relation from channel c' to channel c.

6.1.5 Observation Decomposed/Multiple Observation HMMs

In conventional HMMs, each state can emit one of a finite number of observations that lie on the same feature space, whereas OD/MO-HMMs have multiple observations so that each observation provides a set of finite number of subobservation space that bases on a different feature selection compared with others. Therefore, a state can emit multiple observations (MO-HMMs) or an observation composed with multiple subobservations (OD-HMMs).

Subobservations are assumed to be independent of each other so that one observation space has no common relation to others. The most important feature of OD/MO-HMMs is that states can be still inferred in such a situation in which some of the subobservations are lost during a period of time. This is because remaining active subobservations still carry information that helps model out to assign proper state chain. For instance, [138] uses OD/MO-HMMs in order to model and classify multiagent (interest of multiple users and their interactions among themselves) activity recognition in automatic visual surveillance systems. This method not only reduces the size of feature space but also does not change the feature space even when the number of agents changes.

OD/MO-HMM is characterized as same as HMM except for multiple observations:

- *Observation emission probability*: $\sum_{r=1}^{R} b_j(\vartheta^{(r)} = k^{(r)}) = 1$ where $1 \leq r \leq R$, $1 \leq j \leq N$, $1 \leq k \leq K^{(r)}$, and R is the total number of observations and $K^{(r)}$ is the number of subobservations.

6.1.6 Hierarchical HMMs

HHMMs are the extension of multiple HMMs combined as structured multilevel stochastic processes. In HHMMs, each hidden state is defined as an autonomous probabilistic model itself. Therefore, states can emit either single observation or multiple observations at a time. HHMMs generate these observations by activating substates of a state recursively. A substate may be composed of multiple substates; therefore, recursively activation process continues until reaching a specific state that is called production state. Production states are the only states that actually emit observations. Hidden states, called internal (or abstract) states, do not emit observations. Activation of a substate by an internal state is called vertical state transition. Upon completion of vertical transitions (a vertical transition may yield to have further vertical transitions until reaching actual hidden state), a substate that originated recursive activation process takes control back. Then, a state transition occurs at the same level, which is called horizontal state transition.

A set of states including internal and production states and vertical state transitions produce a tree structure where root state is the top node of hierarchy and leaves are production states.

A state of an HHMM is denoted by $S_t^{(l)} = i$ where i is state index and $l \in \{1, 2, \ldots, L\}$ is hierarchy index. The root is indexed by 1 and production states are by L.

$f_t^{(l)}$ is a binary variable that indicates whether or not there is completion of state transition at level $l - 1$ right before at time t. Therefore, whenever $f_t^{(l)}$ is set, that means HHMM at level $l - 1$ completes and a state transition from $S_{t-1}^{(l)}$ to $S_t^{(l)}$ occurs. Otherwise, state at level l remains same $S_{t-1}^{(l)} = S_t^{(l)}$.

HHMMs are characterized by following elements:

■ Initial state probability of $S_t^{(l)}$, which also means probability of $S_t^{(l)}$, activates $S_t^{(l+1)}$:

$$\Pi^{(l)} = \pi^{(l)}(S_t^{(l+1)} = i) = Pr(S_t^{(l+1)} = i \mid S_t^{(l)}) \qquad (6.2a)$$

is called vertical state transition by entering substate $S_t^{(l+1)}$ through its parent $S_t^{(l)}$.

■ For each internal state $S_t^{(l)} = i$ where $l \in \{1, 2, \ldots, L-1\}$, a horizontal state transition probability is defined:

$$A^{(l)} = a_{ij}^{(l)} = Pr(S_t^{(l+1)} = j \mid S_{t-1}^{(l+1)} = i, S_{t-1}^{(l)}) \qquad (6.2b)$$

where $A^{(l)}$ is state transition matrix and horizontal state transition occurs from state i to state j, which are substates of $S_t^{(l)}$.

■ Each production state $S_t^{(L)}$ can emit observation:

$$B^{(L)} = b_{jk}^{(L)} = Pr(\vartheta_t = k \mid S_t^{(L)} = j) \qquad (6.2c)$$

Finally, system parameters are denoted as

$$\Lambda = \{\lambda^{(l)}\}_{l\in\{1,2,\ldots,L\}} = \{\{\Pi^{(l)}\}_{l\in\{1,2,\ldots,L-1\}}, \{A^{(l)}\}_{l\in\{1,2,\ldots,L-1\}}, \{B^{(L)}\}\} \qquad (6.2d)$$

As indicated in [74,156] and [165], HHMMs are able to correlate structures running almost independent observation sequences while maintaining simplicity and computational tractability among these structures. This feature gives HHMMs to handle statistical inhomogeneous complex sequences such as seen in speech and data processing.

6.1.7 Dynamic Bayesian Networks

DBNs, see Figure 6.2, can be represented as a combination of hierarchical structures and causal–temporal relations among processes simultaneously. Its topology can be identified over three layers named production, relation, and abstract. Production layer consists of several independent state channels. Above this layer, relation layer exists by having close influence with all production layer channels. Top of layers, multiple abstract layers, cover to trigger events by satisfying required relation level with sublayers. In summary, a state transition at any level will initiate a Markov chain at its bottom levels through substates. Detailed studies under this topic can be obtained in [63,155] and [239].

Individual multiple processes, that is, independent multiple Markovian channels, generate different Markovian chains, interactions, and asynchronous manners of influence and then lead state space growing rapidly and becoming intractable/uncorrelated, whereas having assumed that multiple processes run under

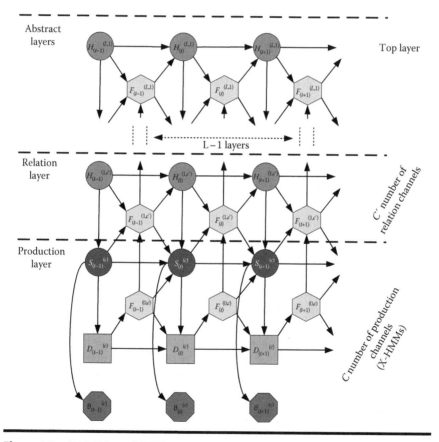

Figure 6.2 HHMMs and DBNs.

context-aware sensing systems, DBNs try to decompose state variables into subsets in order to capture the spatial structure of human activities. Spatial decomposition under DBNs has several advantages:

- Variable states are reduced in terms of complexity of general model and further parameter ambiguity as the increasing number is prevented.
- Using multiple HMMs represents user activities more in detail and exposes internal dynamics explicitly.
- Feature selection is flexible due to individually running but interinfluenced/cooperated channels.

State and observation variables in DBNs at channel c at time t are denoted by $S_t^{(c)}$ and $\vartheta_t^{(c)}$, respectively. $h_t^{(l)}$ denotes interaction state at abstract layer at time t. If $l = 1$, $h_t^{(1)}$ represents a state lying on relation layer. The downward arcs among $S_t^{(c)}$ and $h_t^{(l)}$ variables represent that a state calls its substate.

$f_t^{(l)}$ is a boolean variable that can be valued either 1 or 0. $f_t^{(l)}$ is defined as ending variable since it helps system out to determine how context at time of $t + 1$ will be defined from context at time of t:

- In case of $f_t^{(l)} = 0$, a state on corresponding level will be delivered as same to next time slice:
  - If $f_t^{(0)} = 0$, then production state $S_t^{(c)}$ transits into a new state, $S_{t+1}^{(c)}$.
- On the other hand, when $f_t^{(l)} = 1$, there are two possibilities arisen:
  - If $f_t^{(0)} = 1$, then production state $S_t^{(c)}$ is about to transit an end state. In other words, process has just finished.
  - If $f_t^{(l')} = 0$ where $l' > l$, then a state on layer l' carries itself to next time slice.
  - Otherwise, state switches its context.
- When both $l = 1$ and $l' = 1$, the number of $f_t^{(l)}$ becomes 0, which represents effective height of active hierarchical level.

The upward arcs between $f_t^{(l)}$ variables ensure that system can only change state when lower-level one has finished:

- *Production layer* ($l = 0, c \in C, t = 1 : T - 1$): $S_t^{(c)}$ is a Markov chain with parameters determined by which type of HMM is being followed. This Markov chain is encoded with other existing Markov chains as well as by a set of higher-up state variables, $h_t^{(l')}$.

  Duration state, $d_t^{(l=0,c)}$ or $D_t^{(c)}$ on graph, indicates the remaining duration of productive state. It is added into DBNs to bring semi-Markovian feature to structure. The self-arc on a generative state defines a geometric distribution over waiting times during a specific state. Basically, $d^{(l=0,c)}$ counts how long system stays in a specific state; when residual time hits down to 0, the $f^{(0,c)}$ turns on, $S^{(c)}$ can transit, and duration state, $d^{(0,c)}$, resets. The reason why $S_t^{(c)}$ and $f_t^{(0,c)}$ have no arc is that termination process is deterministic:

$$Pr(D_t^{(c)} = d' \mid D_{t-1}^{(c)} = d, S_t^{(c)} = i, f_{t-1}^{(0,c)} = 1) = p_i(d') \qquad (6.3a)$$

$$Pr(D_t^{(c)} = d' \mid D_{t-1}^{(c)} = d, S_t^{(c)} = i, f_{t-1}^{(0,c)} = 0)$$

$$= \begin{cases} 1, & (d > 1) \wedge (d' = d - 1) \\ 0, & \text{otherwise} \end{cases} \qquad (6.3b)$$

where $f_t^{(0,c)}$ is controlled by $Pr(f_t^{(0,c)} = 1 \mid D_t^{(c)} = d) = 1 - p(d)$. The probability of residual time, d, in a state i can be given by $p(d) = (1-p)p^{d-1}$ where $p = a_{ii}$ is self-state transition probability.

Whenever $S_t^{(c)}$ enters into an end state, it sets $f_t^{(1,c')}$ to 1 to mean process has just finished. This signal notifies that higher-level HMMs can now transit into another state. It also notifies that next chain, $S_{t+1}^{(c)}$, will be initiated (vertical state transition) instead continued to evolve (horizontal state transition):

$$Pr(S_t^{(c)} = j \mid S_{t-1}^{(1:C)} = i, f_{t-1}^{(0,c)} = q, h_t^{(L:1)} = k, D_t^{(0,c)} = d)$$

$$= \begin{cases} \delta(i,j), & (d = 0) \wedge (p = 0) \\ \hat{a}_k^{(c)}(i,j), & (d = 1) \wedge (q = 0) \\ \pi_k^{(c)}(i), & (d = 1) \wedge (q = 1) \end{cases} \qquad (6.3c)$$

where $i \neq j$. Moreover, it is not clearly seen that whether or not channel c has a relation with other running channels; therefore, $S_{t-1}^{(1:C)}$ is used instead of $S_{t-1}^{(c)}$ itself and $\hat{a}$ is used instead of a, which means the production of state transitions might be sourced by other processes (e.g., CHMMs). k notifies a state value that parent node has.

■ *Relation layer* ($l = 1$) and *abstract layer* ($l > 1$) ($1 \leq c' \leq C - 1, l < L, t = 1 : T - 1$): $h^{(l)}$ is a Markov chain with parameters determined by $h^{(1:l-1,c')}$, $S^{(l=0,c)}$, and $f^{(l,c')}$. $f^{(l-1,c')}$ notifies submodel has finished or not. Depending on notification, $h^{(l,c')}$ either transits into another state or remains in the same state.

c' represents a set of joint HMM processes. While network is evolving from lower layers to upper layers, layer l' could be a joint process of some of processes lying over layer $l' - 1$. Therefore, for each network parameter, joint probability has to be considered. For the simplicity, $c' = 1$ is taken to show relations among network parameters better:

$$Pr(h_t^{(l)} = j \mid h_{t-1}^{(l)} = i, f_{t-1}^{(l-1)} = p, f_{t-1}^{(l)} = q, h_t^{(L:l+1)} = k)$$

$$= \begin{cases} \delta(i,j), & p = 0 \\ \hat{a}_k^{(l)}(i,j), & (p=1) \wedge (q=0) \\ \pi_k^{(l)}(j), & (p=1) \wedge (q=1) \end{cases} \quad (6.3\text{d})$$

$f_t^{(l)}$ is also updated by

$$Pr(f_t^{(l)} = 1 \mid h_t^{(l)} = i, f_t^{(l-1)} = p, h_t^{(L:l)} = k) = \begin{cases} 0, & p = 0 \\ a_k^{(l)}(i, end), & p = 1 \end{cases}$$
$$(6.3\text{e})$$

- *Top layer* ($l = L, t = 1 : T - 1$): Top layer has no parent Markov chain evolving. Equations are same as used in relation or abstract layer except for $h_t^{(L:1)} = k$.
- *Initialization* ($l \in L, t = 0$):

$$Pr(S_0^{(c)} = j) = \pi_j^{(c)} \quad (6.3\text{f})$$

$$Pr(h_0^{(l)} = j \mid h_0^{(1:l-1)} = k, S_0^{(0)} = k) = \pi_k^{(l)}(j) \quad (6.3\text{g})$$

- *Termination* ($l \in L, t = T$): $f_T^{(l)} = 1$ means all sub-HMMs have reached their end states. In fact, DBNs never enter an end state. It continues as long as production layer evolves, which depends on $d_t^{(c)}$.

6.2 Evaluation

Hidden process evolves in time, and state sequence is generated by states ordered in successive discrete times:

$$Pr(S^{(c)} \mid \lambda^{(c)}) = \pi_0^{(c)} \prod_{t=1}^{T} \prod_{c'=1}^{C} Pr(S_t^{(c)} \mid S_{t-1}^{(c')}, \lambda^{(c')}) \quad (6.4)$$

While hidden process (6.4) is evolving, each state emits an observation(s); thus, visible sequence is generated correspondingly:

$$Pr(\vartheta^{(c)} \mid S^{(c)}, \lambda^{(c)}) = \prod_{t=0}^{T} \prod_{r=1}^{R} Pr(\vartheta_t^{(c,r)} \mid S_t^{(c)}, \lambda^{(c)}) \quad (6.5)$$

Evaluation problem tries to determine the probability that given observation sequence (6.5) was generated by given model parameters. For the sake of generalization, a comprehensive formula of evaluation problem is given for the stochastic analysis of HMMs in the presence of multiple hidden channels ($1 \leq c \leq C$) and multiple observations ($1 \leq r \leq R$):

$$Pr(\vartheta \mid \lambda) = \sum_{i=1}^{N} Pr(\vartheta \mid S, \lambda) Pr(S \mid \lambda) \tag{6.6}$$

For a specific HMM channel c by analyzing (6.4) through (6.6) together,

$$Pr(\vartheta^{(c)} \mid \lambda^{(c)}) = \sum_{i=1}^{N} Pr(\vartheta^{(c)} \mid S^{(c)}, \lambda^{(c)}) Pr(S^{(c)} \mid \lambda^{(c)})$$

$$= \sum_{i=1}^{N} \left[\pi_0^{(c)} \prod_{r=1}^{R} Pr(\vartheta_0^{(c,r)} \mid \pi_0^{(c)}, \lambda^{(c)}) \right.$$

$$\left. \times \prod_{t=1}^{T} \left[\prod_{r=1}^{R} Pr(\vartheta_t^{(c,r)} \mid S_t^{(c)}, \lambda^{(c)}) \prod_{c'=1}^{C} Pr(S_t^{(c)} \mid S_{t-1}^{(c')}, \lambda^{(c')}) \right] \right] \tag{6.7}$$

where each i is an index of particular hidden state inside of relevant sequence, $S_t^{(c)} = i$.

Let us examine (6.7) now under different topologies of HMMs.

- *HMMs* ($C = 1, R = 1$): Probability of the occurrence of a specific observation sequence

$$Pr(\vartheta \mid \lambda) = \sum_{i=1}^{N} \pi_0 Pr(\vartheta_0 \mid S_0, \lambda) \prod_{t=1}^{T} Pr(\vartheta_t \mid S_t, \lambda) Pr(S_t \mid S_{t-1}, \lambda)$$

$$= \sum_{i=1}^{N} \pi_0 b_j(\vartheta_0 = k) \prod_{t=1}^{T} a_{ij} b_j(\vartheta_t = k) \tag{6.8}$$

- *PaHMMs* ($\{c', c\} \in C, C > 1, c' \perp\!\!\!\perp c, r^{(c)} = 1$): Probability of the occurrence of a specific observation sequence over a defined channel

$$Pr(\vartheta^{(c)} \mid \lambda^{(c)}) = \sum_{i=1}^{N} \pi_0^{(c)} Pr(\vartheta_0^{(c)} \mid S_0^{(c)}, \lambda^{(c)})$$

$$\times \prod_{t=1}^{T} Pr(\vartheta_t^{(c)} \mid S_t^{(c)}, \lambda^{(c)}) Pr(S_t^{(c)} \mid S_{t-1}^{(c)}, \lambda^{(c)})$$

$$= \sum_{i=1}^{N} \pi_0^{(c)} b_j^{(c)}(\vartheta_0^{(c)} = k) \prod_{t=1}^{T} a_{ij}^{(c)} b_j^{(c)}(\vartheta_t^{(c)} = k) \qquad (6.9)$$

■ *FHMMs* ($\{c', c\} \in C, C > 1, c' \perp\!\!\!\perp c, r = 1$): Underlying state transitions are constrained under FHMMs. Through each channel, each state variable evolves according to its own stochastic process:

$$Pr(S^{(c)} \mid \lambda^{(c)}) = \pi_0^{(c)} \prod_{t=1}^{T} Pr(S_t^{(c)} \mid S_{t-1}^{(c)}, \lambda^{(c)}) \qquad (6.10a)$$

and state variable is not coupled to state variable evolving in other channels:

$$Pr(S_t^1, \ldots, S_t^C \mid S_{t-1}^1, \ldots, S_{t-1}^C) = \prod_{c=1}^{C} Pr(S_t^{(c)} \mid S_{t-1}^{(c)}, \lambda^{(c)}) \qquad (6.10b)$$

Through all HMM channels, probability of state occurrence becomes:

$$^{*}Pr(S \mid \lambda) = \prod_{c=1}^{C} \pi_0^{(c)} \prod_{t=1}^{T} Pr(S_t^{(c)} \mid S_{t-1}^{(c)}, \lambda^{(c)}) \qquad (6.10c)$$

Each HMM channel contributes independently to the generation of a common observation sequence:

$$Pr(\vartheta \mid S^{(c)}, \lambda^{(c)}) = \prod_{t=1}^{T} Pr(\vartheta_t \mid S_t^{(c)}, \lambda^{(c)}) \qquad (6.10d)$$

---

* Factorization needs to be introduced with caution since it may result in an exponential growth in parameters such as the size of coupling transition matrices. Therefore, the interaction among metastates can be made by energy level (log probability), refer to [84] or see scalability problem in Section 3.2.3.

A common observation sequence can be represented by combining multiple HMM's outputs with their individual distributions and then by renormalizing the joint result:

$$
{}^{*}Pr(\vartheta \mid \lambda) = \prod_{c=1}^{C} \sum_{i=1}^{N^{(c)}} \pi_0^{(c)} Pr(\vartheta_0 \mid S_0^{(c)}, \lambda^{(c)})
$$

$$
\times \prod_{t=1}^{T} Pr(S_t^{(c)} \mid S_{t-1}^{(c)}, \lambda^{(c)}) Pr(\vartheta_t \mid S_t^{(c)}, \lambda^{(c)})
$$

$$
= \prod_{c=1}^{C} \sum_{i=1}^{N^{(c)}} \pi_0^{(c)} b_j^{(c)} (\vartheta_0 = k) \prod_{t=1}^{T} a_{ij}^{(c)} b_j^{(c)} (\vartheta_t = k) \qquad (6.10e)
$$

On the other hand, PoHMMs multiply individual chain distributions and renormalize them instead of approximating posterior probabilities with a factored distribution. Therefore, exact inference can be executed separately:

$$
Pr(\vartheta \mid \lambda) = \prod_{c=1}^{C} \sum_{i=1}^{N^{(c)}} \pi_0^{(c)} Pr(\vartheta_0 \mid S_0^{(c)}, \lambda^{(c)})
$$

$$
\times \frac{\prod_{t=1}^{T} Pr(S_t^{(c)} \mid S_{t-1}^{(c)}, \lambda^{(c)}) Pr(\vartheta_t \mid S_t^{(c)}, \lambda^{(c)})}{\sum_{k=1}^{K} \prod_{c=1}^{C} Pr(\vartheta \mid \lambda^{(c)})} \qquad (6.10f)
$$

■ *CHMMs* ($\{c', c\} \in C, c > 1, r^{(c)} = 1$): The joint conditional probability of a state transition for a process in CHMMs is given in [30] by

$$
{}^{\dagger}Pr(S_t^{(c)} \mid S_{t-1}^{(1)}, S_{t-1}^{(2)}, \dots, S_{t-1}^{(C)}, \lambda) = \prod_{c'}^{C} Pr(S_t^{(c)} \mid S_{t-1}^{(c')}, \lambda^{(c')}) \qquad (6.11a)
$$

Each HMM channel has its own observation sequence:

$$
Pr(\vartheta^{(c)} \mid S^{(c)}, \lambda^{(c)}) = \prod_{t=1}^{T} Pr(\vartheta_t^{(c)} \mid S_t^{(c)}, \lambda^{(c)}) \qquad (6.11b)
$$

---

* Factorization needs to be introduced with caution since it may result an exponential growth in parameters such as size of coupling transition matrices. Therefore, interaction among meta-states can be made by energy level (log probability), refer to [84], or see scalability problem in Section 3.2.3.

† There is no assumption or condition to constrict the boundaries of equation. Therefore, this is an erroneous formula because RHS does not sum up to 1 to define a proper probability density. Scalability is discussed in Section 3.2.3.

Probability of a certain observation sequence for each channel becomes

$$Pr(\vartheta^{(c)} \mid \lambda^{(c)}) = \pi_0^{(c)} Pr(\vartheta_0^{(c)} \mid S_0^{(c)}, \lambda^{(c)})$$

$$\times \prod_{t=1}^{T} \prod_{c'}^{C} Pr(S_t^{(c)} \mid S_{t-1}^{(c')}, \lambda^{(c')}) Pr(\vartheta_t^{(c)} \mid S_t^{(c)}, \lambda^{(c)})$$

$$= \pi_0^{(c)} b_j^{(c)}(\vartheta_0^{(c)} = k) \prod_{t=1}^{T} \prod_{c'}^{C} a_{ij}^{(c',c)} b_j^{(c)}(\vartheta_t = k) \quad (6.11c)$$

■ *OD/MO-HMMs ($c = 1, r > 1$)*: Since each state emits multiple observations at time t, probability of subobservation occurrences in each time frame is given by

$$ {}^*Pr(\vartheta_t \mid S_t, \lambda) = \prod_{r=1}^{R} (\vartheta_t^{(r)} \mid S_t, \lambda) \quad (6.12a)$$

Probability of observation sequence in the presence of subobservations

$$Pr(\vartheta \mid \lambda) = \sum_{i=1}^{N} \pi_0 Pr(\vartheta_0 \mid S_0, \lambda) \prod_{t=1}^{T} Pr(S_t \mid S_{t-1}, \lambda) Pr(\vartheta_t \mid S_t, \lambda)$$

$$= \sum_{i=1}^{N} \pi_0 \prod_{r=1}^{R} (\vartheta_0^{(r)} \mid S_0, \lambda) \prod_{t=1}^{T} \prod_{r=1}^{R} (\vartheta_t^{(r)} \mid S_t, \lambda) Pr(S_t \mid S_{t-1}, \lambda)$$

$$= \sum_{i=1}^{N} \pi_0 \prod_{r=1}^{R} b_j^{(r)}(\vartheta_0 = k) \prod_{t=1}^{T} \prod_{r=1}^{R} a_{ij} b_j^{(r)}(\vartheta_t = k) \quad (6.12b)$$

■ *HHMMs ($l = L, c = 1, r = 1$)*: A hidden state at level l in HHMMs according to (6.2) is defined as

$$Pr(H_t^{(l)} \mid \lambda) = Pr(H_t^{(l)} \mid Parents(H_t^{(l)})) Pr(H_t^{(l)} \mid H_{t-1}^{(l)}) \quad (6.13a)$$

where *parents*($H_t^{(l)}$) are parents of $H_t^{(l)}$ in graph. Parents can be statistically independent, whereas their influence on child is associated with conditional probability.

---

* There is no assumption or condition to constrict boundaries of equation. Therefore, this is an erroneous formula because RHS does not sum up to 1 to define a proper probability density. Scalability is discussed in Section 3.2.3.

Joint distribution over a layer throughout time

$$Pr(H^{(l)}) = \pi_0^{(l)} \prod_{t=1}^{T} Pr(H_t^{(l)} \mid Parents(H_t^{(l)})) Pr(H_t^{(l)} \mid H_{t-1}^{(l)})$$

$$= \pi_0^{(l)} \prod_{t=1}^{T} A^{(l)} \qquad (6.13b)$$

Joint likelihood distribution becomes

$$Pr(H, S, \vartheta \mid \lambda) = \sum_i \pi^{(L-1)} \prod_{t=1}^{T} Pr(\vartheta \mid H_t^{(L)}, \lambda) Pr(H_t^{(L)} \mid Parents(H_t^{(L)}, \lambda))$$

$$= \sum_i \pi^{(L-1)} \prod_{t=1}^{T} \sum_c \{A^{(L)}\}_{ij} B_j^{(L)}(\vartheta = k) \qquad (6.13c)$$

▪ *Basic DBNs* ($l = 1, c = 2, r = 1$): DBNs are modeled as multilevel stochastic processes to capture activities in hierarchical structure. A high-level activity is decomposed into subset activities indicating simpler activities at low levels, and low-level activities are refined into primitive and productive core activities. Therefore, every state at high level is a taxonomic representation of any semantic state at low level.

By having multilevel structure, hierarchical activities are intuitively represented, and in long term, temporal dependencies are solved among states over abstraction layers according to (6.3).

Dynamic model at second layer, $H_t^{(1)} = (S_t^{(1)}, S_t^{(2)})$, represents temporal interaction (posterior probability) among statistically independent processes at first layer and does not influence processes.

Given dual-channel HMMs, joint likelihood is defined as

$$Pr(H, S, \vartheta \mid \lambda)$$
$$= \pi_0^{(1)} \pi_0^{(2)} Pr(H_0^{(1)} \mid S_0^{(1)}, S_0^{(2)})$$

$$\times \prod_{t=1}^{T} \left[Pr(H_t^{(1)} \mid S_t^{(1)}, S_t^{(2)}, H_{t-1}^{(1)}) \prod_{c=1}^{C} Pr(\vartheta_t^{(c)}, S_t^{(c)}) Pr(S_t^{(c)} \mid S_{t-1}^{(c)}, H_{t-1}^{(1)}) \right]$$

$$(6.14)$$

6.3 Inference

In this section, issues related to inference problem in HMMs including extended HMMs as well are discussed including forward–backward algorithm, decoding algorithm or, in other words, maximum likelihood estimate (MLE) of state sequence, calculation of probabilities and expectations, and maximum a posteriori (MAP) estimation of state and observation.

6.3.1 Learning: Forward–Backward Procedure

Forward and backward algorithms are proposed to find the most likely one-step-ahead or one-step-back state. These algorithms rely on updating weights iteratively in order to decide which state is selected. The weights are α for forward iterations and β for backward iterations. $\alpha(t)$ is probability of current state sequence, S_t generated from one-step-previous state sequence, S_{t-1}. On the other hand, with reverse analogy, $\beta(t)$ is defined as probability of occurrence of S_{t-1} from S_t. Therefore, forward and backward algorithms, as shown in Figure 3.3, return the value of belief while propagating through an HMM, especially for (6.8) through (6.10).

Forward algorithm passes inductively over the chain to compute α_t, which is defined as joint probability of S_t and sequence of observations from ϑ_0 to ϑ_t:

$$\alpha_t = Pr(S_t, \vartheta_0^t \mid \lambda) = \left[\sum_{S_{t-1}} Pr(S_{t-1}, \vartheta_{1:t-1} \mid \lambda) Pr(S_t \mid S_{t-1}, \lambda) \right] Pr(\vartheta_t \mid S_t, \lambda)$$

$$= \left[\sum_{S_{t-1}} \alpha_{t-1} Pr(S_t \mid S_{t-1}, \lambda) \right] Pr(\vartheta_t \mid S_t, \lambda) \qquad (6.15)$$

α_t can be solved inductively by

- *Initialization* $(t = 0)$: $\alpha_0(i) = \pi_i b_i(\vartheta_0 = k)$
- *Induction* $(1 \leq t \leq T - 1)$: $\alpha_t(i) = [\sum_{i=1}^{N} \alpha_{t-1}(i) a_{ij}] b_j(\vartheta_t = k)$
- *Termination* $(t = T)$: $Pr(\vartheta \mid \lambda) = \sum_{i=1}^{N} \alpha_T(i)$

On the other hand, backward algorithm also passes inductively over chain to compute β_t, which is defined as conditional probability of sequence of observations from ϑ_{t+1} to ϑ_T by given S_t:

$$\beta_t = Pr(\vartheta_{t+1:T} \mid S_t, \lambda)$$

$$= \left[\sum_{S_{t+1}} Pr(\vartheta_{t+2:T} \mid S_{t+1}, \lambda) Pr(S_{t+1} \mid S_t, \lambda) \right] Pr(\vartheta_{t+1} \mid S_{t+1}, \lambda)$$

$$= \left[\sum_{S_{t+1}} \beta_{t+1} Pr(S_{t+1} \mid S_t, \lambda) \right] Pr(\vartheta_{t+1} \mid S_{t+1}, \lambda) \qquad (6.16)$$

β_t can also be solved inductively by

- *Initialization* $(t = T)$: $\beta_T(i) = 1$
- *Induction* $(1 \leq t \leq T - 1)$: $\beta_t(i) = \sum_{j=1}^{N} a_{ij} b_j(\vartheta_{t+1} = k) \beta_{t+1}(j)$
- *Termination* $(t = 0)$: $Pr(\vartheta \mid \lambda) = \sum_{i=1}^{N} \alpha_0(i) \beta_0(i)$

At any time t, the evaluation of observation becomes $Pr(\vartheta \mid \lambda) = \sum_{i=1}^{N} \alpha_t(i) \beta_t(i)$.

6.3.2 Extended Forward–Backward Procedure

There can be so many variations proposed for creating fully or partially coupled HMMs and multiple observable HMMs. However, for any HMMs, variation is not a desirable feature because having changing model size and mixture structure makes accurate parameter learning and inference very difficult.

For instance, joint conditional probability of a state transition for a process in CHMMs (6.11) is given:

$$Pr(S_t^{(c)} \mid S_{t-1}^{(1)}, S_{t-1}^{(2)}, \ldots, S_{t-1}^{(C)}, \lambda) = \prod_{c'}^{C} Pr(S_t^{(c)} \mid S_{t-1}^{(c')}, \lambda^{(c')}) \qquad (6.17a)$$

and joint conditional probability of multiple subobservation occurrences in OD/MO-HMMs (6.12) is given:

$$Pr(\vartheta_t \mid S_t, \lambda) = \prod_{r=1}^{R} (\vartheta_t^{(r)} \mid S_t, \lambda) \qquad (6.17b)$$

Note that formulas seem erroneous because RHS does not sum up to 1 to define a proper probability density.

If it is assumed that hidden states in different channels in CHMMs (6.17a) or subobservations in OD/MO-HMMs (6.17b) are independent of one another, (6.11) becomes

$$Pr(S_t^{(c)} \mid S_{t-1}^{(1)}, S_{t-1}^{(2)}, \ldots, S_{t-1}^{(C)}, \lambda) = \mathcal{Z}^{-1} \prod_{c'}^{C} Pr(S_t^{(c)} \mid S_{t-1}^{(c')}, \lambda^{(c')}) \qquad (6.18a)$$

where $\mathcal{Z} = Pr(S_t^{(c)})^{(C-1)}$ and (6.12) becomes

$$Pr(\vartheta_t \mid S_t, \lambda) = \mathcal{Z}^{-1} \prod_{r=1}^{R} (\vartheta_t^{(r)} \mid S_t, \lambda) \qquad (6.18b)$$

where $\mathcal{Z} = Pr(\vartheta_t)^{(R-1)}$.

As indicated in [31] and [134], calculation of normalizing factor, $\mathcal{Z}$, in (6.18a) and (6.18b) is missing because there is no direct parameter to specify interaction.

There is an alternative way (see Appendix Lemma A.1) for formulations (6.18a) and (6.18b), which was first proposed in [194] for higher-order Markov chains to reduce parameter space and to specify the strength of interaction among HMMs. Recall that observation space or hidden state chain is assumed to have no relation to others in traditional HMMs. A contradiction can arise if observation sequence or hidden state chain is claimed to have statistical correlation as seen in CHMMs and OD/MO-HMMs. In either case whether correlation is valid or not, a generic expression can be given according to the following assumption.

- *CHMMs*: A new formulation for (6.11) in a form that joint dependency can be specified as a linear combination of all marginal dependencies:

$$Pr(S_t^{(c)} \mid S_{t-1}^{(1)}, S_{t-1}^{(2)}, \ldots, S_{t-1}^{(C)}, \lambda) = \sum_{c'=1}^{C} \phi_{(c',c)} Pr(S_t^{(c)} \mid S_{t-1}^{(c')}, \lambda^{(c')})$$

$$(6.19)$$

where $\phi_{(c',c)}$ is coupling weight from channel c' to channel c in CHMMs. In other words, how much probability distribution of $S_t^{(c)}$ is affected by each $S_{t-1}^{(c')}$.

- *OD/MO-HMMs*: The problem by changing number of subobservations causes feature length to vary and makes it difficult to obtain the correct order of elements in feature vector. To overcome these drawbacks, (6.12) can be revised by ensuring that subobservations have same length and are dependent on one another, refer to [134] and [138]:

$$Pr(\vartheta_t \mid S_t, \lambda) = \sum_{r=1}^{R} \psi_{(r)} (\vartheta_t^{(r)} \mid S_t, \lambda) \qquad (6.20)$$

where $\psi_{(r)}$ is weight corresponding to emission of subobservations. With this method, probability of existence of multiple observations is expressed as combined probabilities of individual observation rather than their total probability product. Thus, probabilistic dependency among observations is characterized by combinatorial weights.

■ *HHMMs*: Joint likelihood distribution (6.13) at level L becomes

$$Pr(H, S, \vartheta \mid \lambda) = \sum_i \pi^{(L-1)} \prod_{t=1}^{T} Pr(\vartheta \mid H_t^{(L)}, \lambda) Pr(H_t^{(L)} \mid Parents(H_t^{(L)}, \lambda))$$

$$= \sum_i \pi^{(L-1)} \prod_{t=1}^{T} \sum_c (A^{(L)})_{ij} B_j^{(L)} (\vartheta = k) \qquad (6.21)$$

■ *Basic DBNs*: Given the parameter set of DBNs (6.3) and observation sequences $\vartheta = \{\vartheta^{(1)}, \vartheta^{(2)}\}$, the likelihood probability $Pr(\vartheta \mid \lambda)$ in (6.14) is given with state sequences of $\{H^{(1)}, S^{(1)}, S^{(2)}\}$:

$$Pr(\vartheta, H, S \mid \lambda)$$

$$= \pi_0^{(l)} \prod_{c=1}^{C} [\pi_0^{(c)} b_j^{(c)} (\vartheta_0^{(c)} = k)] \prod_{t=1}^{T} [a_{ij}^{(l)} \prod_{c=1}^{C} a_{ij}^{(c)} b_j^{(c)} (\vartheta_t^{(c)} = k)] \quad (6.22)$$

where $l = 1$ and $C = 2$ are taken for basic DBNs.

6.4 Model for Multiple Sensors Use

Assume that event notifier is a moving frame acting like a queue structure to store new and recent observations. The length of frame is an important system parameter. It can be set fixed or dynamically adjusted. If it is fixed, stored observation sequence may yield to infer either same event or more than one events represented in hidden state sequence. Otherwise, the length can be arranged as long as the inference of same event in hidden state sequence is preserved.

Let $event(c, i, t_s, t_e)$ be denoted as probability of channel c residing in state i from time at t_s to time t_e by having observation sequence of $(\vartheta_{t_s}, \dots, \vartheta_{t_e})$, see Figures 6.3 and 6.4.

A generic equalization of *event* for all types of HMMs is given by

$$event(c, i, t_s, t_e) = \prod_{t=t_s}^{t_e} \prod_{r=1}^{R} Pr(d_t^{(c)} = 1) Pr(\vartheta_t^{(c,r)} = k \mid S_t^{(c)} = i) \qquad (6.23)$$

where semi-Markovian feature is shown by the probability of channel c being in state i at time $(t_e - t_s + 1)$ and probability of observing k by subobservations r in channel c being in state i through given time space.

Assume that channels and subobservations evolve independently; however, subobservations influence the inference of hidden states in corresponding channel and

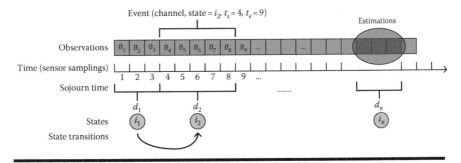

Figure 6.3   Event-based channel evolution.

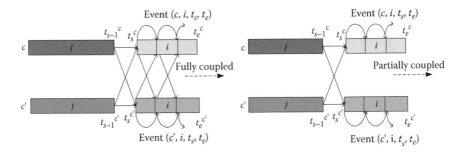

Figure 6.4   Event-based learning (fully/partially coupled channels).

all channels also influence themselves according to which Markovian topology model is being used.

Event-based evaluation problem is solved under two assumptions. The first assumption considers each channel has fully coupled hidden variable, whereas the second one considers coupling only when a state transition happens.

Under these assumptions, likelihood distribution of event structure at channel c (6.23) can be solved by $\alpha_t^{(c)} \cdot \alpha_{(i,t_s,t_e)}^{(c)}$ shows the probability of channel c being in state i from time t_s to time t_e given observation sequence. At $t = 0$, it starts with

$$\alpha_{(i,0,0)}^{(c)} = \pi^{(c)} event(c, i, 0, 0) \tag{6.24a}$$

If each channel is fully coupled,

$$\alpha_{(i,t_s,t_e)}^{(c)} = \left(\prod_{c'=1}^{C} \left(\sum_{j=1}^{N^{(c')}} \left(\sum_{s=t_s^{(c')}=t_e^{(c')}-\Delta^{(c')}}^{t_e^{(c')}} Pr(S_{t+1}^{(c)} = i \mid S_t^{(c')} = j) \alpha_{(j,s,t)}^{(c')} \right) \right) \right)$$
$$\times event(c, i, t_s, t_e) \tag{6.24b}$$

else if each channel needs help from other channels during a state transition,

$$
\alpha_{(i,t_s,t_e)}^{(c)} =
\begin{cases}
\left(\prod_{c'=1}^{C} \left(\sum_{j=1}^{N^{(c')}} \left(\sum_{s=t_s^{(c')}=t_e^{(c')}-\Delta^{(c')}}^{t_e^{(c')}} pR(S_{t+1}^{(c)} = i \mid S_t^{(c')} = j)\alpha_{(j,s,t)}^{(c')} \right) \right) \right) \\
\quad \times event(c, i, t_s, t_s + 1) \\[2mm]
\left(\sum_{i=1}^{N^{(c)}} \left(\sum_{s=t_s^{(c)}=t_e^{(c)}-\Delta^{(c)}}^{t_e^{(c)}} Pr(S_{t+1}^{(c)} = i \mid S_t^{(c)} = i)\alpha_{(i,s,t)}^{(c)} \right) \right) \\
\quad \times event(c, i, t_s + 1, t_e)
\end{cases}
$$

$$(6.24c)$$

Conditions are as follows:

- t flows as $t \leftarrow t + 1$.
- $\Delta^{(c)} = t_e^{(c)} - t_s^{(c)}$ indicates how long a channel remains in the same state.
- $t_e^{(c)} = t$, current time equals the latest time at which a state is being inferred for each channel.
- Whenever a transition occurs over a channel, $t_s^{(c)}$ becomes $t - 1$; otherwise, it remains same. $t_s^{(c)}$ shows starting time at which current inferred state first appears.

On the other hand, likelihood distribution of event structure at channel c can also be solved by $\beta_t^{(c)}$.

At $t = T$, it starts with

$$\beta_{(i,T,T)}^{(c)} = 1 \qquad (6.25a)$$

If each channel is fully coupled,

$$
\beta_{(i,t_s,t_e)}^{(c)} = \left(\prod_{c'=1}^{C} \left(\sum_{j=1}^{N^{(c')}} \left(\sum_{s=1}^{\Delta=t_e-t_s} Pr(S_{t-1}^{(c)} = i \mid S_t^{(c')} = j)\beta_{(j,t=t_s+\Delta-s,t_e^{(c')})}^{(c')} \right) \right) \right)
$$

$$\times\ event(c, i, t_s, t_e) \qquad (6.25b)$$

else if each channel needs help from other channels during a state transition,

$$
\beta^{(c)}_{(i,t_s,t_e)} =
\begin{cases}
\left[\left(\prod_{c'=1}^{C} \left(\sum_{j=1}^{N^{(c')}} \left(\sum_{s=1}^{\Delta=t_e-t_s} Pr(S^{(c)}_{t-1} = i \mid S^{(c')}_t = j)\beta^{(c')}_{(j,t=t_s+\Delta-s,t_e^{(c)})} \right) \right) \right) \right. \\
\qquad \times\, event(c, i, t_e - 1, t_e) \\[2ex]
\left. \left(\sum_{j=1}^{N^{(c)}} \left(\sum_{s=1}^{\Delta=t_e-t_s} Pr(S^{(c)}_{t-1} = i \mid S^{(c)}_t = j)\beta^{(c)}_{(j,t=t_s+\Delta-s,t_e^{(c)})} \right) \right) \right. \\
\qquad \times\, event(c, i, t_s, t_e - 1)
\end{cases}
$$

$$(6.25c)$$

Conditions are as follows:

- t flows as $t \leftarrow t - 1$.
- $\Delta^{(c)} = t_e^{(c)} - t_s^{(c)}$ indicates how long a channel remains in the same state.
- $t_s^{(c)} = t$, current time equals the latest time at which a state is being inferred for each channel.
- Whenever a transition occurs over a channel, $t_e^{(c)}$ becomes $t - 1$; otherwise, it remains same. $t_e^{(c)}$ shows starting time at which current inferred state first appears.

As a conclusion, a generic statistical model is described in this chapter to support proposed frameworks introduced in Chapters 3 and 5 in the case where multiple similar context resources are available. This model consists of a DBN having several layers with running multiple various types of HMMs (channels) in order to represent numerous human actions interconnected via temporal relations in a hierarchy. Bottom layer is modeled to capture atomic activities that are only obtained by sensory observations. Upper layers include high-level (abstract) activities that are formed from atomic activities. Abstract activities reaching up top layer are labeled by desired states (interest). On the other hand, context-aware application may have multiple sensors available to infer a similar context. Thereby, an event-based application model is also proposed by providing learning algorithms for such cases.

Appendix

Lemma A.1 Let X be formed as random processes of $\{x^1, x^2, \ldots, x^m\}$ and y be given as a set of random variables:

$$
\begin{cases}
Pr(X \mid y) = Pr\big(x^{(1)} \mid y\big) \, Pr\big(x^{(2)} \mid x^{(1)}, y\big) \ldots Pr\big(x^{(M)} \mid x^{(M-1)}, \ldots, x^{(1)}, y\big) \\
Pr(X \mid y) = Pr\big(x^{(2)} \mid y\big) \, Pr\big(x^{(3)} \mid x^{(2)}, y\big) \ldots Pr\big(x^{(1)} \mid x^{(M)}, \ldots, x^{(2)}, y\big) \\
\quad \vdots \\
\quad \vdots \\
Pr(X \mid y) = Pr\big(x^{(M)} \mid y\big) \, Pr\big(x^{(1)} \mid x^{(M)}, y\big) \ldots \\
\qquad\qquad\qquad Pr\big(x^{(M-1)} \mid x^{(M)}, x^{(M-2)}, \ldots, x^{(1)}, y\big)
\end{cases}
$$

Based on the preceding equations, $Pr(X \mid y)$ can be rewritten as

$$
Pr(X \mid y) = \sum_{m=1}^{M} w_m Pr\big(x^{(m)} \mid y\big)
$$

where

$$
\begin{cases}
w_1 = \frac{1}{M} Pr\big(x^{(2)} \mid x^{(1)}, y\big) \ldots Pr\big(x^{(M)} \mid x^{(M-1)}, \ldots, x^{(1)}, y\big) \\
w_2 = \frac{1}{M} Pr\big(x^{(3)} \mid x^{(2)}, y\big) \ldots Pr\big(x^{(1)} \mid x^{(M)}, \ldots, x^{(2)}, y\big) \\
\quad \vdots \\
\quad \vdots \\
w_M = \frac{1}{M} Pr\big(x^{(1)} \mid x^{(M)}, y\big) \ldots Pr\big(x^{(K-1)} \mid x^{(M)}, x^{(M-2)}, \ldots, x^{(1)}, y\big)
\end{cases}
$$

are weights to characterize correlation among random processes with the property of $\sum_{m=1}^{M} w_m = 1$.

References

1. ADXL346 3-axis 2 G ultra low power digital accelerometer by analog devices. http://www.analog.com/en/mems-sensors/mems-inertial-sensors/adxl346/products/product.html.

2. Environmental sensor networks: A revolution in the earth system science? *Earth-Science Reviews*, 78(34):177–191, 2006.

3. S. D. Lara, A. J. Prez, M. A. Labrador, and J. D. Posada. Centinela: A human activity recognition system based on acceleration and vital sign data. *Pervasive and Mobile Computing*, 8(5):717–729, 2012.

4. S. Abolfazli, Z. Sanaei, E. Ahmed, A. Gani, and R. Buyya. Cloud-based augmentation for mobile devices: Motivation, taxonomies, and open challenges. *IEEE Communications Surveys Tutorials*, 16(1):337–368, January 2014.

5. G. D. Abowd, A. K. Dey, P. J. Brown, N. Davies, M. Smith, and P. Steggles. Towards a better understanding of context and context-awareness. In *Proceedings of the 1st International Symposium on Handheld and Ubiquitous Computing, HUC '99*, pp. 304–307. London, U.K., Springer-Verlag, 1999.

6. G.-S. Ahn, M. Musolesi, H. Lu, R. Olfati-Saber, and A. T. Campbell. Metrotrack: Predictive tracking of mobile events using mobile phones. In *Proceedings of the 6th IEEE International Conference on Distributed Computing in Sensor Systems, DCOSS'10*, pp. 230–243, Berlin, Heidelberg. Springer-Verlag, 2010.

7. D. Allemang and J. Hendler. *Semantic Web for the Working Ontologist: Effective Modeling in RDFS and OWL*. Morgan Kaufmann Publishers Inc., San Francisco, CA, 2008.

8. E. Altman. *Constrained Markov Decision Processes: Stochastic Modeling*. Stochastic Modeling Series. Taylor & Francis Group, Boca Raton, FL, 1999.

9. M. Armbrust, A. Fox, R. Griffith, A. D. Joseph, R. Katz, A. Konwinski, G. Lee, et al. A view of cloud computing. *Communications of the ACM*, 53(4):50–58, April 2010.

10. L. Atzori, A. Iera, and G. Morabito. The internet of things: A survey. *Computer Network*, 54(15):2787–2805, October 2010.

11. M. Azizyan, I. Constandache, and R. R. Choudhury. Surroundsense: Mobile phone localization via ambience fingerprinting. In *Proceedings of the 15th Annual International Conference on Mobile Computing and Networking, MobiCom '09*, pp. 261–272, New York, NY, ACM, 2009.

12. A. Badii, M. Crouch, and C. Lallah. A context-awareness framework for intelligent networked embedded systems. In *2010 Third International Conference on Advances in Human-Oriented and Personalized Mechanisms, Technologies and Services (CENTRIC)*, pp. 105–110, August 2010.

13. M. Baldauf, S. Dustdar, and F. Rosenberg. A survey on context-aware sys. *International Journal of Ad Hoc and Ubiquitous Computing*, 2(4):263–277, 2007.

14. X. (Jeff) Ban and M. Gruteser. Towards fine-grained urban traffic knowledge extraction using mobile sensing. In *Proceedings of the ACM SIGKDD International Workshop on Urban Computing, UrbComp '12*, pp. 111–117, New York, NY, ACM, 2012.

15. D. Bandyopadhyay and J. Sen. Internet of things: Applications and challenges in technology and standardization. *Wireless Personal Communications*, 58(1):49–69, 2011.

16. L. Bao and S. S. Intille. Activity recognition from user-annotated acceleration data. In A. Ferscha and F. Mattern, eds., *Pervasive Computing*, volume 3001 of *Lecture Notes in Computer Science*, pp. 1–17. Springer, Berlin, Germany, 2004.

17. D. Barber. *Bayesian Reasoning and Machine Learning*. Cambridge University Press, Cambridge, U.K., March 2011.

18. V. S. Barbu and N. Limnios. Reliability of semi-Markov systems in discrete time: Modeling and estimation. In K. B. Misra, ed., *Handbook of Performability Engineering*, pp. 369–380. Springer, London, U.K., 2008.

19. L. E. Baum, T. Petrie, G. Soules, and N. Weiss. A maximization technique occurring in the statistical analysis of probabilistic functions of Markov chains. *The Annals of Mathematical Statistics*, 41(1):164–171, 1970.

20. A. Beach, M. Gartrell, X. Xing, R. Han, Q. Lv, S. Mishra, and K. Seada. Fusing mobile, sensor, and social data to fully enable context-aware computing. In *Proceedings of the Eleventh Workshop on Mobile Computing Systems Applications, HotMobile '10*, pp. 60–65, New York, NY, ACM, 2010.

21. P. Bellavista, R. Montanari, and D. Tibaldi. Cosmos: A context-centric access control middleware for mobile environments. In *Mobile Agents for Telecommunication Applications*, Vol. 2881, pp. 77–88. Springer, Berlin, Germany, 2003.

22. F. B. Abdesslem, A. Phillips, and T. Henderson. Less is more: Energy-efficient mobile sensing with senseless. In S. Banerjee, ed., *ACM MobiHeld'09*, pp. 61–62, 2009.

23. J. L. Bentley, D. F. Stanat, and E. Hollins Williams Jr. The complexity of finding fixed-radius near neighbors. *Information Processing Letters*, 6(6):209–212, 1977.

24. M. Berchtold, M. Budde, D. Gordon, H. R. Schmidtke, and M. Beigl. Actiserv: Activity recognition service for mobile phones. In *Proceedings International Symposium on Wearable Computers (ISWC)*, pp. 1–8, October 2010.

25. E. M. Berke, T. Choudhury, S. Ali, and M. Rabbi. Objective measurement of sociability and activity: Mobile sensing in the community. *The Annals of Family Medicine*, 9(4):344–350, 2011.

26. C. Bettini, O. Brdiczka, K. Henricksen, J. Indulska, D. Nicklas, A. Ranganathan, and D. Riboni. A survey of context modelling and reasoning techniques. *Pervasive and Mobile Computer*, 6(2):161–180, 2010.

27. J. A. Bilmes et al. A gentle tutorial of the EM algorithm and its application to parameter estimation for Gaussian mixture and hidden Markov models. *International Computer Science Institute*, 4(510):126, 1998.

28. J. Blum and E. Magill. M-psychiatry: Sensor network for psychiatric health monitoring. In *9th Annual Postgraduate Symposium the Convergence of Telecommuncations, Networking and Broadcasting*, Liverpool, U.K., June 2008.

29. C. Bolchini, C. A. Curino, E. Quintarelli, F. A. Schreiber, and L. Tanca. A data-oriented survey of context models. *SIGMOD Record*, 36(4):19–26, December 2007.

30. M. Brand. Coupled hidden Markov models for modeling interacting processes. 1997.

31. M. Brand, N. Oliver, and A. Pentland. Coupled hidden Markov models for complex action recognition. In *IEEE Computer Society Conference on Computer Vision and Pattern Recognition*, pp. 994–999, June 1997.

32. A. D. Brown and G. E. Hinton. Products of hidden Markov models. In *Proceedings of the Artificial Intelligence and Statistics*, pp. 3–11, 2001.

33. P. J. Brown, J. D. Bovey, and X. Chen. Context-aware applications: From the laboratory to the marketplace. *IEEE Personal Communications*, 4(5):58–64, October 1997.

34. H. Bruce, G. Raffa, L. LeGrand, J. Huang, B. Keany, and R. Edgecombe. An extensible sensor based inferencing framework for context aware applications. In *IEEE International Conference on Computer Science and Information Technology*, pp. 2878–2883, 2010.

35. O. Cappé, E. Moulines, and T. Ryden. *Inference in Hidden Markov Models* (Springer Series in Statistics). Springer-Verlag New York, Inc., Secaucus, NJ, 2005.

36. L. Capra, W. Emmerich, and C. Mascolo. Carisma: Context-aware reflective middleware system for mobile applications. *IEEE Transactions on Software Engineering*, 29(10):929–945, October 2003.

37. A. Carroll and G. Heiser. The systems hacker's guide to the galaxy energy usage in a modern smartphone. In *Proceedings of the Fourth Asia-Pacific Workshop on Systems*, pp. 1–7. New York, NY, ACM, 2013.

38. F. Casamassima, E. Farella, and L. Benini. Context aware power management for motion-sensing body area network nodes. In *Proceedings of the Conference on Design, Automation and Test in Europe Conference and Exhibition (DATE), 2014*, pp. 1–6, Leuven, Belgium, March 2014.

39. K.-H. Chang, M. Y Chen, and J. Canny. Tracking free-weight exercises. In *UbiComp 2007: Ubiquitous Computing*, pp. 19–37. Springer, Berlin, Germany, 2007.

40. G. Chatzimilioudis, A. Konstantinidis, C. Laoudias, and D. Zeinalipour-Yazti. Crowdsourcing with smartphones. *IEEE Internet Computer*, 16(5):36–44, September–October 2012.

41. H. Chen, T. Finin, A. Joshi, L. Kagal, F. Perich, and D. Chakraborty. Intelligent agents meet the semantic web in smart spaces. *IEEE Internet Computing*, 8(6):69–79, November 2004.

42. M. Chen, S. Gonzalez, A. Vasilakos, H. Cao, and V. C. Leung. Body area networks: A survey. *Mobile Networks and Applications*, 16(2):171–193, April 2011.

43. Y.-P. Chen, J.-Y. Yang, S.-N. Liou, G.-Y. Lee, and J.-S. Wang. Online classifier construction algorithm for human activity detection using a tri-axial accelerometer. *Journal of Applied Mathematics and Computing*, 205(2):849–860, 2008.

44. J. Choi and R. Gutierrez-Osuna. Using heart rate monitors to detect mental stress. In *International Workshop on Wearable and Implantable Body Sensor Network '09*, pp. 219–223, Washington, DC, June 2009.

45. Y. Chon and H. Cha. Lifemap: A smartphone-based context provider for location-based services. *IEEE Pervasive Computing*, 10(2):58–67, April 2011.

46. D. Chu, N. D. Lane, T. T.-T. Lai, C. Pang, X. Meng, Q. Guo, F. Li, and F. Zhao. Balancing energy, latency and accuracy for mobile sensor data classification. In *Proceedings of the 9th ACM Conference on Embedded Networked Sensor Systems, SenSys '11*, pp. 54–67, New York, NY, ACM, 2011.

47. G. Ciuperca and V. Girardin. Estimation of the entropy rate of a countable Markov chain. *Communications in Statistics-Theory and Methods*, 36(13–16):2543–2557, 2007.

48. L. Cloth, M. R. Jongerden, and B. R. Haverkort. Computing battery lifetime distributions. In *37th Annual IEEE/IFIP International Conference on Dependable Systems and Networks (DSN)*, pp. 780–789, 2007.

49. L. Martin and T. L. Martin. Balancing batteries, power, and performance: System issues in CPU speed-setting for mobile computing. PhD thesis, Carnegie Mellon University, Pittsburgh, PA, 1999.

50. S. Consolvo, D. W. McDonald, T. Toscos, M. Y. Chen, J. Froehlich, B. Harrison, P. Klasnja, A. LaMarca, L. LeGrand, and R. Libby. Activity sensing in the wild: A field trial of UbiFit garden. In *Proceedings of the SIGCHI Conference on Human Factors in Computing Systems, CHI '08*, pp. 1797–1806, New York, NY, ACM, 2008.

51. A. Corradi, M. Fanelli, and L. Foschini. Implementing a scalable context-aware middleware. In *IEEE Symposium on Computers and Communications, 2009 (ISCC 2009)*, pp. 868–874, July 2009.

52. T. M. Cover and J. A. Thomas. *Elements of Information Theory (Wiley Series in Telecommunications and Signal Processing)*, 2nd edn. Wiley-Interscience, July 2006.

53. D. Craig. Cognitive prosthetics in Alzheimer's disease: A trial of a novel cell phoned-based reminding system. *Elsevier Alzheimer's & Dementia*, 6(4):1552–5260, 2010.

54. G. D'amico, J. Janssen, and R. Manca. Duration dependent semi-Markov models. *Applied Mathematical Sciences*, 5(42):2097–2108, 2011.

55. D. Danilov, R. A. H. Niessen, and P. H. L. Notten. Modeling all-solid-state Li-ion batteries. *Journal of Electrochemical Society*, 158(3):A215–A222, 2011.

56. O. Davidyuk, J. Riekki, V. M. Rautio, and J. Sun. Context-aware middleware for mobile multimedia applications. In *Proceedings of the Third International Conference on Mobile and Ubiquitous Multimedia in MUM 04*, pp. 213–220. ACM Press, 2004.

57. G. Deodatis and M. Shinozuka. Auto-regressive model for nonstationary stochastic processes. *Journal of Engineering Mechanics*, 114(11):1995–2012, 1988.

58. A. K. Dey. Understanding and using context. *Personal and Ubiquitous Computing*, 5(1):4–7, 2001.

59. S. Dhar and U. Varshney. Challenges and business models for mobile location-based services and advertising. *Communications of ACM*, 54(5):121–128, May 2011.

60. M. Doyle and J. Newman. Analysis of capacity-rate data for lithium batteries using simplified models of the discharge process. *Journal of Applied Electrochemistry*, 27:846–856, 1997.

61. M. Doyle, T. F. Fuller, and J. Newman. Modeling of galvanostatic charge and discharge of the lithium/polymer/insertion cell. *Journal of Electrochemical Society*, 140(6):1526–1533, 1993.

62. R. O. Duda, P. E. Hart, and D. G. Stork. *Pattern Classification*, 2nd edn. Wiley-Interscience, New York, 2000.

63. T. V. Duong, H. Bui, D. Q. Phung, and S. Venkatesh. Activity recognition and abnormality detection with the switching hidden semi-Markov model. In *IEEE Computer Society Conference on Computer Vision and Pattern Recognition (CVPR)*, pp. 838–845, Washington, DC, IEEE Computer Society, 2005.

64. S. R. Eddy. Hidden Markov models. *Current Opinion in Structural Biology*, 6(3): 361–365, 1996.

65. S. B. Eisenman, E. Miluzzo, N. D. Lane, R. A. Peterson, G.-S. Ahn, and A. T. Campbell. The bikenet mobile sensing system for cyclist experience mapping. In *Proceedings of the 5th International Conference on Embedded Networked Sensor Systems, SenSys '07*, pp. 87–101, New York, NY, ACM, 2007.

66. D. Ejigu, M. Scuturici, and L. Brunie. An ontology-based approach to context modeling and reasoning in pervasive computing. In *Fifth Annual IEEE International Conference on Pervasive Computing and Communications Workshops, 2007 (PerCom Workshops '07)*, pp. 14–19, March 2007.

67. Y. Ephraim and N. Merhav. Hidden Markov processes. *IEEE Transactions on Information Theory*, 48:1518–1569, 2002.

68. M. Ermes, J. Parkka, and L. Cluitmans. Advancing from offline to online activity recognition with wearable sensors. In *IEEE EMBS'08*, pp. 4451–4454, August 2008.

69. I. A. Essa. Ubiquitous sensing for smart and aware environments. *IEEE Personal Communications*, 7(5):47–49, 2000.

70. C. F. Chiasserini, R. R. Rao, and Senior Member. Energy efficient battery management. In *IEEE INFOCOM'00*, pp. 396–403, 2001.

71. M. Fahim, I. Fatima, S. Lee, and Y.-K. Lee. Daily life activity tracking application for smart homes using android smartphone. In *4th International Conference on Advanced Communication Technology '12*, pp. 241–245, February 2012.

72. P. Fahy and S. Clarke. Cass a middleware for mobile context-aware applications. In *Workshop on Context Awareness, MobiSys*, 2004.

73. D. Figo, P. C. Diniz, D. R. Ferreira, and J. M. Cardoso. Preprocessing techniques for context recognition from accelerometer data. *Personal Ubiquitous Computer*, 14(7):645–662, October 2010.

74. S. Fine, Y. Singer, and N. Tishby. The hierarchical hidden Markov model: Analysis and applications. *Machine Learning*, 32:41–62, 1998.

75. J. Forstadius, O. Lassila, and T. Seppanen. Rdf-based model for context-aware reasoning in rich service environment. In *Third IEEE International Conference Pervasive Computing and Communications Workshops*, pp. 15–19, IEEE, 2005.

76. J. H. Friedman. Regularized discriminant analysis. *Journal of the American Statistical Association*, 84(405):165–175, 1989.

77. J. Froehlich, T. Dillahunt, P. Klasnja, J. Mankoff, S. Consolvo, B. Harrison, and J.A. Landay. Ubigreen: Investigating a mobile tool for tracking and supporting green transportation habits. In *Proceedings of the SIGCHI Conference on Human Factors in Computing Systems, CHI '09*, pp. 1043–1052, New York, NY, ACM, 2009.

78. T. F. Fuller, M. Doyle, and J. Newman. Relaxation phenomena in lithium-ion-insertion cells. *Journal of Electrochemical Society*, 141(4):982–990, 1994.

79. R. K. Ganti, N. Pham, H. Ahmadi, S. Nangia, and T. F. Abdelzaher. Greengps: A participatory sensing fuel-efficient maps application. In *Proceedings of the 8th International Conference on Mobile Systems, Applications, and Services*, pp. 151–164, New York, NY, ACM, 2010.

80. R. K. Ganti, F. Ye, and H. Lei. Mobile crowdsensing: Current state and future challenges. *IEEE Communications Magazine*, 49(11):32–39, November 2011.

81. D. Garlan, D. P. Siewiorek, A. Smailagic, and P. Steenkiste. Project aura: Toward distraction-free pervasive computing. *IEEE Pervasive Computing*, 1(2):22–31, April 2002.

82. J.-L. Gauvain and C.-H. Lee. Maximum a posteriori estimation for multivariate Gaussian mixture observations of Markov chains. *IEEE Transactions on Speech and Audio Processing*, 2(2):291–298, 1994.

83. Z. Ghahramani. Hidden Markov models. In *An Introduction to Hidden Markov Models and Bayesian Networks*, pp. 9–42. World Scientific Publishing Co., Inc., River Edge, NJ, 2002.

84. Z. Ghahramani and M. I. Jordan. Factorial hidden Markov models. *Machine Learning*, 29(2–3):245–273, November 1997.

85. C. Gomez-Otero, R. Martinez, and J. Caffarel. Climapp: A novel approach of an intelligent HVAC control system. In *Iberian Conference on Information Systems and Technologies '12*, pp. 1–6, June 2012.

86. T. Gu, H. K. Pung, and D. Q. Zhang. A service oriented middleware for building context aware services. *Journal of Network and Computer Applications*, 28(1):1–18, 2005.

87. B. Guo, L. Sun, and D. Zhang. The architecture design of a cross-domain context management system. In *Eighth IEEE International Conference on Pervasive Computing and Communications Workshops (PERCOM Workshops), 2010*, pp. 499–504, March 2010.

88. S. C. Hageman. Simple pspice models let you simulate common battery types. *Electronic Design News*, 38:117–129, 1993.

89. M. Hall, E. Frank, G. Holmes, B. Pfahringer, P. Reutemann, and I. H. Witten. The WEKA data mining software: An update. *ACM SIGKDD Explorations Newsletter*, 11(1):10–18, 2009.

90. T. Halpin. Object-role modeling: Principles and benefits. *International Journal of Information System Modeling and Design (IJISMD)*, 1(1):33–57, 2010.

91. J. Han, E. Haihong, G. Le, and J. Du. Survey on NoSQL database. In *Sixth International Conference on Pervasive Computing and Applications (ICPCA), 2011*, pp. 363–366, October 2011.

92. Y. Hanai, J. Nishimura, and T. Kuroda. Haar-like filtering for human activity recognition using 3d accelerometer. In *IEEE 13th Digital Signal Processing Workshop and 5th IEEE Signal Processing Education Workshop*, pp. 675–678, January 2009.

93. Z.-Y. He and L.-W. Jin. Activity recognition from acceleration data using AR model representation and SVM. In *International Conference on Machine Learning and Cybernetics '08*, Vol. 4, pp. 2245–2250, July 2008.

94. Z. He and L. Jin. Activity recognition from acceleration data based on discrete consine transform and SVM. In *IEEE International Conference on Systems, Man and Cybernetics*, pp. 5041–5044, October 2009.

95. M. A. Hearst, S. T. Dumais, E. Osman, J. Platt, and B. Scholkopf. Support vector machines. *Intelligent Systems and Their Applications, IEEE*, 13(4):18–28, 1998.

96. A. Henpraserttae, S. Thiemjarus, and S. Marukatat. Accurate activity recognition using a mobile phone regardless of device orientation and location. In *International Conference on Body Sensor Networks (BSN), 2011*, pp. 41–46, May 2011.

97. K. Henricksen, J. Indulska, and A. Rakotonirainy. Modeling context information in pervasive computing systems. In *Proceedings of the First International Conference on Pervasive Computing, Pervasive '02*, pp. 167–180. Springer, Berlin, Germany, 2002.

98. K. Henricksen, J. Indulska, and A. Rakotonirainy. Generating context management infrastructure from high-level context models. In *Fourth International Conference on Mobile Data Management (MDM)—Industrial Track*, pp. 1–6, 2003.

99. J. Herrera, D. Work, R. Herring, X. Ban, Q. Jacobson, and A. Bayen. Evaluation of traffic data obtained via GPS-enabled mobile phones: The mobile century field experiment. *Transportation Research Part C*, 18(4):568–583, August 2010.

100. R. Hoekstra. Representing social reality in owl 2. In E. Sirin and K. Clark, eds., *OWLED*, vol. 614, *CEUR Workshop Proceedings*. CEUR-WS.org, 2010.

101. R. Honicky, E. A. Brewer, E. Paulos, and R. White. N-smarts: Networked suite of mobile atmospheric real-time sensors. In *ACM SIGCOMM'08*, pp. 25–30, 2008.

102. K. Hornik, M. Stinchcombe, and H. White. Multilayer feedforward networks are universal approximators. *Neural Networks*, 2(5):359–366, 1989.

103. S. Hu, H. Wei, Y. Chen, and J. Tan. A real-time cardiac arrhythmia classification system with wearable sensor networks. *Sensors*, 12(9):12844–12869, 2012.

104. C. J. Huberty and S. Olejnik. *Applied MANOVA and Discriminant Analysis*. Wiley Online Library, 2005.

105. B. Hull, V. Bychkovsky, Y. Zhang, K. Chen, M. Goraczko, A. Miu, E. Shih, H. Balakrishnan, and S. Madden. Cartel: A distributed mobile sensor computing system. In *Proceedings of the 4th International Conference on Embedded Networked Sensor Systems, SenSys '06*, pp. 125–138, New York, NY, ACM, 2006.

106. N. Husted and S. Myers. Mobile location tracking in metro areas: Malnets and others. In *Proceedings of the 17th ACM Conference on Computer and Communications Security, CCS '10*, pp. 85–96, New York, NY, ACM, 2010.

107. T. Huynh, M. Fritz, and B. Schiele. Discovery of activity patterns using topic models. In *Proceedings of the 10th International Conference on Ubiquitous Computing*, pp. 10–19, New York, NY, ACM, 2008.

108. D.-W. Jang, B. K. Sun, S.-Y. Cho, S. Sohn, and K.-R. Han. Implementation of ubiquitous health care system for active measure of emergencies. In *Sixth International Conference on Advance Language Processing and Web Information Technology '07*, pp. 420–425, August 2007.

109. L. C. Jatoba, U. Grossmann, C. Kunze, J. Ottenbacher, and W. Stork. Context-aware mobile health monitoring: Evaluation of different pattern recognition methods for classification of physical activity. In *IEEE Conference on Engineering in Medicine and Biology Society*, pp. 5250–5253, August 2008.

110. B. S. Jensen, J. E. Larsen, K. Jensen, J. Larsen, and L. K. Hansen. Estimating human predictability from mobile sensor data. In *IEEE International Workshop on Machine Learning for Signal Processing*, pp. 196–201, August 2010.

111. I. Jolliffe. *Principal Component Analysis*. Wiley Online Library, 2005.

112. M. R. Jongerden and B. R. H. M. Haverkort. Battery modeling. Technical report, January 2008.

113. E. Jovanov, A. O'Donnell Lords, D. Raskovic, P. G. Cox, R. Adhami, and F. Andrasik. Stress monitoring using a distributed wireless intelligent sensor system. *IEEE Engineering in Medicine and Biology Magazine*, 22(3):49–55, May–June 2003.

114. E. Jovanov and A. Milenkovic. Body area networks for ubiquitous healthcare applications: Opportunities and challenges. *Journal of Medicine System*, 35(3): 1245–1254, 2011.

115. I. Kaj and V. Konane. Analytical and stochastic modelling of battery cell dynamics. In K. Al-Begain, D. Fiems, and J.-M. Vincent, eds., *Analytical and Stochastic Modeling Techniques and Applications*, Vol. 7314 of *Lecture Notes in Computer Science*, pp. 240–254. Springer, Berlin, Germany, 2012.

116. S. Kang, J. Lee, H. Jang, H. Lee, Y. Lee, S. Park, T. Park, and J. Song. Seemon: Scalable and energy-efficient context monitoring framework for sensor-rich mobile environments. In *ACM MobiSys'08*, pp. 267–280, 2008.

117. T. P. Kao, C. W. Lin, and J. S. Wang. Development of a portable activity detector for daily activity recognition. In *IEEE ISIE'09*, pp. 115–120, 2009.

118. A. Katasonov, O. Kaykova, O. Khriyenko, S. Nikitin, and V. Y. Terziyan. Smart semantic middleware for the internet of things. In *ICINCO-ICSO*, pp. 169–178, INSTICC Press, 2008.

119. C. D. Kidd, R. Orr, G. D. Abowd, C. G. Atkeson, I. A. Essa, B. MacIntyre, E. Mynatt, T. E. Starner, and W. Newstetter. The aware home: A living laboratory for ubiquitous computing research. In *Proceedings of the Second International Workshop on Cooperative Buildings. Integrating Information, Organizations, and Architecture*, pp. 191–198, Springer, Berlin, Germany, 1999.

120. E. Kim, S. Helal, and D. Cook. Human activity recognition and pattern discovery. *IEEE Pervasive Computing*, 9(1):48–53, January–March 2010.

121. M. Kim, D. Kotz, and S. Kim. Extracting a mobility model from real user traces. In *25th IEEE International Conference on Computer Communications. Proceedings*, pp. 1–13, April 2006.

122. K. Ellebæk Kjær. A survey of context-aware middleware. In *International Multi-Conference on IASTED: Software Engineering*, pp. 148–155, 2007.

123. M. Knappmeyer, S. L. Kiani, C. Fra, B. Moltchanov, and N. Baker. Contextml: A lightweight context representation and context management schema. In *IEEE International Symposium Wireless Pervasive Computing (ISWPC)*, pp. 367–372, May 2010.

124. A. Krause and C. Guestrin. Optimal nonmyopic value of information in graphical models: Efficient algorithms and theoretical limits. 2005.

125. A. Krause, M. Ihmig, E. Rankin, D. Leong, S. Gupta, D. Siewiorek, A. Smailagic, M. Deisher, and U. Sengupta. Trading off prediction accuracy and power consumption for context-aware wearable computing. In *IEEE International Symposium on Wearable Computer*, pp. 20–26, 2005.

126. J. Krumm and E. Horvitz. Predestination: Inferring destinations from partial trajectories. In *ACM UbiComp'06*, pp. 243–260, 2006.

127. R. Krummenacher and T. Strang. Ontology-based context modeling. In *Proceedings Third Workshop on Context-Aware Proactive Systems (CAPS 2007)*, p. 22, June 2007.

128. J. R. Kwapisz, G. M. Weiss, and S. A. Moore. Activity recognition using cell phone accelerometers. *SIGKDD Exploration Newsletter*, 12(2):74–82, March 2011.

129. K. Lahiri, A. Raghunathan, S. Dey, and D. Panigrahi. Battery-driven system design: A new frontier in low power design, 2002.

130. O. D. Lara and M. A. Labrador. A mobile platform for real-time human activity recognition. In *IEEE CCNC'12*, pp. 667–671, January 2012.

131. F. Lefvre, C. Montaci, and M.-J. Caraty. On the influence of the delta coefficients in a hmm-based speech recognition system. In *International Conference on Speech Science and Technology*, ISCA, December 1998.

132. J. Lester, T. Choudhury, and G. Borriello. A practical approach to recognizing physical activities. In K. P. Fishkin, B. Schiele, P. Nixon, and A. Quigley, eds., *Pervasive Computing, Lecture Notes in Computer Science*, vol. 3968, pp. 1–16. Springer Berlin Heidelberg, 2006.

133. S. E. Levinson. Continuously variable duration hidden Markov models for automatic speech recognition. *Computer Speech and Language*, 1(1):29–45, March 1986.

134. X. Li, M. Parizeau, and R. Plamondon. Training hidden Markov models with multiple observations—a combinatorial method. *IEEE Transactions on Pattern Analysis and Machine Intelligence*, 22(4):371–377, April 2000.

135. L. Liao, D. Fox, and H. Kautz. Extracting places and activities from GPS traces using hierarchical conditional random fields. *International Journal of Robotics Research*, 26(1):119–134, January 2007.

136. C.-W. Lin, Y.-T. C. Yang, J.-S. Wang, and Y.-C. Yang. A wearable sensor module with a neural-network-based activity classification algorithm for daily energy expenditure estimation. *IEEE Transactions on Information Technology in Biomedicine*, 16(5): 991–998, September 2012.

137. C. Liolios, C. Doukas, G. Fourlas, and I. Maglogiannis. An overview of body sensor networks in enabling pervasive healthcare and assistive environments. In *Proceedings of the 3rd International Conference on Pervasive Technologies Related to Assistive Environments, PETRA '10*, pp. 43:1–43:10, New York, NY, 2010.

138. X. Liu and C. Chua. Multi-agent activity recognition using observation decomposed hidden Markov model. Vol. 24, pp. 166–175, Newton, MA, Butterworth-Heinemann, February 2006.

139. H. Lu, W. Pan, N. D. Lane, T. Choudhury, and A. T. Campbell. Soundsense: Scalable sound sensing for people-centric applications on mobile phones.

140. H. Lu, J. Yang, Z. Liu, N. D. Lane, T. Choudhury, and A. T. Campbell. The jigsaw continuous sensing engine for mobile phone applications. In *ACM Proceedings of the 8th ACM Conference on Embedded Networked Sensor Systems, SenSys '10*, pp. 71–74, New York, NY, ACM, 2010.

141. T. Luckenbach, P. Gober, S. Arbanowski, A. Kotsopoulos, and K. Kim. Tinyrest—A protocol for integrating sensor networks into the internet. In *Proceedings of REALWSN Workshop on Real-World Wireless Sensor Networks*, 2005.

142. N. Maisonneuve, M. Stevens, M. E. Niessen, P. Hanappe, and L. Steels. Citizen noise pollution monitoring. In *Proceedings of the 10th Annual International Conference on Digital Government Research: Social Networks: Making Connections between Citizens, Data and Government*, pp. 96–103, Digital Government Society of North America, 2009.

143. J. F. Manwell and J. G. McGowan. Lead acid battery storage model for hybrid energy systems. *Solar Energy*, 50(5):399–405, 1993.

144. C. Mascolo, L. Capra, and W. Emmerich. Mobile computing middleware. *Advanced Lectures in Networks*, pp. 506–510, 2002.

145. U. Maurer, A. Smailagic, D. P. Siewiorek, and M. Deisher. Activity recognition and monitoring using multiple sensors on different body positions. In *International Workshop on Wearable and Implantable Body Sensor Networks*, pp. 4–116, April 2006.

146. M. A. Mendoza, N. P. de la Blanca, and M. J. Marin-Jimenez. Pohmm-based human action recognition. In *10th Workshop on Image Analysis for Multimedia Interactive Services (WIAMIS)*, pp. 85–88, May 2009.

147. E. Miluzzo, C. T. Cornelius, A. Ramaswamy, T. Choudhury, Z. Liu, and A. T. Campbell. Darwin phones: The evolution of sensing and inference on mobile phones. In *Proceedings of the 8th International Conference on Mobile Systems, Applications, and Services, MobiSys '10*, pp. 5–20, New York, NY, ACM, 2010.

148. E. Miluzzo, N. D. Lane, S. B. Eisenman, and A. T. Campbell. Cenceme: Injecting sensing presence into social networking applications. In *Proceedings of the 2nd European Conference on Smart Sensing and Context, EuroSSC '07*, pp. 1–28, Berlin, Heidelberg, Springer-Verlag, 2007.

149. E. Miluzzo, N. D. Lane, H. Lu, and A. T. Campbell. Research in the app store era: Experiences from the cenceme app deployment on the iphone, 2010.

150. D. Minnen, T. Westeyn, D. Ashbrook, P. Presti, and T. Starner. Recognizing soldier activities in the field. In *International Workshop on Wearable and Implantable Body Sensor Networks*, pp. 236–241, Springer, Berlin, Germany, 2007.

151. P. Mohan, V. N. Padmanabhan, and R. Ramjee. Nericell: Rich monitoring of road and traffic conditions using mobile smartphones. In *ACM SenSys'08*, pp. 323–336, 2008.

152. A. Monteiro, G. V. Smirnov, and A. Lucas. Non-parametric estimation for non-homogeneous semi-Markov processes: An application to credit risk, 2006.

153. S. C. Mukhopadhyay and O. A. Postolache. *Pervasive and Mobile Sensing and Computing for Healthcare: Technological and Social Issues*, Vol. 2. Springer Verlag, Berlin, Germany, 2012.

154. M. Mun, S. Reddy, K. Shilton, N. Yau, J. Burke, D. Estrin, M. Hansen, E. Howard, R. West, and P. Boda. Peir: The personal environmental impact report, as a platform for participatory sensing systems research. In *Proceedings ACM/USENIX International Conference on Mobile Systems, Applications, and Services*, 2009.

155. K. Murphy. Dynamic Bayesian networks: Representation, inference and learning. PhD thesis, July 2002.

156. K. Murphy and M. Paskin. Linear time inference in hierarchical HMMs, 2001.

157. R. Murty, A. Gosain, M. Tierney, A. Brody, A. Fahad, J. Bers, and M. Welsh. Citysense: An urban-scale wireless networking testbed. In *IEEE Int'l Conference on Technologies for Homeland Security*, pp. 583–588, 2008.

158. T. D. Nielsen and F. V. Jensen. *Bayesian Networks and Decision Graphs.* Springer, New York, 2009.

159. D. Panigrahi, S. Dey, R. Rao, K. Lahiri, C. Chiasserini, and A. Raghunathan. Battery life estimation of mobile embedded systems. In *Fourteenth International Conference on VLSI Design*, pp. 57–63, 2001.

160. A. Pantelopoulos and N. G. Bourbakis. A survey on wearable sensor-based systems for health monitoring and prognosis. *IEEE Transactions on Systems, Man, and Cybernetics*, 40(1):1–12, January 2010.

161. A. Papliatseyeu and O. Mayora. Mobile habits: Inferring and predicting user activities with a location-aware smartphone. Vol. 51 of *Advances in Soft Computing*, pp. 343–352. Springer, Berlin, Germany, 2009.

162. J. Parkka, M. Ermes, P. Korpipaa, J. Mantyjarvi, J. Peltola, and I. Korhonen. Activity classification using realistic data from wearable sensors. *IEEE Transactions on Information Technology in Biomedicine*, 10(1):119–128, January 2006.

163. R. Pawula. Generalizations and extensions of the Fokker-Planck-Kolmogorov equations. *IEEE Transactions on Information Theory*, 13(1):33–41, January 1967.

164. D. Peebles, H. Lu, N. D. Lane, T. Choudhury, and A. T. Campbell. Community-guided learning: Exploiting mobile sensor users to model human behavior. AAAI Press, 2010.

165. D. Q. Phung, T. V. Duong, S. Venkatesh, and H. H. Bui. Topic transition detection using hierarchical hidden Markov and semi-Markov models. *MULTIMEDIA '05*, pp. 11–20, ACM, 2005.

166. R. W. Picard, E. Vyzas, and J. Healey. Toward machine emotional intelligence: Analysis of affective physiological state. *IEEE Transactions on Pattern Analysis and Machine Intelligence*, 23(10):1175–1191, October 2001.

167. P. Prekop and M. Burnett. Activities, context and ubiquitous computing. *Computer Communications*, 26(11):1168–1176, 2003.

168. B. Priyantha, D. Lymberopoulos, and J. Liu. Littlerock: Enabling energy-efficient continuous sensing on mobile phones. *IEEE Pervasive Computer*, 10(2):12–15, April–June 2011.

169. A. Purohit, Z. Sun, F. Mokaya, and P. Zhang. Sensorfly: Controlled-mobile sensing platform for indoor emergency response applications. In *10th International Conference on Information Processing in Sensor Networks '11*, pp. 223–234, April 2011.

170. M. L. Puterman. *Markov Decision Processes: Discrete Stochastic Dynamic Programming.* 1st edn. John Wiley & Sons, Inc., New York, 1994.

171. R. Pyke. Markov renewal processes: Definitions and preliminary properties. *The Annals of Mathematical Statistics*, 32(4):1231–1242, 1961.

172. J. R. Quinlan. Induction of decision trees. *Machine Learning*, 1(1):81–106, 1986.

173. M. Quwaider and S. Biswas. Body posture identification using hidden Markov model with a wearable sensor network. pp. 19:1–19:8.

174. M.-R. Ra, J. Paek, A. B. Sharma, R. Govindan, M. H. Krieger, and M. J. Neely. Energy-delay tradeoffs in smartphone applications. In *Proceedings of the Eighth International Conference on Mobile Systems, Applications, and Services, MobiSys '10*, pp. 255–270, New York, NY, 2010.

175. L. R. Rabiner. A tutorial on hidden Markov models and selected applications in speech recognition. *Proceedings of the IEEE*, 77(2):257–286, February 1989.

176. K. K. Rachuri, M. Musolesi, and C. Mascolo. Energy-accuracy trade-offs in querying sensor data for continuous sensing mobile systems. 2012.

177. K. K. Rachuri, M. Musolesi, C. Mascolo, P. J. Rentfrow, C. Longworth, and A. Aucinas. Emotionsense: A mobile phones based adaptive platform for experimental social psychology research. In *Proceedings of the 12th ACM International Conference on Ubiquitous Computing, Ubicomp '10*, pp. 281–290, New York, NY, USA, ACM, 2010.

178. D. Rakhmatov and S. Vrudhula. Energy management for battery-powered embedded systems. *ACM Transactions on Embedded Computing Systems*, 2:277–324, 2003.

179. D. N. Rakhmatov and S. B. K. Vrudhula. An analytical high-level battery model for use in energy management of portable electronic systems. In *IEEE/ACM International Conference on Computer Aided Design*, pp. 488–493, 2001.

180. C. Randell and H. Muller. Context awareness by analysing accelerometer data. In *The Fourth International Symposium onWearable Computers*, pp. 175–176, October 2000.

181. R. Rao, S. Vrudhula, and D. N. Rakhmatov. Battery modeling for energy-aware system design. *Computer*, 36(12):77–87, December 2003.

182. V. Rao, G. Singhal, A. Kumar, and N. Navet. Battery model for embedded systems. In *International Conference on VLSI Design*, pp. 105–110, 2005.

183. N. Ravi, N. Dandekar, P. Mysore, and M. L. Littman. Activity recognition from accelerometer data. In *17th Conference on Innovative Applications of Artificial Intelligence (IAAI)*, pp. 1541–1546. AAAI Press, 2005.

184. S. Reddy, K. Shilton, G. Denisov, C. Cenizal, D. Estrin, and M. Srivastava. Biketastic: Sensing and mapping for better biking. In *Proceedings of the SIGCHI Conference on Human Factors in Computing Systems, CHI '10*, pp. 1817–820, New York, NY, ACM, 2010.

185. A. Rehman, M. Mustafa, I. Israr, and M. Yaqoob. Survey of wearable sensors with comparative study of noise reduction ECG filters. *International Journal of Computing and Network Technology*, 1(1):45–66, 2013.

186. D. Riboni and C. Bettini. Cosar: Hybrid reasoning for context-aware activity recognition. *Personal Ubiquitous Computer*, 15(3):271–289, March 2011.

187. Daniele Riboni and Claudio Bettini. Cosar: Hybrid reasoning for context-aware activity recognition. *Personal and Ubiquitous Computing*, 15(3):271–289, March 2011.

188. T. Rodden, K. Cheverst, K. Davies, and A. Dix. Exploiting context in HCI design for mobile systems. In *Workshop on Human Computer Interaction with Mobile Devices*, pp. 21–22, Citeseer, 1998.

189. M. Roman, C. Hess, R. Cerqueira, A. Ranganathan, R. H. Campbell, and K. Nahrstedt. A middleware infrastructure for active spaces. *IEEE Pervasive Computing*, 1(4): 74–83, October 2002.

190. M. Román, C. Hess, R. Cerqueira, A. Ranganathan, R. H. Campbell, and K. Nahrstedt. A middleware infrastructure for active spaces. *IEEE Pervasive Computer*, 1(4):74–83, 2002.

191. P. Rong and M. Pedram. An analytical model for predicting the remaining battery capacity of lithium-ion batteries. Vol. 14, pp. 441–451, 2003.

192. D. Salber, A. K. Dey, and G. D. Abowd. The context toolkit: Aiding the development of context-enabled applications. In *Proceedings of the SIGCHI Conference on Human Factors in Computing Systems, CHI '99*, pp. 434–441, New York, NY, ACM, 1999.

193. M. Sama, D. S. Rosenblum, Z. Wang, and S. Elbaum. Model-based fault detection in context-aware adaptive applications. In *Proceedings of the 16th ACM SIGSOFT International Symposium on Foundations of Software Engineering, SIGSOFT '08/FSE-16*, pp. 261–271, New York, NY, ACM, 2008.

194. L. K. Saul and M. I. Jordan. Mixed memory Markov models: Decomposing complex stochastic processes as mixtures of simpler ones. *Machine Learning*, 37(1):75–87, October 1999.

195. B. N. Schilit and M. M. Theimer. Disseminating active map information to mobile hosts. *IEEE Network*, 8(5):22–32, 1994.

196. F. S. Schnatter. *Finite Mixture and Markov Switching Models*. Springer Verlag, New York, 2006.

197. K. Shafiee, V. C. M. Leung, and R. Sengupta. Request-adaptive packet dissemination for context-aware services in vehicular networks. In *IEEE Vehicular Technology Conference (VTC Fall)*, pp. 1–5, 2012.

198. Q. Shi, L. Wang, L. Cheng, and A. Smola. Discriminative human action segmentation and recognition using semi-Markov model. In *IEEE Conference on Computer Vision and Pattern Recognition*, pp. 1–8, June 2008.

199. K. Shilton. Four billion little brothers?: Privacy, mobile phones, and ubiquitous data collection. *Communication of ACM*, 52(11):48–53, November 2009.

200. M. Shin, P. Tsang, D. Kotz, and C. Cornelius. Deamon: Energy-efficient sensor monitoring. In *6th Annual IEEE Communications Society Conference on Sensor, Mesh and Ad Hoc Communications and Networks*, pp. 1–9, June 2009.

201. D. Siewiorek, A. Smailagic, J. Furukawa, A. Krause, N. Moraveji, K. Reiger, J. Shaffer, and F. L. Wong. Sensay: A context-aware mobile phone. In *Proceedings of the 7th IEEE International Symposium on Wearable Computers, ISWC '03*, p. 248, Washington, DC, IEEE Computer Society, 2003.

202. P. Siirtola and J. Rning. Recognizing human activities user-independently on smartphones based on accelerometer data. *International Journal of Interactive Multimedia and Artificial Intelligence*, (5):38–45, 2012.

203. M. Skubic. A ubiquitous sensing environment to detect functional changes in assisted living apartments: The tiger place experience. *Elsevier Alzheimer's & Dementia*, 6(4):1552–5260, 2010.

204. V. Srinivasan and T. Phan. An accurate two-tier classifier for efficient duty-cycling of smartphone activity recognition systems. In *Proceedings of the Third International Workshop on Sensing Applications on Mobile Phones, PhoneSense '12*, pp. 11:1–11:5, New York, NY, ACM, 2012.

205. K. G. Stanley and N. D. Osgood. The potential of sensor-based monitoring as a tool for health care, health promotion, and research. *The Annals of Family Medicine*, 9(4): 296–298, 2011.

206. M. Stikic, D. Larlus, S. Ebert, and B. Schiele. Weakly supervised recognition of daily life activities with wearable sensors. *IEEE Transactions on Pattern Analysis and Machine Intelligence*, 33(12):2521–2537, December 2011.

207. T. Strang and C. Linnhoff-Popien. A context modeling survey. In *Workshop Proceedings*, 2004.

208. L. Sun, D. Zhang, B. Li, B. Guo, and S. Li. Activity recognition on an accelerometer embedded mobile phone with varying positions and orientations. In *Proceedings of the 7th International Conference on Ubiquitous Intelligence and Computing, UIC'10*, pp. 548–562, Berlin, Heidelberg, Springer-Verlag, 2010.

209. P. TalebiFard and V. C. M. Leung. Context-aware dissemination of information and services in heterogeneous network environments. *Journal of Ambient Intelligence and Humanized Computing*, 3:1–13, 2013.

210. R. Tan, J. Gu, Z. Zhong, and P. Chen. Metadata management of context resources in context-aware middleware system. *Web Info. Sys. and Mining*, pp. 350–357, 2012.

211. E. M. Tapia, S. S. Intille, W. Haskell, K. Larson, J. Wright, A. King, and R. Friedman. Real-time recognition of physical activities and their intensities using wireless accelerometers and a heart rate monitor. In *Proceedings of International Symposium on Wearable Computers*, pp. 1–4, 2007.

212. A. Thiagarajan, L. Ravindranath, K. LaCurts, S. Madden, H. Balakrishnan, S. Toledo, and J. Eriksson. Vtrack: Accurate, energy-aware road traffic delay estimation using mobile phones. In *Proceedings of the 7th ACM Conference on Embedded Networked Sensor Systems, SenSys '09*, pp. 85–98, New York, NY, ACM, 2009.

213. O. Thomas, P. Sunehag, G. Dror, S. Yun, S. Kim, M. Robards, A. Smola, D. Green, and P. Saunders. Wearable sensor activity analysis using semi-Markov models with a grammar. *Pervasive and Mobile Computing*, 6(3):342–350, June 2010.

214. H.-L. Truong and S. Dustdar. A survey on context-aware web service systems. *International Journal of Web and Information System*, 5(1):5–31, 2009.

215. L. T. Vinh, S. Lee, Hung X. Le, H. Q. Ngo, H. I. Kim, M. Han, and Y.-K. Lee. Semi-Markov conditional random fields for accelerometer-based activity recognition. *Applied Intelligence*, 35(2):226–241, October 2011.

216. A. Viterbi. Error bounds for convolutional codes and an asymptotically optimum decoding algorithm. *IEEE Transactions on Information Theory*, 13(2):260–269, 1967.

217. C. Vogler and D. Metaxas. Parallel hidden Markov models for American sign language recognition. In *Proceedings of the Seventh IEEE International Conference on Computer Vision*, Vol. 1, pp. 116–122, 1999.

218. K. Wagstaff, C. Cardie, S. Rogers, S. Schrödl et al. Constrained k-means clustering with background knowledge. *Machine Learning* 1:577–584, 2001.

219. X. H. Wang, D. Q. Zhang, T. Gu, and H. K. Pung. Ontology based context modeling and reasoning using owl. In *Proceedings of the Second IEEE Annual Conference on Pervasive Computing and Communications Workshops, 2004*, pp. 18–22, March 2004.

220. Y. Wang, B. Krishnamachari, Q. Zhao, and M. Annavaram. Markov-optimal sensing policy for user state estimation in mobile devices. In *Proceedings of the 9th ACM/IEEE International Conference on Information Processing in Sensor Networks, IPSN '10*, pp. 268–278, New York, NY, ACM, 2010.

221. Y. Wang, J. Lin, M. Annavaram, Q. A. Jacobson, J. Hong, B. Krishnamachari, and N. Sadeh. A framework of energy efficient mobile sensing for automatic user state recognition. In *Proceedings of the 7th International Conference on Mobile Systems, Applications, and Services, MobiSys '09*, pp. 179–192, New York, NY, ACM, 2009.

222. K. Weinberger, J. Blitzer, and L. Saul. Distance metric learning for large margin nearest neighbor classification. *Advances in Neural Information Processing Systems*, 18:1473, 2006.

223. M. Weiser. The computer for the 21st century. *Scientific American*, 265(3):94–104, 1991.

224. L. R. Welch. Hidden Markov models and the Baum-Welch algorithm. *IEEE Information Theory Society Newsletter*, 53(4):10–13, 2003.

225. W. Wibisono, A. Zaslavsky, and Sea Ling. Comihoc: A middleware framework for context management in MANET environment. In *24th IEEE International Conference on Advanced Information Networking and Applications (AINA), 2010*, pp. 620–627, April 2010.

226. A. Wood, J. Stankovic, G. Virone, L. Selavo, Z. He, Q. Cao, T. Doan, Y. Wu, L. Fang, and R. Stoleru. Context-aware wireless sensor networks for assisted living and residential monitoring. *IEEE Network*, 22(4):26–33, July–August, 2008.

227. F.-J. Wu, Y.-F. Kao, and Y.-C. Tseng. From wireless sensor networks towards cyber physical systems. *Pervasive and Mobile Computer*, 7(4):397–413, 2011.

228. P. Yan, I. Lin, M. Roy, E. Seto, C. Wang, and R. Bajcsy. In *Wireless Internet Conference (WICON)*, March 2010.

229. Z. Yan, D. Chakraborty, A. Misra, H. Jeung, and K. Aberer. SAMMPLE: Detecting semantic indoor activities in practical settings using locomotive signatures. In *Proceedings of the 16th IEEE International Symposium on Wearable Computers (ISWC)*, pp. 37–40, New York, NY, IEEE, 2012.

230. Z. Yan, V. Subbaraju, D. Chakraborty, A. Misra, and K. Aberer. Energy-efficient continuous activity recognition on mobile phones: An activity-adaptive approach. In *International Symposium on Wearable Computers (ISWC)*, pp. 17–24, June 2012.

231. Z. Yan, V. Subbaraju, D. Chakraborty, A. Misra, and K. Aberer. Energy-efficient continuous activity recognition on mobile phones: An activity-adaptive approach. In *Proceedings of International Symposium on Wearable Computers*, 2012.

232. J. Yang, H. Lu, Z. Liu, and P. P. Boda. Physical activity recognition with mobile phones: Challenges, methods, and applications. In *Multimedia Interaction and Intelligent User Interfaces*, Advances in Pattern Recognition, pp. 185–213, Springer, London, U.K., 2010.

233. H. Yoon, Y. Zheng, X. Xie, and W. Woo. Social itinerary recommendation from user-generated digital trails. *Personal and Ubiquitous Computing*, 16:469–484, 2012.

234. S.-Z. Yu and H. Kobayashi. A hidden semi-Markov model with missing data and multiple observation sequences for mobility tracking. *Signal Processing*, 83(2):235–250, 2003.

235. O. Yurur, C. H. Liu, X. Liu, and W. Moreno. Adaptive sampling and duty cycling for smartphone accelerometer. In *IEEE 10th International Conference on Mobile Ad-Hoc and Sensor Systems (MASS), 2013*, pp. 511–518, IEEE, 2013.

236. O. Yurur and W. Moreno. Energy efficient sensor management strategies in mobile sensing. In *XVIII ISTEC General Assembly 2011*, May 2011.

237. L. A. Zadeh. Fuzzy logic, neural networks, and soft computing. *Communications of the ACM*, 37(3):77–84, 1994.

238. P. Zappi, C. Lombriser, T. Stiefmeier, E. Farella, D. Roggen, L. Benini, and G. Tröster. Activity recognition from on-body sensors: Accuracy-power trade-off by dynamic sensor selection. In R. Verdone, ed., *Wireless Sensor Networks, Lecture Notes in Computer Science*, Vol. 4913, pp. 17–33. Springer Berlin, Heidelberg, 2008.

239. W. Zhang, F. Chen, W. Xu, and Z. Cao. Decomposition in hidden Markov models for activity recognition. In *International Conference on Multimedia Content Analysis and Mining (MCAM)*, pp. 232–241, Springer-Verlag, Berlin, Germany, 2007.

240. J. Zheng, D. Simplot-Ryl, C. Bisdikian, and H. T. Mouftah. The internet of things. *IEEE Communication Magazine*, 49(11):30–31, November 2011.

241. V. W. Zheng, Y. Zheng, X. Xie, and Q. Yang. Towards mobile intelligence: Learning from GPS history data for collaborative recommendation. *Artificial Intelligence*, 184–185:17–37, June 2012.

242. S. Zhong and J. Ghosh. A new formulation of coupled hidden Markov models. 2001. Technical Report.

243. S. Zhong and J. Ghosh. HMMS and coupled HMMS for multi-channel EEG classification. In *International Joint Conference on Neural Networks'02*, Vol. 2, pp. 1154–1159, 2002.

244. C. Zhu and W. Sheng. Human daily activity recognition in robot-assisted living using multi-sensor fusion. In *IEEE International Conference on Robotics and Automation*, pp. 2154–2159, May 2009.

245. X. Zhu. Semi-supervised learning literature survey. 2006.

246. Z. Zhuang, K.-H. Kim, and J. P. Singh. Improving energy efficiency of location sensing on smartphones. In *ACM MobiSys'10*, pp. 315–330, 2010.

Index

199